ON
THE
OTHER
HAND

ON THE OTHER HAND

by

Rachel Adams

HARPER & ROW, PUBLISHERS

NEW YORK, EVANSTON, AND LONDON

FIRST EDITION

D–N

LIBRARY OF CONGRESS CATALOG CARD NUMBER: 62-14519

With gratefulness from my heart to all
who have so enriched my life: my family, my friends,
and especially my husband

With sincere appreciation to
Marguerite Hoyle Munson
for her help in editing these pages

Contents

Illustrations

ON
THE
OTHER
HAND

i

Retrospect

As far back as I can remember I have wanted to write a book, largely through the desire to share with others the joy I knew as a child while growing up in one of the loveliest spots of rural New England. The obsession continued to grow as my life became more involved following my marriage to an indomitable young woodsman who later found it impossible to resist the challenge of politics as it affected his town and state and, ultimately, his nation. Crowded and exciting days filled my life for nearly twenty years while my husband served as town representative to the General Court of New Hampshire, as congressman to Washington from New Hampshire's Second District, as governor, and then in a nation-wide political campaign which resulted in the election of Dwight D. Eisenhower as President. During President Eisenhower's first term in office, and through part of his second term, my husband was the Assistant to the President—a position differing from any previous job in the executive branch of the White House. There had been presidential assistants in the past but none with the breadth of power with which the President invested Sherman Adams.

As a child, lacking nearby playmates, I depended largely on my imagination and ingenuity to make the days more exciting. During the summer boarder season I had plenty to keep me interested but in the off-season I sometimes found that my imagination needed recharging. I tried desperately to stimulate it by sitting in front of the large mirror in the living room and concentrating on passing through the looking-glass as Alice did. It didn't work then but years later it seemed to me that I had almost done just that, for I found myself, quite suddenly, in an unfamiliar world of Presidents, Kings, Queens and palaces. There were mad-hatters too, and all kinds of entrancing and lovable creatures. And I found, as Alice did, that once one is through the looking-glass one has to put up with what one finds there, and it is not all tea parties.

Of all my experiences during the years I was trying to keep up with my energetic husband, the Washington interlude was the most interesting, though the weeks on the campaign train offer close competition; indeed, I think if I could relive just one experience I would hop aboard the "Eisenhower Special." I would, however, stock up on extra-special vitamins before setting out. I often recall too the inaugurations we participated in, the many adventures with protocol, and the endless series of official or informal parties. And how can anyone like us, accustomed to well-plowed roads, forget the tie-ups in traffic after a three-inch snowfall?

For a few years the Washington interlude furnished a pleasant and exciting contrast to our somewhat more sedate life in the country. Now our usual winter attire is in keeping with our interest in skiing and other outdoor activities—a distinct change from white tie and tails for the Governor and an evening gown of fragile material for me. Where we had glittering chandeliers we now have sparkling snow crystals. And instead of being part of a roomful of colorful people and conversation we now share the ski slopes with other brightly clad outdoor enthusiasts. During the warmer months we can be found on a golf course, bridle paths, mountain trails, fishing streams, or even working in our hayfield and gardens.

I am thoroughly happy to be back in the New England countryside once again. I believe my husband feels the same way, for this is the New England where we were born and where we grew up. Our common admiration for the out-of-doors drew us together forty years ago. We have brought up three girls and a boy, and they, like us, appreciate country living. And now our grandchildren are following in our ski and snowshoe tracks—or even breaking trail at times!

Undoubtedly there are people who wonder how a man who has

always been as relentlessly active as my husband has been can be content with a sort of "country gentleman" role, especially after so many years of public life. I feel that his return to a less exhausting and tense schedule is all for the best. He has always possessed an overabundance of energy and what is familiarly known as "drive." It has not diminished because he is no longer deep in politics. The days are still full, and that is the way it will be as long as he lives. Instead of working behind a desk or at a conference table, he is now out-of-doors for the better part of the day. The tenseness that built up over a number of years, while he was trying to achieve perfection at his several jobs, has mellowed into an appreciation of things he thought he had no time for in his younger days. It was extremely hard for him to leave a job unfinished, as he had to when he left the White House, but just as his departure undoubtedly relieved the minds of persons directly and indirectly responsible for his resignation so was my mind relieved that he would no longer have to expend himself, both mentally and physically, to such limits as had been his custom for some time.

I am glad I had the Washington experience, even while remembering the unpleasant bits. It was a part of the full and interesting life I have been privileged to live. Both the Governor and I have warm recollections of the many true friends who stayed close in all kinds of weather, and we will always remember with gratitude the exciting and fascinating events of which we were a part during his political career.

Memory is a sorting house and as time goes by we consciously or unconsciously separate the wheat from the chaff. The wheat we store away while the chaff disappears with the breeze.

ii

The Way It Was

I have been told that it was one of those rare June mornings. My father opened the screen door of the big white house up the hill from the lake, walked out on the spacious veranda, down the steps, and took the path to the road. Then he saw that the rosebush was full of the first white blossoms of the year. It was an old-fashioned variety that Mother had brought from "the old place" when she and Father came to Belmont, Vermont, to live. Quickly he cut a bouquet and returned to the house. (Father always did things quickly. He was always a few paces ahead of Mother when they were out walking. In church he was generally ahead of the organist. He painted quickly and the tunes on his violin had a fast tempo.) Entering the west corner bedroom he handed the roses to my mother, who was lying in bed with her new daughter beside her.

Not only was it a perfect June day, it was also Sunday, and it pleased my mother in particular that I had been born on the Sabbath day. Hopefully she often reminded me in later years that "the child that is born on the Sabbath day is brave, and bonny, and good and gay."

Young Thomas Brown was just beginning his career as a doctor in that horse-and-buggy era. Many years later he told me that Father handed him $5 for assisting me into the world. It was the regular fee for a confinement at that time.

As the years went by I felt very lucky to have parents who all but idolized me, and who lived in what I was sure was the most beautiful place on earth. My parents weren't the only ones who literally welcomed me with open arms. Harold, a twelve-year-old brother,

4

and two slightly younger sisters, Edna and Kathleen, showered me with affection and care all through my growing-up years.

Mother was of Irish ancestry, blue-eyed and dark-haired, with a peaches-and-cream complexion. Her name, before she married, was Mary Louise Sheehan, and she was one of seven children. She married Eddie White from up Belmont way. He had come down to Cuttingsville, where Mary lived, to work in the Carriage Shop. Edward White wasn't a large man. His father, Deacon John, was taller. So were his brothers, William and Milton. There wasn't much weight on him either. It never had a chance to catch up with him. He worked hard and fast all day in the shop decorating sleighs and carriages. In the evenings he was always ready for whatever fun the quiet country life of those days afforded.

Though very proud of his pretty bride and deeply in love, he would not take up her faith. So Mary, bless her, attended the Baptist church with Eddie. Later she encouraged her children to go to the same church though she did insist that I be christened by an Episcopal clergyman—the same man who, years later, was to confirm me and to perform my marriage ceremony.

That Baptist church was a familiar place in the early years of my life. It was there that I learned the Beatitudes—word for word— and enjoyed church suppers, which, including Aunt Lizzie Mead's "always perfect" whipped cream cake, and Fanny Thomas' famous George Washington pie, cost all of fifteen cents. And there were Wednesday night socials in the vestry, with games following a full-course baked bean supper.

Over at the dance hall at the foot of the lake on Saturday evenings things were different but, as long as all behaved themselves tolerably well, an evening of square dancing and waltzing was lots of fun. Ezra Titus fiddled for some of those lively evenings. He did things a little differently from others—he held the fiddle between his knees and bowed with his left hand, and if he saw a couple getting a square all messed up because they didn't know how to do it, he would stop the music and straighten them out. Often, as the evening wore on and the dance hall became warmer and warmer, Ezra would reach under his chair for the ever-present jug of cider every chance he had. One winter evening when the cider jug had been popular some of the boys lifted Ezra in his chair, fiddle and all, and set him on top of the hot stove. Ezra kept right on fiddling.

The village got most excited when gypsies came to town. Old wagons, full of dirty children and grownups would be spotted on the outskirts of the village by some alert farmer's wife and she would lose no time in cranking the wall telephone to give the general alarm. Questions from other members on the party line would fly at her over the wires. "Which way they goin'?" "How many be they?" Others wouldn't wait to ask questions—they'd high-tail it out to the pasture to get the stock in and then see that everything that could be was locked up tight.

Town Meeting Day was another excitement. Everybody came to town on *that* day unless there was a blizzard. They came to settle things as peacefully as possible—to vote for selectmen, school-board members, road commissioner, and so on. The ladies of both the Baptist and Methodist churches put on a huge meal at noon—trying to outdo what each expected the other group was doing. And when the voters started coming down the road from town meeting the Methodist ladies would stand at the windows of their vestry and beckon to the hungry voters to come to *their* dinner instead of going up the hill to where the Baptist ladies had their tables well loaded also.

I wasn't very old when I learned that Memorial Day was one of the most important days of the year. All the girls who had white dresses and long white cotton stockings wore them to school for the exercises. Black stockings were more in evidence, however, along with the inevitable high-laced black shoes. A big wide bow for the hair was another cherished addition to the ensemble of a little girl intent on hoping she could remember her Decoration Day piece as she stood up front in the schoolroom, facing parents and friends. Through the wide-open doors leading to the entry came the delicious scents of early spring flowers. Pails of water held bunches of lilacs, violets, and adders'-tongues. There was a neatly tied bouquet for each pupil, to be carried, after the speaking was over, as they marched through the village and up the hill to the cemetery. There we walked to the graves of those who had fought in the Civil War and laid our bunches of blossoms under the fluttering American flags. Afterwards we followed my father with his drum across to Wesley Priest's house, where that old soldier never failed to hand out oranges and bananas to the school children who had carried out the ceremony of remembering.

A severe illness one winter when I was very young undoubtedly had much to do with the freedom I enjoyed later. During that illness I spent many weeks on the old Chippendale sofa near the tall living-room stove. My favorite song was "Jesus Wants Me for a Sunbeam"—my rendering of which tore at my mother's heart, worried as she was about me.

I remember vividly the visits of the old doctor. Along the latter part of the afternoon the sound of sleigh bells would signal his arrival. Mother would put down her mending and get up out of the rocking chair beside me. She knew who was coming, just as she knew when the mailman was nearby or the ice teams were passing.

After driving his tired horse into the yard the doctor would remove the frayed and weary-looking buffalo robe from his knees and put it over the seat of the sleigh to keep out the blowing snow, and place a blanket on the horse. Then he would pick up the worn and sagging medicine bag and come up onto the porch—stomping with each step to remove as much snow as possible. Mother would hand him the broom and suggest perhaps he would like to brush off his overshoes before he came inside.

After taking my temperature and putting another bottle of foul-tasting liquid on the stand he would answer Mother's questions regarding the health of any neighbors who were ill. Then, giving last-minute instructions for my care, he would wind the knitted scarf around his neck and put on the heavy overcoat, which already had filled the room with a good rich horse odor. Tired, and stooping a little, not from the weight of his bag but from the many years of being a country doctor, he would leave the house—his last call before supper. As he opened the door the horse would turn its head and give a welcoming whinny and a vigorous shake that made the sleigh bells ring. We would continue to hear the bells to the top of the hill, jingling in a cadence suggesting that the horse knew he was on the way to the barn.

The doctor's tonic apparently worked, for the following spring found me out-of-doors. My mother had been told to "keep her out in the fresh air and sunshine." As days grew into weeks, and weeks grew into years, nothing could have suited me better. Occasionally Mother tried to keep me inside long enough to teach me a little housekeeping, but that activity held little interest for me and I cut all the corners I could in order to be free again. One inside job I enjoyed, however. That was helping Father bring in the wood each winter evening. It took several trips from the winter kitchen out through the summer kitchen, past the aromatic barrels of Baldwin apples in the shed, to where the wood was piled. The odd and frightening shadows that danced on the walls as we made our way with the lantern kept me close to Father.

On Saturday nights we made an extra trip to get enough butter-nuts out of the barrel to keep us busy until bedtime. Father would get an old flatiron, turn it upside down and, with a hammer, crack the practically shockproof butternuts. With pans full, and a nut pick for everyone, we found our favorite places in the living room. Mine was the Chippendale sofa, until I had found the last piece of butter-nut meat; then I climbed into Father's lap. His old reed rocker kept time now fast, now slow, according to the nature of the story he was relating to Mother, undoubtedly something he had heard at the store when he went to get the mail.

I relished too the aroma of the one 7-20-4 cigar that Father smoked each night. Even now a whiff of cigar smoke works like a magic carpet, as does snow blowing in my face, or the song of the white-throated sparrow or the rippling of a finally ice-free little brook in the spring.

That we didn't have many of the things we would have liked, nor some of the things we needed, bothered me very little. I had few playthings, as a youngster, of the kind that are bought at a store, and I needed none, for my imagination and the outdoors kept me thoroughly occupied and happy. Mother showed me how to make cornhusk dolls and I played at mud pies back of the summer kitchen where the spring sun melted the snow early. I hunted for bits of broken colored glass and having found some couldn't have been happier if I had found a perfect and gorgeous Turk's-cap on the sands of Florida. My freedom was somewhat curtailed when I started going to the one-room district school which was down the road a bit from our house. Having to sit so long in one place was not to my liking. There were compensations, however, such as being allowed to ring the bell if I was the first to arrive, or to pass out the pencils which had been collected and sharpened the night before. Then, too, someone always had to take the pail and go to a nearby house for drinking water, which was placed on the shelf in the corner of the schoolroom where the dipper hung.

In the wintertime the ink bottles had to be collected from the desks at the end of the day and set close to the chunk stove to keep from freezing during the night. There were times, however, when the fire went out and the ink froze anyway. Then the next morning after a good roaring fire got going there would be a wonderful commotion as the forgotten ink bottles blew their tops and the thawing ink went flying in every direction.

If the boy who was building the fire that winter had been at his job early enough, the heat from the stove, which stood near the center of the room, would have chased the cold at least to the edges by the time the last bell rang. There was little lingering in the entry as pupils quickly hung up their coats and brought in their wet mittens to be placed as close to the hot fire as was safe. But there were many winter days when it was impossible to warm the room any distance from the stove. Then the older boys would bring in sturdy chunks from the woodshed and the children would form a circle around the stove, teetering on the chunks while trying to keep their minds on lessons.

The teachers in those district schools of a half-century and more ago more than earned their meager pay. The big boys were "big" not only to us smaller children but often to the teacher as well. They were farm boys for the most part. Their schooling was often interrupted, for the farm work had to be done, and the boys kept right on growing while they lost time in school. Smart was the schoolmarm who knew how to keep them from taking over.

Several years before I was born my family had begun to take summer boarders. Some became "regulars," and new names were added to the big black-covered ledger each year. I have sometimes wondered whether the feverish activity in late spring of "getting ready for the boarders" and the subsequent bustle, after they arrived, of keeping them well fed and entertained wasn't responsible for my desire to have something exciting happening all the time. I am certain it did a great deal to condition me for my later life when I accompanied my husband back and forth across the country during his years of political activity. As soon as the snowbanks around the house had almost disappeared, Mother would get the urge to start spring housecleaning. All the rugs and carpets were taken outdoors and given a good beating. The summer kitchen was opened up little by little and, as the days grew warmer and warmer, it was used more and more. Storm windows came off and windowpanes were washed. Then, as warmer days approached, Father would give the porch a coat of paint, and about the same time he could be found around the boathouse getting the boats ready to "go on." The dock usually needed attention after a long winter of being locked in the ice, and as soon as school was out I lost no time in joining him.

Long before I was born, when the family moved to Belmont, Father went into the paper-hanging business. He was also a painter, and for a number of years he decorated the inside of churches with stencils or, at times, freehand work. During his travels around the countryside on different jobs he became interested in antiques and about the time I entered my teens he bought a Ford and scoured the surrounding territories for treasures from the past. He studied the old designs and restored many which would have been lost forever but for his cleverness. He was probably the first to advertise an assortment of authentic stencils for sale. With the accompanying instructions an interested buyer could "do over" his own prized possessions. Now, though he had long since given up paper hanging and painting, he had more work than he could keep ahead of, for he was also turning out reproductions of early American chairs, tables and mirrors. After many lean years of intermittent work, traveling here and there, his artistic nature had finally found a profitable outlet. He was creating, and at the same time doing much to secure the heritage of the past for others to enjoy. His youthful ambition to be a landscape artist was almost forgotten as he painstakingly sought out an old design hidden under many layers of paint.

Whether I was born with the same desire to paint or whether I acquired it I do not know, but at times it has been an obsession—generally to be pushed aside to make way for more demanding activities.

iii

An Enchanted Summer

The beginning of the twenties found me enrolled in Northfield Seminary at East Northfield, Massachusetts. Although the tuition was low, even for those days, it would be no easy task to make the required payments. Nevertheless, my mother felt I would benefit by the supervision and discipline such a school afforded, so in due course there I was, standing in a long line of girls on Registration Day. It was hot and I knew no one at the school. As my parents drove away I felt very much alone and it didn't take me long to realize that I was going to have less freedom than ever before in my life.

Mother would not have felt so happy about my being there if she had known about my roommate, a girl from Boston who was much more sophisticated and experienced than I. She was a lot of fun but not exactly the type I needed—someone to encourage in me a degree of diligence. Her lessons came easy. Mine seemed to come hard, or not at all—a circumstance that worried me a little. But somehow I got through the first year and in June, of 1922, I boarded the northbound train, along with many other students. At Bellows Falls, Vermont, I changed to the Rutland train. My destination was Mount Holly station—two miles from Belmont and home.

The trip seemed interminable only because I could hardly wait to get home. Long before the whistle blew for Mount Holly I was standing near the vestibule door, my suitcases beside me. I hoped Mother would be "filled up" with reservations for the summer and that many of the regulars would be returning. I also hoped there would be some young men around, but I hardly expected such good luck.

The train came to a halt and I descended the steps, with the conductor's help, and landed on the cinders beside the track. It was good to be in the fresh air again, I thought, as I looked to see if there was anyone to meet me. As I picked up the suitcases I saw Tad Priest sauntering over to retrieve the mailbags. There wasn't anyone else around so I put my luggage into his dilapidated car and soon we were chugging up the steep hill toward Belmont. Tad had been meeting trains and carrying the mail for many years. He never had much to say but I tried hard to get him to talk about something. By the time we had reached the dugway I had given up and was happily anticipating reaching the top of the hill where I could get the first view of the lake. It would be flat going then, past the old Barrett place on the left where the best lilacs grew, and on to the Meads' place on the right which had been built by Abraham Jackson, one of the Quakers who had helped settle the town.

As we turned up the driveway to Lake View Cottage, Mother and Father appeared. How good they looked—how wonderful to be home again! There was a feeling of excitement and suspense as they helped me carry my things to my room. They hoped I would be surprised—and I was! My room had been "freshened up," as Father called it. After Mother was sure I had noticed all the improvements and told me what she thought would interest me most about current affairs in the little village, she started downstairs and then returned to my door.

"You will have to wait on table until the other girls arrive for the summer," she said, not without a trace of hopefulness that I would be willing. She didn't like to put me to work as soon as I arrived but I set her mind at ease. My apprenticeship in helping with summer boarders had begun at a very tender age when my job had been to ring the rising bell, then the first and last bell for meals. Now that I was older I enjoyed waiting on table. I liked the little white aprons but I liked best serving Mother's cooking. I took as much pride in the compliments that I was asked to convey to her in the kitchen as if I had prepared the food myself.

The first Sunday after I returned home was cloudy and cool. One of the guests, a young woman from New York, had invited to dinner the young man who had given her a ride back from church in another village. He had accepted, and his little Model T runabout was parked across the road in front of the house when I returned from services at the Baptist church.

I hurried upstairs to make myself more presentable for waiting on table. I was most anxious to see what kind of young man—with a car —had been found around these parts. Mother had told me he was employed at a mill in the next village. As I stood in the kitchen waiting for the tray to be loaded I was a typical seventeen-year-old, smoothing out my little white apron and glancing in the mirror numerous times. Then I opened the door a crack and saw that our boarder and her guest had entered the dining room and were about to sit down.

I quickly picked up the tray and carried it into the dining room. After setting it on the serving table, I was introduced to her guest by our boarder. His name was Sherman Adams and he had an engaging smile.

For the rest of that meal I did the best job of waiting that I was capable of, and was more than pleased to see how thoroughly he appreciated Mother's stewed chicken and baking-powder biscuits, mashed potatoes and boiled onions. I had no qualms about the dessert. Everybody liked my mother's apple pies, though few were lucky enough to get a second piece, since the first was always of good size. But Sherman Adams had a second piece. Soon after, he got into his little car and disappeared in the direction of Healdville.

A few days passed, and I began to think he would never appear again; then one evening his Ford stopped out front. "Just going by and thought I'd stop," he said. I supposed he had come to call on our boarder but he seemed interested only in talking to me. He continued to stand on the grass by the front porch. I sat on the railing. It was well along in the evening and the June bugs and moths were bombarding the glass of the lighted carriage lamp on the post at the corner of the steps.

After a few pleasantries he asked me if I thought I might like to go out with him some evening.

"What is there to do around here?" he asked.

"Well," I answered, trying to appear not the least bit excited, "about the only thing to go to is a square dance on Saturday nights."

"I don't know anything about square dancing," he said.

"You could learn, couldn't you?" I asked hopefully.

"Would you teach me?"

"Sure!" I answered, without even decent hesitation.

The following night Sherman Adams and I walked down to the Odd Fellows' Hall where the orchestra was tuning up. He was more than I had dared hope for on the train journey home from school. He even negotiated the intricate steps of the square dances with such ease that I suspected he knew more about them than he had let on. As I entered the house after saying good night I had a feeling that it might be a pretty good summer after all.

Sherman had other interests, I learned as the days went by. On the occasional visits he made to our house during the next few weeks I discovered he was taking his new job very seriously. He was generally too tired to go out in the evening. Everyone worked Saturdays, so that left only Sundays and an evening now and then for finding a little fun in that very quiet countryside. That he was not serious about any of the other girls in nearby towns whom he called on now and then made me feel a little better. And when, later, he came to Belmont on all his time off I was quietly overjoyed.

One particular day Sherm drove me to Hanover, New Hampshire, to show me the college that had meant so much to him. We returned to that lovely Dartmouth campus again later in the summer to attend a service in the church where as a student he had sung in the choir.

When the Belmont people found out Sherm had a wonderful baritone voice he was invited to sing at a Baptist service. The years he had spent as a boy soprano in St. Stephen's Episcopal Church in Providence, Rhode Island, where his family lived, had rather weaned him away from the Baptist hymns that he had heard almost as soon as he first opened his eyes in the little corner bedroom of his grandfather's parsonage in East Dover, Vermont, and when he finally agreed to take part in a Belmont service it wasn't any Baptist hymn that he charmed his audience with—it was Gounod's "Ave Maria." It was the first time I had heard him sing, and I was deeply impressed.

I knew very little about classical music but when my aunt Ella, who spent her summers in Belmont, was enthusiastic about Sherm's singing, I was delighted, for my aunt Ella knew all about such things. It was in her house that I had first heard an operatic recording, although I had been introduced much earlier to classical records in my sister Edna's home. Aunt Ella had bought one of the first little victrolas and played her records over and over.

My mother loved to sit with Aunt Ella and listen to excerpts from *Lucia* and other operas. Father wasn't so interested. He generally thought of an errand he had to do, or he would find a rocker on the far end of the porch and light up one of his 7-20-4 cigars. When, somewhat later, Mother finally succeeded in persuading him to buy a victrola, it was with the promise that he wouldn't have to listen to any of "that stuff." So Mother had to be careful about choosing the first four records. "Oh, Promise Me" and "Humoresque," "Liebestraum" and "Berceuse" were all we had for a number of months. Father wasn't much impressed with her selections but eventually came to tolerate them. His favorite music had always been any of Stephen Foster's melodies. He was greatly pleased when someone presented him with a record called "Cohen on the Telephone." As soon as any visitor arrived, especially kinfolk, he would wind up the little motor in the oak box and settle down in his chair with a satisfied grin on his face. I am sure he got a kick out of playing it often, for he knew it bothered his wife.

When Sherm realized his kind of music would find at least a couple of ready listeners in our house he brought up some of his records and we played them when Father was working in his shop. Sherm had, as a boy and later as a college student, been a charmed listener in the grand era of opera. He was an accomplished pianist even during his high school days and that training together with the musical education he had received as a choirboy strongly colored the rest of his life.

The blue skies of June gave way to the thunderstorms and the clatter of mowing machines of July's sultry days. August came hot on July's heels but with what seemed like a lessening of pace. The hay was nearly all in. The flies kept up their vigil by the screen doors of the kitchens, and their buzz and the hum of other insects only added to the quietness of the little village. Everybody felt relaxed. There didn't seem to be any sign of hurry anywhere. Even the white sails of a boat in the middle of the lake seemed to have given up hope of interesting the light breezes that now and then came near enough only to tease a little. The store steps were empty, and up in the cemetery on the hill there wasn't a sign of movement except for an occasional flutter of the faded American flags on the soldiers' graves. The only noise that softly staccatoed the tranquillity of those late-summer days was the even tap-tap-tap of a hammer as someone, not too far away, replaced worn-out shingles on a barn roof.

The idyllic summer passed quickly. There would never be another summer like it. First things became past experiences to be relived again in days to come—but only in memory.

September came, and with it the feeling of aloneness I always felt as the last of the summer boarders and friends left. It was only a fleeting sensation, however, a sort of hang-over from all previous years. It was different now. I would be going back to Northfield Seminary—and I wouldn't have to go by train. Sherm would drive me back in the Studebaker roadster he had recently bought.

Our first trip in that auto had been to the Rutland County Fair. It was my idea. Sherm had never been to a county fair and I thought he didn't enjoy it as much as I did. In fact he seemed to get the most pleasure out of watching me have fun. We tried a few of the chance places along the midway and he won a doll, which he quickly handed to me; I am sure he had never, even remotely, envisioned himself walking along the midway of a fair loaded down with the ludicrous loot that is generally collected. I came to realize as time went on how foreign anything of that nature was to his make-up. He had early been introduced to a way of life that emphasized holiness, duty, and application. His grandfather, the Reverend Cyrus Sherman, with whom Sherm had spent his summers in the East Dover parsonage, saw to that.

Sherm's first job as a youngster was down at the water mill below his grandfather's house. He was well pleased with himself for earning a penny a hundred for piling chair stock. If he got in ahead of the other boys—and when there was enough water in Rock River —he could earn as much as fifteen cents a day.

There was "a pretty good pool up about a hundred yards from the mill." It was there that "old man Perkins, frock coat and all, baptized his flock, as the tails of his coat floated out on the water with the current." Sherm's grandmother had heard all about her young grandson's joining the Episcopal church in Providence and of his singing in the choir, and the next summer when he came to spend his vacation in the little Vermont village where he had been born she took him down to the bank of the pool. "The Baptizing Hole" it was called by many of the local folks. As the very old lady and the very young man stood on the grassy bank watching the solemn gathering waist-deep in the cool waters, the grandmother said to the boy at her side, "Don't you think that's a little more like baptizin' than getting a little water sprinkled on your head!"

Then there were Marcus Adams and Sarah, his wife—Sherm's grandparents on his father's side. "They had more children than religion—thirteen that lived to grow up, mostly boys." But the time came when Grandmother Adams felt the need of "gettin' religion." Old Mark didn't care whether she prayed or not—he continued to take a dim view of religious matters and Sarah's new interest amused him. The farm and the necessity of keeping his large family provided for took up all his time and attention.

Old Mark had a little fun once in a while when the right kind of situation presented itself. He was a great hand to bet. He'd bet on the weight of sheep, or when the ice would go out in the spring, or just about anything. One hot summer day he and four of his boys were on top of a load of hay, coming around the corner by Halliday's store. Mark cramped the wagon too hard and the whole thing tipped over, burying one of the boys—the rest jumped free. When Mark saw one of his boys was missing he yelled excitedly to his son Herb, "Betcha five dollars, by God, it killed him—take my bet?"

Old Mark lost his bet, but the story went down in the annals of East Dover.

By the end of the summer I was not at all eager to return to the Seminary. Sherm was responsible for that feeling. He was also responsible for my promise to work hard at the piano as well as my other studies. I knew my limitations and by that time I also knew his strong feeling about doing things right and I doubted whether I would be able to measure up to his standards of perfection.

On the day I was to leave, my suitcases and boxes were stowed in the Studebaker. The family would be glad, I was sure, to have me safely back within campus limits. The busy summer had been hard on them. Along with all the work connected with the care and entertainment of the summer boarders they had the added worry of me. My brothers and sisters had not had an auto to take them hither and yon for an evening of fun. It was a new experience for my parents to have a child disappear down the road in a cloud of dust with a young man and know she wouldn't be likely to return for several hours. But Sherm was always considerate of Mother's anxiety. He seldom failed to tell her just where we were going and when we could be expected back. She came to have faith in him as a good companion for her youngest child but just the same I think she was glad to see me going back to school.

It wasn't customary in those days for a seminary student to be returned for a new semester by a young, attentive male escort. Parents, brothers and sisters were very much in evidence—even aunts, uncles and cousins—but to be brought back by a beau was most untraditional. In fact, a few years earlier it would have been considered extremely improper.

The approach of a young man anywhere near a girls' dormitory always caused a flurry of excitement. I had taken this into consideration when I planned our arrival. Wanting to show off my beau and the new Studebaker roadster to as many as possible, I directed Sherm to drive to the south entrance of East Hall. It was as I had hoped. Since it was late in the afternoon, most of the girls had already returned and the steps and the white wooden railing of the large veranda were crowded with a gay, chattering flock of excitable femininity.

I could hardly wait for the squeals that I knew would be forthcoming as soon as my friends spotted me getting out of the car. It was a supreme moment. I had set the stage the best I knew how— and I couldn't wait for the audience to get their first look at my leading man. (That I would be "props" manager and, to some degree, public relations agent, as over the years the show went on, never occurred to me then.)

After leaving my luggage in the hall, we returned to the car. I tried to think of something to talk about to prolong the period before saying good-by, but it wasn't any use. I knew it was nearly time for the warning bell for dinner. All of a sudden, with a look of determination which I was to become well acquainted with, Sherm said, "Good-by," and then gave me a boyish grin. He turned on the ignition, shifted into low gear, and the car wound slowly down the long driveway. I climbed the long steps toward weeks of studies, discipline and girls, girls, girls.

iv

And Then We Were Married

During our visits to the Dartmouth College campus earlier in the summer Sherm had told me about the day he first arrived in Hanover. The Reverend Cyrus Sherman had steered the Model T Ford to the side of the road at College Hall, facing the campus. Then he set the hand brake and slowly stepped to the ground. It had been a long trip for an old man, nearly seventy-five miles. It was early afternoon on a lazy September day. Across the street the rocking chairs on the porch of the inn were all filled, and the railing was well sprinkled with students. It was Registration Day for freshmen at Dartmouth College.

The Reverend Mr. Sherman had brought his grandson, Sherman Adams, up from East Dover, Vermont, to start his college career. A steamer trunk and a few dollars was all the new freshman had, along with his credentials from Hope High School in Providence. With these in his hand he went in search of the Administration Building. He had made no formal application; he simply arrived, presented his high school record, and received a handshake and a welcome from the new president, Ernest Martin Hopkins.

At seventeen Sherm was well equipped with a studious mind, a love for the out-of-doors, and a better-than-average baritone voice. The ability to get things done even at that youthful age soon became apparent to those who knew him.

He was brown from a summer's work in the hay fields near his grandfather's home. His slightness of frame belied his ability to take on any job. He was wiry and very fit.

After registering he looked up his room. Finding his new quarters quite bare, he went in search of secondhand furniture.

"It didn't take me long!" he later told me. "I found a rickety desk and two old chairs and I was all settled!"

Sherm hadn't been on the Hanover scene long before someone asked him if he was going to try out for the Glee Club. He said he guessed he would and in a short time he appeared at Dr. Clapp's studio for a tryout. The professor sat down at the piano and struck a C.

"Which way are we going?" he asked. "Up or down?"

"Down," was the answer.

The professor went on to strike the notes B, and A, and G, and F, and Sherm followed him—down to low C.

The professor smiled and said, "Come around to the next rehearsal!"

The first time Sherm sang with the Glee Club on tour was in New York, and he has always enjoyed watching the expression on listeners' faces when he tells them that he made his debut in Carnegie Hall; the explanation that it was with quite a sizable group of other boys follows later.

Right after his Commencement in 1920, which followed four years of hard study and activity in several organizations, particularly in the Dartmouth Outing Club, Sherm tossed his diploma into a large wooden chest which was already quite full of an assortment of items, including winter clothes, a couple of old trail markers, some puttees— a souvenir of his Marine training at Parris Island in 1918—and a bulging scrapbook with the Dartmouth seal on the cover. The scrapbook contained, among the usual clippings, pictures, ticket stubs, and dance programs, numerous concert programs, reminders of evenings at the opera when singers like Caruso, Scotti, Alda, Schumann-Heink and others were thrilling audiences everywhere.

With his few belongings Sherm left immediately for the summer's work. The Appalachian Mountain Club had again hired him to build and clear trails in the White Mountains of New Hampshire, as it had in other summer vacations during his college career. His principal contribution, an A.M.C. member later told me, was in locating and opening the south part of the Kinsman Ridge trail from North Kinsman Mountain to Lost River. "The work was supervised by a member of the club but Sherm was always given much of the credit for the location of the trail and, of course, the actual clearing of the trail was done by him. As a matter of fact," he added, "Adams' reputation as a good trail man persisted for many years with later members of the trail crew. If a man felt that he had done a particularly good job, he would say that 'Sherm Adams couldn't have done it better.' "

Most of his work that first summer after graduation was near the village of Lincoln, a paper mill town with extensive logging operations. The possibility of a job for the future in that kind of country interested him, and on one of his trips into the village he decided to see if there might not be an opening for him somewhere. He was told that Martin A. Brown was the man to see. Mr. Brown, when approached, told Sherm yes, there was a job he could have—one that it was hard to find anyone to take—a job as a member of the "runner crew."

Sherm accepted on the spot, and in September found himself in Boston rounding up men to work in the woods. Until the following January he "ran" men out of Boston to feed the lumber camps in Lincoln and Beebe River, New Hampshire, Eagle Lake in Maine, and Healdville, Vermont, making two or three trips a week with groups he had rounded up. If he had men to deliver in Healdville, he would usually take them up on the afternoon train. As the train neared the station early in the evening, Sherm would herd his charges into the vestibule, and as the train came to a stop would encourage them to get off. They would be taken into custody by the foreman of the Black River Lumber Company and Sherm would continue on to Rutland, where he boarded the midnight train back to Boston.

As a rule the men were fairly easy to handle. Occasionally there would be one who wasn't entirely sure he wanted to be included on the excursion. One evening in deep winter, the engine of "the eight-o'clock" train was winding its way up the steep grade toward the Healdville station. Its whistle sounded for many miles across the frozen and quiet countryside. Sherm had all his little group assembled —or so he thought. Counting them off just to make sure, he found that two were missing. As the train began to slow down for the stop, Sherm ran through the train and found the missing men hiding in the vestibule next to the baggage car. The train had just started to move away from the station when Sherm opened the door and pushed the two dissenters off into a snowbank; then he jumped and landed on top of them—"and that they didn't like," he later told me. The men had planned to "jump their fare" and get to Rutland.

A few of the men who found themselves in the woods, either by intent or by persuasion, stayed all winter. Then there were those who didn't last overnight. Some had never been out of Boston, and some had never seen a spruce tree or a sawmill, or had more than a speaking acquaintance with an ax. Many of the best men were from Lithuania, Russia, and Poland, men who had learned how to work, as had others of French, Irish, and Italian origin. There were tough and trouble-some men, and there were kind and co-operative ones too. Many couldn't read or write, and in some instances their names were some-thing they had dreamed up.

Lumber camps often had three shifts—one with men arriving, one with men working, and the third with men leaving. Sherm's job for a number of months was to keep them coming. He must have im-pressed his boss, for late in the spring of 1921, Mr. Brown asked him if he would like to do some scaling at the Healdville operation. Be-cause of the spring slump the company had decided to close the em-ployment office in Boston.

Sherm had been getting $40 a week while "running" men. The new job offered only $75 a month, with room and board, but he was glad of a chance to get out of the city and into the woods and lost no time in checking out of his little room in Boston and settling down in the company house in Healdville.

Arthur Estey was a scaler at the Healdville operation and he also worked in the mill when he was needed. He and his wife, and numerous small children, went to live in the company house near the sawmill a few months after Sherm was made manager. Arthur's wife, Leona, had come into my life much earlier. She had been a pink-cheeked girl of eighteen when she went to work for my mother the summer I was born. Her pleasant disposition and diligence had made her a favorite of Mother's, and when I was christened I was given the middle name of Leona.

As scaler, Sherm spent the daytime up on the mountain near the camps, or where the crews were yarding logs, or at the mill. Not many months later he was offered the job of treasurer and that work he took care of in the evenings. It must have been quite a change for a former choirboy, student of music, and grandson of a Baptist preacher, to find himself in his early twenties working with men some of whom were twice his size and in some cases with many times his experience. Not only working with them but in charge of them.

Quiet and studious by nature, he must have found it necessary to appear tough. He had always had great determination and if he tackled a job he finished and did it well. It is not surprising that over a period of years the day-after-day supervision of the rough-hewn and sometimes unpredictable lumberjacks would work changes in a man like Sherm. The boy who had diligently practiced at the piano hour after hour was now having to prove he could be just as tough as the toughest lumberjack, and as the years passed, his natural gentleness and light touch were more and more overshadowed by the brusqueness and inflexibility called forth by the heavier and heavier demands on his abilities. He talked to the men in the kind of language they were familiar with. He said little but what he said they understood. There was seldom any letup. Holidays were workdays and very often Sundays also. There were no regular vacations—ever. If work let up, he might take a few days for a quick trip somewhere.

As a youngster, and especially during his teens, he was undoubtedly somewhat sensitive about his size. With his overabundance of drive he must have wished that he had the build of an athlete. Perhaps he even envied those with a more imposing physique. Then when the opportunity came to take charge of a group of big, husky men with at least the appearance of brute strength, he could only match and conquer by his obsession for getting a job done, no matter how tough it was. Time and again he could call on his abundant storehouse of energy when giants twice his size were demanding a rest.

Sherm delighted in exhibiting his ablity to outwalk and outwork any who thought they were a match for him. There were few who tried to best him. His reputation spread fast.

There were others who had a great respect for Sherm in those earlier days. One of them was the fellow who, during prohibition, had a still in the nearby hills. He let it be known on several occasions, with a noticeable degree of admiration, that Adams was the only one who had been able to find his place of business. That was one of Sherm's problems—finding out where the lumberjacks were getting their moonshine.

Many days were something more than just hard. One abnormal winter there wasn't any snow in the woods until well into January, and there were a million feet of logs to get out before the snow left. Sherm scoured the countryside for enough teams to get the job done. Finally he located the thirty teams and sleds needed and they went to work, making two trips a day. By mid-April, when the snow left, the logs were all down off the mountain.

And then there was the day when Sherm arrived back at the cookhouse just before supper—and found no meal ready for the hungry men who would soon be coming in. What he did find was a cook—drunk again. Sherm grabbed the bottle and poured what remained down the sink. The cook lost no time—even in his partial stupor. Picking up a dish he dashed outside the building to catch what he could as the liquor trickled out the end of the open pipe.

There were intervals of crisp enjoyment too. When the conditions were good, Sherm would take his skis up the mountain to whatever job he was working on and when it was time to head back to camp he would go whizzing down those icy logging roads "about a mile a minute." The road from Camp No. 2 was his favorite run.

That rough and busy life was what Sherm returned to after he had said good-by to me at Northfield Seminary. My days that followed were simply those of a schoolgirl—a schoolgirl, I will have to admit, who knew little about applying herself with any degree of diligence to the task of studying.

My room that particular year was on the south side of East Hall. When the window was open, during the afternoon and evening, my mind was often distracted from my algebra and English assignments by the strains of some of Sherm's favorite compositions. I had a time for piano practice too, for I had promised Sherm I would work harder in order to be able to accompany him when he was invited to sing. I tried to improve, and to some extent I did, but I never attained the degree of perfection he hoped for.

I had been back at school only a few weeks when I saw the familiar roadster winding slowly up the drive to East Hall. I knew Sherm would be trying to spot me among the groups of girls who were also waiting to see him. Not many young men were allowed to visit students. Only the older girls could "entertain" during certain hours—under chaperonage—on specific days.

Sherm had written that he hoped I could go for a ride with him when he came to see me. He didn't realize that would be about as impossible as my getting an A in music. Of course, if we took a teacher along we could take a short trip and that was what we decided to do. I went in search of one of the younger instructors who said she would be glad to go with us. We dutifully drove her to a store where she said she had an errand to do. And we dutifully waited, while discussing the more interesting prospect of driving off without her. For a Dartmouth graduate to be chaperoned every minute while calling on his girl was a bit unusual. Sherm didn't enjoy those gatherings in the parlor of East Hall, especially if some other couple had got there first and taken over the window seat in the far corner of the room. I didn't either but I could be happy simply knowing he was there.

As Christmastime drew near, I crossed each day off the calendar. In some of his letters Sherm had hinted at a surprise, and Mother had said something about a surprise too. In one letter Sherm suggested that the surprise was "terrible," and that perhaps I shouldn't come home at all. The next letter gave me reason to believe that I would love it.

At last the day arrived. The platform at the station was crowded with excited girls, some waiting for the southbound train and others, like me, anxiously watching for the northbound engine to come in sight. When I reached Mount Holly station, Tad Priest was there to meet me. I knew how happy the folks would be to have me back. The weeks had been lonesome for them, even though Sherm had been a frequent visitor. Many Sundays he had skied over from Healdville, four miles away, to visit my family and have dinner with them.

I hadn't been in the house very long before someone came up onto the porch. Mother knew it was Sherm. I hadn't expected him so soon. He came in out of the winter day's early darkness to the 25-watt brightness of the winter kitchen. It had been a long time since he had held me close and now he wrapped his arms around me as I buried my face in the coonskin collar of his brown corduroy jacket.

Finally he asked if I wanted to see the surprise, saying I would probably want to go back to school right away. Mother looked pleased, so I wasn't at all worried.

Leading the way out to the woodshed, Sherm held the lantern high. I saw two adorable Eskimo puppies. I was delighted. To think I was to have *two* puppies all my own! Sherm had found out during the first few weeks he had known me that I was very fond of animals, always wanting to bring home stray dogs and cats.

Getting the puppies was only one of the many endurance tests that Sherm put himself through over the years. Early December was extremely cold but nevertheless he had borrowed Dan Fenn's horse and sleigh and invited another millworker to go along for the ride. With a lantern under the robe to help keep them warm, they drove nearly twenty miles to North Clarendon to pick up the puppies— and then turned around and drove the same distance back and left the puppies with my mother. Father was willing to let her have complete charge of them—he had had too many unpleasant experiences with animals. He never forgot the time our ram butted him into the grain barrel as he was trying to get out the last measureful, and the time he traded for a horse, for little or nothing, which promptly ran away with him. There had been numerous other unpleasant experiences with cats, dogs, horses, and sheep over the years and Father wasn't going to get mixed up with a couple of Eskimo puppies.

Evenings and Sundays during that Christmas holiday we went for sleigh rides under a sparkling sky along country roads or we snow-shoed across the cold whiteness of the fields and pastures and over the hills. But many evenings we spent around the cozy fire in the living room, reading or listening to records.

Sherm decided some of those hours afforded a good chance to im-prove my acquaintance with the classics—especially those he was particularly fond of, so I obediently sat on the Chippendale sofa beside him as he read from the first book he had selected. It didn't hold my interest; I watched the flickering flames of the fire and was miles away in thought most of the time as, in his wonderful voice, he covered page after page. But the evening came when he thought it was time to question me to see how much I had absorbed. I could remember almost nothing. Exasperated at my lack of co-operation, he immediately opened the door of the stove and without a word threw in the book. The first book-burning in Belmont, very likely. Later, we bought another copy of the book—Ballantyne's *Ungava*.

At the end of my vacation I returned again, by train, to the Seminary. I tried harder to concentrate, I practiced my piano lessons with greater industry, but the letters I received from Sherm were undoubtedly the only bit of scholarly wisdom that I fully absorbed. They were generally brief and in beautiful order.

By the time St. Patrick's Day arrived I was home again for vacation. Sherm seemed to like the brand of Irishness I possessed and appar-ently he thought it was a good day to do something special. He had gone to Rutland and asked that I meet him at the evening train. That he had gone to Rutland to buy an engagement ring never entered my mind. And when he put it on my finger later that evening I was a deeply thrilled seventeen-year-old.

Sherm was to be sent to Lincoln, New Hampshire, the following summer. His days in Healdville were over, for the Black River Lumber Company was about to close its books for good. The timber on Lud-low Mountain had been used up.

We decided to be married that summer, and I went back again to the Seminary for the final term, wearing the diamond and fervently wishing my school days were already over.

We were married in the Baptist church in Belmont. My sister Kathleen, an accomplished seamstress, had made my wedding dress and fashioned my veil. Classmates from the Seminary and a cousin were bridesmaids, Sherm's sister was maid of honor, and one of his college friends was best man. I walked down the aisle with Father, as the organist pumped away on the old Estey organ. The man waiting for me beside the former Bishop of Vermont was the only person I was conscious of. He looked different, somehow. The first chance I had after the ceremony, as we greeted friends in the vestibule, I asked my husband what had happened to his hair.

"I cut it," he said.

As I learned afterward, he had cut it himself. When Leona Estey saw what he had done, she was exasperated and wanted to know what he "had gone and done that for just before he was going to get married." Sherm said it was the season—he "always" cut his hair short for the hot weather and working in the woods—and besides it suited a life of servitude. So he had taken a pair of shears and cut as far back as he could reach—unconventional maybe, but very comfortable.

Following the small reception in the living room of the house where I was born, we started on our honeymoon in the Studebaker roadster. We had almost a week before Sherm had to begin his new work for the Parker-Young Company in Lincoln, where we were to live for a few weeks in the hotel until the house across the street was ready for occupancy. Now he was to show me the wonderful mountains of New Hampshire which he had come to love. He still had a great deal of respect and admiration for the Green Mountains of Vermont, our native state, but the rugged, above-timber peaks of the White Mountains offered more of a challenge. He had already climbed all the major mountains and many of the smaller ones. During his Dartmouth Outing Club days and when he was doing work for the

Appalachian Outing Club, he had often made record-breaking trips over the trails, frequently alone.

Ours wasn't the "breakfast in our room" type of honeymoon I had heard about but certainly didn't expect. I had known Sherm long enough to learn that a new day was a specific challenge and he couldn't wait to get going. We were among the first to appear for breakfast at the inns where we stayed, and we were ready for our evening meal long before closing time; and we were glad to retire early after the exhausting days of hiking and riding over the dusty mountain roads.

Early in the week we had visited Fadden's Store in North Woodstock. Sherm insisted that I have a proper pair of hiking boots and Fadden's would be the place to find them. High-laced affairs they were, and with wool knickers and sweaters they completed the sensible attire for a female hiker in that era. Sherm had started early to see that I was well shod in order to keep up with him. (After we had been married a few years I learned to take along a pair of walking shoes whenever I started on a trip with Sherman Adams. I might think I was headed for a sedate convention, but if, on the way, we came anywhere near a battlefield it was off with the high heels and on with the low.)

Sherm thought we should climb at least one mountain on our honeymoon, and a good one, he decided, would be Mt. Osceola. So we found the road that followed the Mad River up to Waterville Valley. The day we had chosen was a real mountain day. As far as the eye could see there were mountains in every direction. It wasn't as cool as I should have liked it to be for a stiff climb; however, I had had little chance to show Sherm what a good hiker I thought I was, and I had every intention of keeping up with him even while I entertained some doubt that I could. Nor was I too pleased that he had invited another hiker who was staying at the inn to accompany us. Along with the overabundance of black flies, I considered him just a little unwelcome.

I've never forgotten that first White Mountain climb, and last autumn when my husband took off for the top of Osceola with numerous grandchildren and neighbors' small fry, I said, "I'll meet you on the other side of the mountain with the car." I've climbed many mountains, lots of them higher than Osceola, but none that left such a lasting impression of swarms of murderous black flies and a relentless sun.

One morning following that first Osceola trip we took the road to Lost River, one of the state's best known tourist attractions. On the way we stopped to look at Indian Leap, by Agassiz Basin. Indian stories had always fascinated me, and the story connected with that formation of rocks—of how the braves used to jump across the high place above the swirling waters—delighted me. Long before we married, Sherm had given me a picture of himself on snowshoes—standing on the huge snowdrift that bridged the space between the rocks. Indian Leap would always bring back memories of that exuberant youth on snowshoes—full to the top of his knitted cap with the joy of the out-of-doors. He was laughing, but the stance he held long enough for the click of the camera shutter indicated that every muscle was waiting impatiently to take off.

At Lost River we donned "coveralls" for an exhaustive inspection of every cave and tunnel, and later in the day on our way to Franconia Notch we found a welcome relief from the day's heat in the damp, cool shadows of the Flume Gorge. The many different mosses clinging to the cliffs dripped beads of moisture onto the stream far below. Innumerable crevasses sheltered ferns. The boardwalk and steps were soaked in places by the brook in its frantic effort to get out into the sunlight again. Old Mrs. Guernsey, if she could return out of the deep past, would find the "pretty place" quite different from the way it looked when she discovered it while searching for a lost cow. That was a long time ago—when Indian moccasin tracks could be found and when the brook was abundantly blessed with brown trout.

Following a winding path through the deep woods we came to The Pool, and glanced down on its beauty from high on a rickety bridge which vibrated with every step we took. Sherm led the way down to the water's edge where we were surrounded by cool mist and secluded shadows. He knelt and caught a handful of the chilled water—he never could resist a chance to sample the streams he came across in the woods.

Later, as the sun sank behind the Great Stone Face, we looked up from the shadows of the Notch to that noble profile whose awesomeness has hushed boisterous tourists into quietness and evoked in others an uncontrollable desire to put on paper the thoughts and feeling inspired by that handiwork of God.

As we continued slowly on we passed the Profile House on the west side of the Notch. It was an old and dignified landmark that had welcomed guests and travelers back in the stagecoach days and later when the first cars steamed and toiled up the curving gravel road. It was near dinnertime, but the celebrated hospitality of the impressive Profile House was not for us. Sometime, perhaps, but right then it certainly was not within the limited means of a young woodsman and his bride.

Love, I found, could get along just so long without food. Sherm was beginning to feel the same emptiness, and we decided it was about time to start looking for an inn. Our search ended almost as soon as we entered into the village of Franconia. A neat large frame house, guarded by tall pines and just across the road from Gale River, attracted us and we turned the Studebaker into the driveway.

While we were eating, fire engines screamed past. Then more and more cars and fire engines, all heading in the direction from which we had recently come. It was a large fire, as we soon found out—another old landmark was being quickly consumed by wind-swept flames. We would never be able to enter the Profile House; in a few hours all that was left of the big hotel and numerous cottages was smoking ruins.

The Lincoln Years

On August 6 the five-minutes-of-seven whistle at the paper mill blew as usual, followed by the seven-o'clock blast. Our life in Lincoln had officially started. That whistle would, for a great many years, remind me of my housewifely duties. As the years went by, those early morning toots ceased to bother us—we had already been up for some time. But to the ears of a very young and new bride that unfamiliar sound was not welcome. It reminded me that I was now on my own for a long day—the honeymoon was over.

I felt terribly alone in my new surroundings. I didn't know a soul. After making much of the housekeeping of our one room on the third floor of the Lincoln Hotel, and unpacking some of our wedding gifts, I tried to think what I might do to help pass the time until Sherm returned at noon.

My husband had left the car for me to use but I didn't care about going for a ride by myself. Finally I decided I would find the company store and buy the tube of toothpaste Sherm had asked me to get, and I would stop at Susie Sharon's house and leave some laundry for her to do.

Sherm had shown me where Susie lived and on the way to the store I knocked at her door. It was wonderful, I thought, to have the laundry done without any effort on my part. Still, I couldn't get rid of a sort of guilty feeling that I should be doing it myself.

Susie finally answered my knock. She looked me over without a word; so this was that young Adams' new wife what was living up at the hotel. Susie, I found out in time, never greeted anyone with open arms, nor with anything akin to warmheartedness. When someone appeared at her house with a bundle of laundry she begrudgingly opened the door and gave no greeting—just looked through her visitor with a somewhat disdainful air. She was seldom sure she could do the work but she'd see.

Early I decided I'd try to get Susie warmed up. I showed an interest in her house, or at least what I could see of it with newly ironed shirts and linens hanging from every available spot, praised her work, and admired the tubs of flowers that filled her tiny yard and which were, apparently, her only joy. The old washtubs of geraniums and petunias brought us to a better understanding of each other. We grew to be good friends.

Having disposed of the laundry with instructions *not* to starch my husband's shirts, I walked on to the company store. The August sun was well above Loon Mountain and was already warming the cement sidewalk. It was going to be a hot day.

I glanced down toward the station. The train had just arrived. Perhaps the mail would be sorted, I thought, by the time I had bought the toothpaste.

Mounting the steps of the Parker-Young Company general store I had to step around several millworkers, men whose shift came later in the day. For them the store steps were a place to gather while settling world affairs and waiting for the mail to be sorted.

As I left the store my ears caught the sounds so typical of a paper mill town. Steam was rushing upward from the digester stacks of the mill across the street. Number 5 engine was busily traveling up and down the tracks in the yard. The largest smokestack of all was sending out a cloud of black smoke which trailed into nothingness as it vanished over Loon Mountain to the southeast.

I smelled the accumulation of sulphur fumes, the coal-burning engine, the sawdust and the pungent odor of the softwood logs. Living in a mill town was going to be a new experience for me but I already could tell I was going to like it.

Descending the steps of the store I tried to look nonchalant as I glanced at the little silver watch Sherm had given me the previous Christmas. I always had such a nice feeling when I looked at it. Except for the gold thimble that Mother had given me on my sixteenth birthday, it was the nicest gift I had ever received. I hoped the watch would suggest it was time for the mail to be ready, but mostly I was dreading weaving my way among the step-sitters. After I got out of hearing they would probably make some remarks about the girl Sherm Adams had married. I was glad when I had negotiated the descent and was on the way to the post office. But there again I found groups standing around talking and waiting. I felt like exhibit A. Having grown up in a small village I knew perfectly well that I was spotted as a newcomer at once, and wished I were back in the seclusion of the little hotel room on the third floor.

There wasn't any mail for the Sherman Adamses. Not even a card from Mother. Well, I had just seen her the day before—there hadn't been quite time for mail to arrive from Belmont.

I walked back to the hotel feeling somehow that I belonged in Lincoln. My first errand at the one department store had accomplished more than I thought it would. The buying of the toothpaste hadn't, however, helped to make me feel less lonely, and so, reverting to a childish habit, I had also bought a roll of cinnamon Necco wafers. After closing the door of our room behind me, I placed the toothpaste on the little shelf above the washbowl where Sherm would be sure to see it. Then I looked around the room at our new possessions, which were mostly wedding presents. The painted wooden candlesticks added something to the bureau. The Maxfield Parrish print wasn't hung yet and neither was the large photograph of the Great Stone Face. The new toaster with the flop-down sides still had a shiny, virginal look. Sherm's wooden chest was in the corner—still unexplored. There were still some wedding gifts that hadn't been unpacked. Sherm had suggested we leave them done up until we moved across the street to the first floor of the company house.

I went to the one window and held the white scrim curtains aside as I looked down on the service entrance of the hotel. The ice wagon was standing near the kitchen door. The forlorn white horse looked even more forlorn because of the decrepit straw hat which was pulled onto its head. The two ears that protruded through slits in the straw were upright but everything else about the horse seemed to sag. It was getting warmer and little streams of water dropped from the edges of the cart onto the gravel and immediately disappeared.

Turning back into the room, I again looked at my watch. It was ten-thirty. What could I now do to pass the time until noon? Sherm would be back then to eat lunch with me. He would have about three-quarters of an hour before leaving for work again.

Finding nothing to do in our room I went down to the lobby. Mr. Morgan, the manager, was friendly and seemed to sense that I was lonely. He asked me if I had seen much of the village and I told him that I had just returned from the store and the post office.

"Well, I guess you have seen just about everything then." He laughed.

I bought some postcards showing White Mountain scenes and again climbed the two flights of stairs to our room. There I squeezed as many words as possible onto each of the cards. By the time I had finished it was barely eleven-fifteen. Never had I known time to pass so slowly.

Finally I decided to go down to the porch and find a rocking chair near the south end where I could watch for my husband; perhaps he would be early. I settled myself with a magazine and as I disinterestedly turned a page now and then I glanced in the direction of Main Street, longing to see a tanned young man turn the corner and walk toward the hotel.

After I had thumbed through the magazine several times, the twelve-o'clock whistle blew. Men started appearing from the direction of the mill. Tall men, short men, old men, young men, some of them coming up the steps to the hotel, some going on by. I began to get panicky—and then there he was. I didn't know it then but that was the way it would always be. When I needed him most, he would always be there.

"Hi, Bob," was all the greeting I got. It was all I expected. We went to our room, where he washed up—but not until he had taken me in his arms and kissed me. Oh, how good he smelled. He had been in the lumberyard all morning. The sun, sawdust, and pitch had worked together to make him a living part of the out-of-doors. He was the trees, the sunshine, the brooks, and the breeze.

We ate at the long table where other mill and office workers sat. The food was served family style and was good, and plentiful. There was little talking. There was little time for conversation. Nearly everyone was absorbed in the meal and looking forward to a chance to read the daily paper and have a smoke before returning to his afternoon's work.

One by one they left the table and finally we, too, had eaten the last crumb of excellent apple pie, which I thought was almost as good as my mother's. Sherm ran up the stairs to our room for his hat, then he gave me a kiss and was off again. He had not gone very far when the piercing sound of the five-minutes-of-one whistle entered every corner, backyard and inch of that little village between the hills. It entered the room on the third floor where I was alone again for what seemed like an eternity.

I thought of the lake in Belmont and wondered what my friends were doing on such a lovely day. Probably they were off on a picnic, or maybe fishing, or going for a hike, and here I was tied down by a whistle. The man-sized dinner I had indulged in, along with the lazy feeling that the August day encouraged, made me sleepy. The mountain climbing and all the excitement of the previous week probably had something to do with my weariness too. I curled up on the brown metal bed and finished the roll of Necco wafers while I contemplated my newly found way of life. In a few moments I was fast asleep.

Lincoln, the village that has been "home" to us ever since that day, was hewn from the forest in 1892 by a group of approximately one hundred persons from the little community of Zealand, New Hampshire. In horse-drawn lumber wagons they made a 20-odd-mile trek to Lincoln, on the other side of the Pemigewasset wilderness to the southwest.

The leader of those hardy and weather-beaten travelers was James E. Henry—who in later years would be referred to as "old J.E.," the "old man," or "the lumber king." He has been gone many years now but his fame will last for generations. Those who worked for old J.E. knew him to be a hard taskmaster. He was "a foxy old fellow" and "Gorry, you couldn't fool him on horses!" He undoubtedly knew good men when he saw them, too, for the crew that came to Lincoln on that early fall day had all the necessary qualities needed for the vigorous work they were going to do. And about the many tales regarding "the old man's" tightfistedness during his reign as lumber king, those same followers would comment "some's true, some isn't."

Good timber was getting scarce around Zealand and old J.E. had looked down on the Pemigewasset wilderness from the top of his Zealand possessions and decided what he saw looked good. He would move to greener forests. With him were his three sons and his wife—and a gathering of indomitable men including woodsmen, blacksmiths, storekeepers, sawyers, and those who could accommodate themselves to almost any kind of work.

The largest family was James Boyle's. He had left St. Giles, Canada, in 1879 to work as woods boss for J.E., and it was his seven sons, along with other men, who later helped their father clear the site for the village of Lincoln.

Old Jim Doherty also was a necessary member of the hard-working crew that followed J.E. to more abundant timber. And after the village was well established, with a preponderance of Boyles and Doyles—and a smattering of Dohertys—old Jim let it be known that "the B'yles is good people, an' the D'yles is good people, but not a one of 'em has a thing on the D'yertys!" And that's about the way it was with all of that group of men who helped in building the new village; they were all good, hard-working, God-fearing people— intent on earning their small wages in order to take care of their fast-growing families.

Young Jack Boyle had been told about the many mountain goats to be seen around the mountains on the way to Lincoln but "all I see was plinty o' rocks," he told listeners in later years. And when the party reached their destination there was little else to see except forests. There were only three farmhouses in the area which would become the village. The women and children crowded in with the owners of these homes. The men slept wherever they could—under trees, in tents, or in the fields. Old J.E. slept on a mattress on the floor of the harness shop for a while, as soon as it had been built.

All haste was made to put up the necessary buildings before cold weather set in. As soon as the first houses were up the families moved in. There "were no windows, so the squirrels and chipmunks moved in, too, and helped themselves to what they wanted!" As with the Puritans, that first winter was a hard one. There was a lot of cold weather and the snow was five feet deep. But from some of those who endured it we learn that there was plenty to eat and everyone was happy, for everyone was busy and "there wasn't much time for grumbling."

Within a few months land was cleared and streets were laid out. Sawdust from the busy sawmill was hauled in dumpcarts to make the streets less muddy. Two or three pork barrels were placed along the first street in front of the houses to hold water brought from the springs and streams. The sound of the ax and the crosscut and the falling of big trees could be heard climbing higher and higher up the mountains as the little community continued to grow.

The early days of Lincoln—or Henryville as it was called during its beginning—were rugged. There was little time for amusement or relaxation. The hours were long and the pay was small. Many times those working on the railroad wouldn't get home until early morning—"and they were lucky if they got a dollar a day. There was no half-time and no time-and-a-half—them was long, long days," Jack Boyle recalled.

The progress of the new village was sprinkled with adversity—but like the knitting of a healthy broken bone it grew stronger with each affliction. The disastrous fire of 1907 leveled many of the new homes on Main Street and in the upper part of the village. The store and the big barn where the horses were kept—and where the fire started—went in the blaze. The fire roared with the prevailing wind up toward the Pemigewasset wilderness. The rains which fortunately came were all that saved the new evergreen empire for old J.E.

Before the fire there had been an epidemic of typhoid fever because of the lack of sanitation. The new doctor quickly insisted that the town must provide a sewerage system and a better source of drinking water. Another year there was diphtheria. One of the woods camps was full of it. Old J.E. was riding in the engine on one of his inspection trips into the woods. The engineer reached up to a shelf and took down a bottle of whiskey. Old J.E. got pretty excited and wanted to know just what the engineer was going to do with it. "Drink it!" he said. "I don't feel so good—might be I'm agittin' the diphtheria!"

The brakes on those early log trains were set by hand. Coming off the mountain with a heavy load, it was sometimes hard to set the brakes quickly enough. Transportation was in fact still hazardous, perhaps even more so with the coming of the railroads than when the stagecoaches were clattering over the twisting, hilly, rut-filled roads. Old Jerry Johnson and Ira Muzzey were drivers of the first order on the stagecoach run back and forth to the Profile House in Franconia Notch—but each of them tipped over with their coach and broke a leg.

The winters gave plenty of trouble too. Old Billy McGee, driver of the snow-roller from the Woodstock-Lincoln town line to Lafayette Campground would sometimes be gone eighteen hours before he and the six-horse hitch had conquered the lonely stretch of drifts and falling snow. Sometimes, the new water pipes in the village froze. The little school was none too warm. Bad accidents deep in the woods, caused by an ax, or a horse perhaps, sent the doctor hopping the special log train to give first aid, and then, if necessary, to bring the injured back to the little hospital for further treatment.

By the time we arrived in Lincoln it had mellowed and grown less like a frontier town. But life in the woods and at the lumber camps was still rugged and full of tough lumberjacks. There were big heavy-set editions of Paul Bunyan and there were the smaller wiry types. There were good ones and bad ones. And, as in all other woods operations, there was always a group "coming in" and a group "going out." The food, or the lodgings, or the long hours could be the excuse for starting "down the track." More often it was just the desire to go somewhere else.

To keep the numerous camps equipped with a full crew—and to see that those men earned their pay—was for a number of years the job of my husband. I, and others, often wondered how a man with his background found himself in one of the toughest "boss" jobs in the country. All day long it was his business to keep the insatiable mills supplied with a never-ending flow of pulpwood and logs. If he was lucky to get home early enough at night he liked to listen to one of our recorded symphonies—perhaps a Beethoven, or maybe it would be one by Brahms. It was always early to bed, for at five-thirty in the morning our alarm clock would ring. We seldom took an evening off for partying—the days were too long and full of hard work. And it was many years before Sherm took advantage of a holiday. There was always something to check up on, Sundays not excepted. Many were the hours of overtime that were simply part of the job, and there were nights, too, when tractors bogged down, woods horses were sick, timberland fires were raging, floods were menacing the dams, or there were cars to be loaded with pulpwood. As with all outdoor operations, the job often had to be carried on in the most adverse kind of weather and under extremely difficult and trying circumstances. I remember well the night my husband returned from a timber cruising trip into the Hancock Valley. It was during a real cold spell in winter after the unseasonable thawing of the Pemigewasset River, and he had to wade across. He arrived home with his heavy woolen woodsman's pants frozen stiff. I took some heavy-duty shears and slit the frozen trousers; it was the only way he could get them off. Such experiences were in the line of duty. His husky fellow workers soon found out that what Adams was short on in height and breadth he more than made up for in endurance and accomplishment.

Now most of the scars on the mountains where the big timber was removed so many years ago have filled in with fast-growing, less desirable forestation. There are still traces of old logging roads here and there which the elements and time work hand in hand unceasingly to obliterate. Most of the attainable soft woods are gone. Only in high, inaccessible places are there still virgin specimens. These even the woodsmen of a day now past were unable to wrest from their granite-fortified heights. Most of the woods horses have disappeared from the Pemigewasset wilderness, too. Gone, also, is the East Branch and Lincoln Railroad, where the busy little Baldwin, Climax, and Shay engines used to tug and pull at the heavy loads of logs in fall, winter, and spring.

For nearly a year after our marriage we lived on the first floor of the house across the street from the hotel; then we moved into a small house farther up Church Street and next door to the Union church. The second floor of our first home had been occupied by a classmate of Sherm's and his bride. Mary Marden and I started housekeeping together, had our first daughters the following year, and now our grandchildren are having good times in the same village.

Our daughter Jean was born when her sister Marian was barely fourteen months old. With two babies so near the same age, I was busy. My twentieth birthday came just a month after Jean was born, and there were many days when I found it hard to be tied down to the everlasting routine of diapers, formulas, laundry, and the usual house-work. During those days, particularly after being inside the better part of a long winter, I would find excuses now and then to get away. Frequently Mary and I would put our babies into the car and go in search of the signs of spring. We might be looking for arbutus, spring lambs, the last of the sugaring season at some familiar sugarhouse, or perhaps a picnic spot beside a still-swollen stream. We journeyed quite far on some occasions and, as happens when one is completely absorbed, we sometimes lost track of the passage of time—and were late in getting home to prepare the evening meal. It was one of those occasions that gave rise to the story of the garage. That particular story, like many others, has been tossed around for so long that it is hardly recognizable any more. Here are the facts.

My husband, who would have been out in the fresh air since early morning, usually came home tired and hungry. One could hardly blame him for being annoyed when I was late just once too often. He suggested that I stay at home for a while.

The following morning he went to work without leaving the keys to the garage. Whether he meant to be sure that I didn't take to the road that day or whether he forgot, I never inquired. I simply decided that I would take the car out and that I would be back well before he returned.

It was an old garage, with room for two cars. At first I thought I could, with considerable patience, move the car sideways until I could back it out of the adjoining empty stall, but I soon found it couldn't be done. I looked at the lock again. The screws that held it were loose in the well-weathered wood of the doors. I decided upon a new attack. Getting into the driver's seat I gently bumped the rear of the car against the doors. After one or two such proddings the screws holding the lock gave way and the doors swung open. Off we went in search of more springtime, and the car was back in the garage, with the lock in place, well before Sherm returned. I never mentioned the affair to him and to this day I do not know whether he knew the car had been out of the garage, or whether he had meant to take the keys with him—which I think he did.

After living in the little white house for two years we moved into a very large three-storied house on Pollard Road (which in recent years has been made into five apartments). The fifteen spacious rooms, with high ceilings and what seemed like a quarter of an acre of porches, gave me no worries. To have plenty of room, both inside and out, for our fast-growing family was our immediate concern. I did all my own work and I remember especially the fifty-seven windows that I endeavored to clean twice a year.

Our blonde Sally arrived just a few months before we moved into the large house. I remember good old Dr. Burtt appearing at the little white house following my telephone call early in the morning and saying, "Guess you and me better take a little trip down to the hospital."

He helped me down the snowy steps and into his car. Nurse Billings opened the door of the little Lincoln Hospital as we slowly climbed the steps, and the old doctor still had his hand under my arm.

I had not awakened Sherm before leaving. He was sleeping the sleep of a hard-working out-of-doors man. I knew his mother, who had come to help, would look after him and the two little girls.

Sherm always had a way of appearing when I needed him most. I didn't feel that I needed him that night. But I recall very well a time when I was feeling very lonely and far away from everyone whom I loved—except my first baby daughter, then only a few days old. It was late in March and the road familiarly known as the Notch Road, which connected the towns of Lincoln and Franconia, on opposite ends of the Franconia Range of mountains, would not be open until warmer weather had melted the snow. In the Notch proper the drifted snow was still deep and most of the fifteen miles between Lincoln and Franconia could be negotiated only on snowshoes or skis. My husband, who had been with me when the baby was born, decided he had to see us again.

After work he started out on the 21-mile trip on skis, probably not giving much thought to visiting hours at the hospital. The nurses were trying to cheer me up late in the evening when I heard his voice, and then came the unmistakable sounds of his ski boots as he came down the corridor to my room. He had made his way through the trackless Notch, hopped a horse-drawn sled for a few miles through Franconia, and then continued on his skis until he reached the hospital—considerably after visiting hours.

One January, a few years after we moved into the big house, we had extremely cold weather. The thermometer registered 40 or more below zero for several nights. The one radiator in the big kitchen wasn't adequate, even in ordinary winter weather, so we had to be sure to keep a fire in the coal stove overnight.

Whoever "fixed the fire" on one of those very cold nights did a poor job for when I went to the kitchen at 5:30 the following morning the fire was out. I had no idea it had been so cold throughout the night—and I had no idea the kitchen was as cold as it later proved to be. I was used to a cold kitchen until I had the fire going good.

After turning on the electric stove and starting breakfast I got another fire going in the coal stove as soon as I could. A moment later there was a snap and a swish—the pipes to the hot-water tank behind the stove had burst and cold water was pouring out at an alarming rate. Sherm came running at my call and shut off the main water supply, but most of the water in the tank had spread over the floor.

While waiting for their breakfast the three little girls had fun sliding on the fast-forming ice on the kitchen floor. A friend from New Jersey who was visiting us at the time was a wonderful guest, thoroughly amused at the treatment her north country friends were showering her with!

In the spring of 1936 Sherm made a miscalculation which was just short of disastrous. It had to do with a horse. Following the winter's work in the woods, horses belonging to the company were either put out to pasture for several months of reconditioning or were sold, if possible, depending on the qualities, good or bad, of each particular horse. That spring there was a gray horse whose disposition was such that the woods boss thought it best to let someone else have him.

One afternoon, late in March, a man appeared who was interested in buying any of the woods horses that were for sale. He thought the flea-bitten gray horse looked as if it might be something he could use, and questioned Sherm about him. Sherm's answer was to go up to the side of the horse and suggest that it move to show that it was still full of spark. But the horse continued to stand as if in a daze, one rear hip lower than the other and the hoof turned under. Sherm glanced around the yard and spotted a good-sized stick. Walking determinedly back to the horse, he placed a well-aimed whack on its statue-like rear end. The result was fast and accurate. After its lightning-quick action, the horse sauntered off to a likely-looking bunch of the previous summer's grass. But Sherm lay on the ground with a mean-looking red wound in the shape of a horseshoe exactly in the center of his forehead and just above his eyes.

After only thirteen years of married life it was very upsetting to have my husband carried into the house and carefully laid on the couch, his face almost unrecognizable. In an almost inaudible voice he said, "I got kicked, Bob, but I'll be all right!" (For many years he called me Bob—a nickname I had picked up in my early teens.)

As I looked at him and wondered whether he was going to recover, my strength and courage were fortified by the presence of old Dr. Burtt and Nora Parent, the district nurse—a team that was hard to beat in those days. Nevertheless, there were many times while Sherm was recuperating that I worried for fear there might be some lasting trouble as a result of his injury. However, as months passed it became apparent that the healing process had worked miraculously to obliterate the damage to flesh and bone.

During those years in Lincoln while our three daughters and one son were growing up, we encouraged them to become acquainted with the national forests and state parks in our vicinity. With such vast playgrounds, I was seldom at a loss for something interesting for the children to do. I probably should add that I was as much interested in exploring the trails, rivers and mountains as were the children and their friends. I could generally be counted on to overlook any housework that needed attention in favor of the first fishing trip of the season that our son Sam and his friends suggested. Our girls were climbing enthusiasts, especially the two older ones. Sally, the youngest, had to be encouraged to the top of the hills with well-spaced administrations of jelly beans until she reached the ripe climbing age of six.

Each of the four seasons had a particular attraction. It was early springtime when I filled the car with small children and drove to Waterville, where my husband had been busy on the log drive in the Mad River since early in the morning. It was exciting to watch the big head of water, which had been released from the flash dams upstream, come rushing down to flush out the wood and carry it down toward the log-pond in Campton. Sometimes we were invited to join the river drivers for midmorning lunch—a huge meal cooked at a portable camp near the river for hardy and hungry men. The men on the log drive were served four meals, breakfast at 4:30, then the midmorning lunch, another one at 2:00 P.M., and the evening meal at 7:00. I was always up to get my husband's breakfast and Sherm would be home for supper unless some part of the equipment was out of order or there were logs that had to be driven as long as there was light to see by.

Summers passed swiftly with numerous excursions to beaches some miles distant or overnight hikes into the mountains and all the many other things to do that are peculiar to country living.

The days of autumn brought renewed joy—and a fresh determination to add more peaks to our already imposing list of conquered heights. The brilliant foliage, the clear and bracing days, often teased me away from a basketful of ironing or other household chores. To ease my guilty conscience, considering the work left undone, I could only explain that the venture had been worthy from my point of view because it gave the children something to do and added to their out-of-doors experience. It was my firm belief that no one should discourage the gleam in a youngster's eye when he felt the call of a rocky trail up into the clouds or the rippling of a trout brook. It was too bad that Sherm couldn't have joined us more often. The very few times when he did accompany us, the trip was a great deal more worthwhile and enjoyable, for he knew every trail and mountain peak and had a quiet way of passing on his knowledge of the out-of-doors.

While I was growing up in Vermont, winter was near at hand when the wood was piled in the woodshed and the house was banked with a tremendous accumulation of dried leaves and evergreen boughs. There would be a coating of ice on the lake too. The early days of winter in Lincoln were signaled by the cold wind which blew into the valley from the top of Mount Moosilauke to the northwest and by the glistening frost clinging to every twig and limb on the trees high up the mountainsides. It was then we would watch for the skies to become overcast with the soft, quiet clouds that could mean the first snowflakes of the season. How glad I have been that our children could grow up knowing the thrill of the first snowfall in the country— the excitement of sleigh rides, the energy-bursting fun of square dances, and the swift, exhilarating descent of a ski slope.

vi

Politician's Wife

We had been married about sixteen years when my husband decided to enter politics. At the insistence of his boss and the townspeople, he ran for and was elected to a seat in the New Hampshire General Court. The town of Lincoln has always had a predominance of Democrats—and without their votes Sherm, a registered Republican, would never have been launched on a political career.

During the months when the legislature was in session he would drive the seventy-five miles to the State House in Concord every Monday and return to Lincoln on Thursday evening. While he was away I found plenty to keep me busy. I continued to be the chairman of the Red Cross chapter and the leader of the Girl Scout troop which I had been interested in for many years. A more recent addition to my efforts in community service was membership on the school board. And it was during those years that I helped to organize the local chapter of the American Legion Auxiliary.

Occasionally I would go to Concord for special gatherings connected with my husband's work with the legislature. As time went by, he became much in demand as an after-dinner speaker and that meant considerable traveling around the state. Those days were my initiation into the world of politics.

Following the first two years as Representative, Sherm thought he would like to return to the legislature, so in 1942 he made his second bid for the support of the town voters. He again won easily and was later elected Speaker of the House of Representatives. During those months I visited the state capital more often, taking the children on several occasions to the gallery of the House Chamber to watch their father preside over the largest governing body in the world except for the House of Commons in Great Britain. (Within a few years, however, following an amendment proposed at the Constitutional Convention, it was voted that the New Hampshire legislature should not exceed four hundred members.) Sherm's remarkable memory served him well. Seldom was he unable immediately to "recognize" any one of those four hundred and thirty solons—or the town that each one represented.

Those days were the beginning of the banquet circuit which, for the most part, consisted of cold, soggy turkey, canned peas, and the inevitable canned fruit cup, along with a slice of ice cream for dessert. There were, now and then, events at which the menu turned out to be something totally unexpected and delicious. If I was lucky enough, when sitting at the head table, to have an interesting dinner partner all else could be forgiven, but if I had cold turkey on each side of me as well as in front, and in addition had to listen to lengthy speeches, it was a long, long evening.

Another entree which was very popular at that time was ham with raisin sauce. Often we had had it several times within a short period. One evening as we left for a supper and meeting in New London I casually remarked to the Governor, as we made ourselves comfortable in the back seat of the car, "I do hope they aren't having ham with raisin sauce tonight." We arrived at the hall just in time to be seated at the table. As my plate was placed in front of me the Governor said in a voice which I wished had been quieter, "Just what you ordered, Plum!" (I had ceased to be "Bob" some years ago.)

My husband became increasingly interested in government at the state level and I became more and more accustomed to hard chairs for long hours. When on infrequent occasions there was cold turkey on either side of me, I learned that it could generally be warmed up. Luckily there were very few times over many years when I was anything but happy with my dinner partner.

Having spent my whole life in a small village, it was fun to get out to any kind of large gathering around the state. I loved the excitement of the political powwows, the friendliness of the Republican teas, and the bustle and speeches, and new hats at the women's luncheons. Political life seemed fine to me—as long as all I had to do was listen—appear interested—look pleasant—and be ready to go anywhere at any time. The speechmaking I was glad to leave to those more competent.

After two terms as Representative to the General Court, Sherm campaigned for a seat in the House of Representatives in Washington and was elected Congressman from the Second District of the State of New Hampshire. The first real break with what had been our way of life came early in January of 1945, when we packed our car and, with our two youngest children, Sally who was seventeen and seven-year-old Sam, started the 600-mile journey to Washington. At that time our oldest daughter, Marian, was in her first year at the Juilliard School of Music and Jean was a senior at Northfield Seminary (now called Northfield School for Girls). They were already looking forward to vacations and the chance to visit us in Washington.

We had no house to move into on our arrival. We had been promised an apartment, which was not yet ready, so we took rooms in one of the downtown hotels on Pennsylvania Avenue—very handy for the Inaugural Parade of President Roosevelt.

Rationing was in full swing; there was rationing of gas, meat, and among other things there was rationing of hotel rooms. After our allotted number of days the management notified us that our time was up and we would have to leave. Our apartment still wasn't ready and the new Congressman and his family went through a few hectic hours until permission was finally given us to stay another day or two, though we had to move to other rooms.

When we at last did get into our apartment we furnished it with only what was necessary, for we planned to go home as often as we could and had no intention of staying in Washington indefinitely. As for my husband's office—I still remember the many hours when, with my shoes off, I stood on the divan or the backs of the heavy leather-covered chairs to hang the many Currier and Ives "green curtain series" of former Presidents which he felt he must have in his outer room. There were other long hours when I helped the office force address envelopes—though I never did get on the payroll!

I found being the wife of a congressman thoroughly exciting, and like most of the others I joined the Congressional Club, where the wives of congressmen and of other high officials in government fore-gathered. Besides the Friday afternoons, when there were special programs, there were weekly Red Cross surgical dressing classes. I worked with other members on several projects which added thousands of dollars to the club treasury and I found the charming rooms and the friendly atmosphere a delightful place to entertain friends from my home state. But the best part of the club was the lasting friendships that I made. I found the women, who came from all parts of the country, extremely interesting and friendly. I loved to hear the Southern women talk and it wasn't long before I could tell a South Carolinian, a Georgian, or a Texan simply by listening.

While Sherm concentrated on his work, which included member-ship on the House Labor Committee, my special duty was to take care of constituents from New Hampshire. I never tired of driving en-thusiastic visitors down to Mount Vernon or over to the Masonic Memorial in Alexandria, Virginia, or to any of the numerous other national shrines which were on the list of "musts."

I'll never forget one time at Mount Vernon, and I doubt if the constituents whom I was shepherding will either! As we passed through the ancient kitchen of Washington's home, I noticed a chair resembling one of mine at home which had burned places on the back made, so I had been told, by candles that had been placed too close. I wondered if that old chair, just beyond the heavy rope that was stretched across the room, had similar markings and my curiosity was too much for me. I looked around to see if anyone would mind and seeing no one but my two constituents, who were absorbed in other items, I reached across the rope and barely tipped the chair to look at the back. The din, clatter, and pandemonium that resulted transfixed me. My constituents looked at me in horror as much as to say, "Now, what have you done?"

We weren't alone long. A guard whipped into the room, went directly to the chair and changed its position ever so little, and the alarm immediately stopped ringing. I had a few very bad moments. I wondered where he would take me and hoped I would be allowed to go home for the night. I even wondered what Congress would do about it. The guard didn't seem to be interested in my explanation. He looked disdainfully down at me and said, "Maybe that will teach you to leave things alone!" My guests and I continued our tour of Mount Vernon—walking carefully and keeping our hands behind us.

Less harrowing but almost as embarrassing was the day one spring when the State of Virginia had an unexpected syrup season. The luscious liquid didn't appear from any of the maples—it dripped from the electric light fixture on the ceiling of the kitchen in the apartment under ours. The young Australian bride of an Army man was thoroughly surprised to find something that smelled and tasted so good coming from her ceiling light. I was called downstairs to see if I could figure out what was happening. I was as much distressed as she was surprised, for I immediately thought of the glass gallon jar of new maple syrup that my husband had brought back from New England the previous night and placed on the bottom shelf of our kitchen closet, which was directly over her light fixture. My fears were confirmed when I rushed upstairs and saw the cracked jar with only a few inches of golden Grade A syrup left.

On weekends we took the children to the art galleries and the museums. The new National Airport was a favorite place, too, for all of us. Then there were concerts, and on Sundays Sherm sang in the choir of the Washington Cathedral where we worshiped. Living in the capital city was a new and delightful experience but they were tiring years for my conscientious husband.

During his term as congressman he was urged by friends and members of his party back home to run for governor of New Hampshire. I never asked him, but I assumed at the time that he felt he should stay in Washington, now that the voters of the Second District in New Hampshire had shown their approval of him, for at least more than one term. Still, the call to serve as governor was difficult to resist. Sherm was finding the Washington climate hard to adjust to. Air conditioning was almost unheard of at the time, and he was not used to spending the better part of every day in an office. He had no chance for outdoor exercise, and he missed that. He didn't take up golf until a year or two later, when we were back in Concord.

When, at last, he did decide to run for governor, he chose well, for considering the course of events he was in the right spot at the right time to spearhead the Eisenhower Crusade in its earliest stages. One evening during a whirlwind tour for votes he made a speech in one of the little villages in the western part of the state. The night was hot, and hotter still in the upstairs auditorium of a public building, and all the windows were opened. As my husband, in good form and excellent voice, told the gathering why they should vote for him and other Republicans on the ticket, he was gratified by the clapping—more than he had expected. It encouraged him to lengthier and greater praise of the Republican party and the effort that he knew would be made by the local voters at the polls. Just before he ended his speech someone clapped at the wrong place and he suddenly realized with amusement that it was mosquitoes that had been getting most of the attention. They had entered in hordes through the open windows.

He didn't win that first battle for the governorship, but he lost by only a few votes—257, to be exact. After the inevitable recount there were two things to do—find a job and figure out how to win in the next election two years from then.

His job during that period was with the American Pulpwood Association of New York. It was as its representative that he became well acquainted with many members of the Canadian government and men who were connected with the pulp and paper industry in that country.

When the time came to start actively campaigning again he was ready with a strong organization of men and women throughout the state. It was a rugged few months, for Sherm left no loopholes whereby he would stand a chance of losing another election. In fact, we were so completely worn out following the November election that put him in the governor's chair that we even accepted an invitation to sample the hospitality of a well-known hotel at Miami Beach. Ordinarily my husband wouldn't have considered Florida under any conditions—a vacation to him meant mountains and streams, certainly not a plush hotel.

We flew to Miami and were driven to the hotel where, after he had finished unpacking, the Governor-elect fell into a deep sleep, which lasted several hours. It was most unusual for him to be sleeping in the middle of the day—but it was not unusual for him to have decided to win that election at any cost of strength and effort.

After that week in Florida, which, by the way, was one of the few really completely relaxing vacations we ever had, we flew back to New Hampshire to get ready for the opening of the state legislature early in January. The Governor-elect had many problems to work on in the weeks ahead in preparation for his new job. One of those problems he gave to me to try to solve. New Hampshire is one of several states that has no permanent governor's residence. A number of chief executives in the past have had homes in the vicinity of the state capital or within fairly easy driving distance. Our home was seventy-five miles north, too far to commute.

We didn't feel we could afford the kind of place we would have liked, where we could entertain as governor and first lady, and there seemed to be no furnished house in our price range. Finally, after I had searched for weeks, a friend suggested that we look at her mother-in-law's house on Ridge Road. We found it to be conveniently located. Also, it was not too large for me to manage without a maid. The owner obligingly went to live with her son and family and we moved in just a few days prior to the Governor's inauguration.

The 6th of January in 1949 was not one of those clear crisp New England winter days. The clouds hung low and were full of wetness. Still, the doors to the Eagle Hotel in Concord, New Hampshire, swung busily as guests from all corners of the state arrived for the coffee hour. It was Inaugural Day. My husband was about to start his first term as governor of the Granite State.

We left our Ridge Road house and entered the rooms assigned to us in the Eagle Hotel. Early on this Inauguration Day the L. Sherman Adamses from Wellesley, Massachusetts—no relation but practically the same name—sent two huge boxes of gorgeous orchids for the new

Governor's family. Later, when the second inaugural came around, they again generously provided the blooms which they had raised. So, well bedecked with huge white blossoms, I preceded the Governor to the dining room to greet our fifty guests.

The Governor's councilors and their wives, the staff and their wives, and our children, plus many friends, made up the gathering. After being fortified with coffee and pastries, the guests departed for the State House across the street. I was taken into custody by an aide and led the group of councilors' wives to the floor of the House, but not before I had paused at the top of the Capitol steps to watch my husband start his walk from the Eagle Hotel to the Capitol building where he was to deliver his Inaugural Address to the legislature.

The five members of the Governor's Council followed him—all wearing Homburgs, as was he. The Governor had announced that he had no intention of wearing a tall silk hat. As fas as he was concerned, the other gentlemen in the party could wear what they wanted. It was a break with New Hampshire tradition—and one that would affect the style of a Presidential Inauguration in the not too distant future.

After he had delivered his message to the lawmakers, we adjourned to the Governor's chambers, where we stood in line with the councilors and their wives. Former Governors were first in line to greet us; after them came the State House officials, legislators, and old and new friends. It was a rugged hour or so, after which we went back to the hotel for a large luncheon.

In the late afternoon we returned to our house on Ridge Road. The new Governor asked for a light supper. He had had a full day, including three meals. I served him tea and toast—and vanilla ice cream with maple syrup. That he accepted the syrup amazed me, for ordinarily he would have no maple syrup on ice cream—on cornbread, yes, or pancakes, to be sure. I mentioned my surprise to our twelve-year-old boy.

"Maybe the day was too much for him," suggested Sam.

The next morning when he came downstairs for breakfast I asked, "How do you feel this morning, Governor?"

"I feel that I'd like to go out and find a new job," he replied, still with a trace of weariness.

With the inauguration festivities out of the way, the Governor got busy on his budget message, working on it all the following Sunday, which we spent at home in Lincoln. My job was to keep anyone from bothering him so that he could give it all his attention.

Back in Concord early the next morning, I found I had a continuous job answering the doorbell, the telephone, and trying to get the housework looked after. Being the wife of a Governor—and a new resident on the street—meant that there was a constant round of tea-parties. Then, too, it seemed that every day a new egg man would appear to see if I didn't want to buy my eggs from him, and the first week all the milkmen in the valley called at my back door. I accepted countless invitations for luncheons, teas, meetings—rarely did I regret—and I was decorated with corsages everywhere I went. I drove my own car on most occasions. The state trooper and the big limousine were for official occasions, the Governor had decreed, and it bothered him to be expected to make use of them at all. Perhaps I was holding my head too high one day thinking of my status—or maybe I just wasn't thinking—anyway I bumped squarely into a parking meter. A most awkward predicament, I thought, for the wife of a governor on the Main Street of Concord.

After that I watched the parking meters and kept my distance. I learned also to watch photographers and not to eat if there was one with a camera pointed in my direction (I felt that I just didn't look well with my mouth open).

Naturally wanting to do all I possibly could to help the Republican cause, I suggested to Viola Adams—again no relation—chairman of the women's division of the Republican State Committee, that I thought it would be nice to have a tea every once in a while for women who might like to come to Concord to visit the legislature. And so it was that the so-called County Teas came into being. The first group of women arrived early in February. They came in time to see the legislature in session, then had luncheon and did some sightseeing, and between three and five o'clock they came to our Ridge

Road home for tea. There were approximately seventy-five women on that first occasion, and the house wasn't really big enough to take care of half that number. I wondered that some resourceful and energetic soul didn't march right down to the legislature and demand that the state provide a roomy if modest residence for its chief executive and his family.

I made the hundreds of cookies, cakes, and sandwiches for those gatherings. I had no regular help—only a couple of waitresses who came in just before the women arrived. It was hard work but it was work that I enjoyed. After the last guest had left, I was generally very weary, but the day was still not done. If there wasn't a banquet or meeting somewhere around the state that we had to attend, often the Governor would bring home an old friend for dinner. I loved having people around—but the most frequently repeated notation in my diary for those "governess" years is "very tired today."

The excitement and the full days kept up for four years—with accelerating tempo as the Eisenhower-for-President campaign got under way during the last year of my husband's second term as governor.

vii

Aboard Ike's Bandwagon

I knew, early in 1951, that the Governor was mulling over the possibility of getting General Eisenhower interested in the Presidency of the United States. As with anything he did, he gave considerable, and cautious, thought to the matter. One thing I knew without being told: once he made up his mind one way or the other—to back Eisenhower or to back Taft—Sherman Adams would be no fence-sitter. If he had elected to join the railbirds he would have had plenty of company, for during the next months there was to be a large vacillating group, wondering whether to fly down into Mr. Taft's early planted field or to take to the General's freshly plowed ground on the other side of the fence.

There were others interested in pulling the Eisenhower bandwagon out from the shadows where it had stood since the Republican Convention in Philadelphia in 1948. Norris Cotton, congressman from New Hampshire's Second District, went to Paris in June, 1951, fervently hoping to arouse the General's interest. He returned to the United States even more certain that Eisenhower had all the qualities that would make him an exceptional candidate of the Republican party. But he had received no go-ahead signal from the General. It was the same with Robert Burroughs, a former National Committeeman from New Hampshire who had become greatly impressed with Eisenhower, and his potentiality as a candidate. Mr. Burroughs also journeyed to Paris in hope of wooing the General with a rosy picture of Eisenhower as Republican candidate for the Presidency.

The reception that Cotton and Burroughs received from Eisenhower was typical of the welcome he gave others who made similar visits. The

General felt complimented and appreciated the interest of those who wanted him to consider being a presidential candidate, but his job with NATO was still unfinished. It was a waste of time to come to Paris for a discussion regarding his availability, he told them, insisting he had already had much more public attention than anyone could want; after his work as head of NATO was finished, he said, he and his wife were looking forward to settling down in a home of their own far away from public life and all that it entailed. "The United States is full of politicians," he said, "many of them good ones, who love the public attention and publicity, and all the reporters and the flash bulbs. Let them have it. I have had enough of that kind of thing."

But in spite of his apparent coldness to the idea, Mr. Cotton and Mr. Burroughs, like the Governor, felt there was still a chance that the General could be induced to think more favorably of it. It was quite obvious that he wasn't going to be pushed into any such undertaking, but perhaps in time he would become more used to the possibility.

As the Republican emissaries returned from Paris following their talks with the General, some well-known facts about Eisenhower were reiterated. The points that he had exceptional ability to inspire great enthusiasm, that where he led men would follow, and that his qualities of personal persuasiveness were without equal were stressed again and again by those who had talked with him.

The question of his public position on internal issues, which kept popping up now and then, didn't seem to bother the Governor unduly. The most important thing was peace, and everyone knew how Eisenhower felt about that greatest of all issues. His dedication to the work he was doing with NATO and his confidence in the part that the United States would take with the rest of the world in achieving that goal had been convincingly demonstrated time and again.

All during that summer of 1951 the soundings in quest of an Eisenhower commitment continued. Toward the end of August, Senator Robert Taft came to New Hampshire to address the legislature, which was still in session, and later in the day a large gathering

at Hampton Beach. My husband regarded Mr. Taft's visit as a political "feeler" and was glad of the chance to know the honorable
gentleman better as he drove him to Hampton following the State
House visit. He had heard much about Mr. Taft's apparent lack of
warmth, but he was pleased to find him companionable and friendly.
"At his best he was a delightful person," I have heard the Governor
say, "but you have to keep your wits sharpened when in serious conversation with him." The Governor was sure the Senator's reputation
for being cold and impersonal was due to intense preoccupation with
matters of importance. My husband would be one of the first to say
that Taft was a great American.

Harold Stassen also came to New Hampshire in August. He was
at that time president of the University of Pennsylvania but was
definitely considering running as a candidate for the Presidency of
the United States. His trip to New Hampshire gave the Governor a
chance to talk with him at length regarding his plans and aims.
Stassen was one of the many who had visited General Eisenhower
in Paris. The General had been as noncommittal with him as he had
been with the rest. Because of the Ike sentiment in New Hampshire,
Stassen said he would not oppose Eisenhower if he became an avowed
candidate; on the contrary, he would support him. But that Eisenhower would ever consent to become a candidate he strongly doubted,
and until he did become available Stassen would go ahead with his
own organization and watch which way the wind blew.

As the summer gave way to autumn the interest in Eisenhower
continued to grow. At the Annual Governors' Conference, which
was meeting in Gatlinburg, Tennessee, that year, my husband announced to his fellow governors and to the rest of the world the
road he intended to take in the forthcoming elections of 1952, saying
he was "almost sure" the General would allow his name to be on
the March primary ballot. His next move was to make sure that all
those who professed an interest in Eisenhower-for-President lost no
time in getting together in a united effort which would put the Ike
show on the road with an impressive send-off.

Back in 1948 a group of Granite State citizens had attempted to interest Eisenhower in the New Hampshire primary. They were disappointed, however, when he withdrew his name and the plan failed. A new law had been enacted since 1948, making New Hampshire one of the few states where voters could mark their ballots to show their specific choice for President. Being the first state in the Union to hold a presidential primary, where delegates to the Republican and Democratic conventions are chosen, New Hampshire was in a unique position to raise the curtain on the Eisenhower Show or the Taft Performance. The voters would be the deciding factor.

The Governor believed that the General was a Republican—but it certainly was true that he had never said so publicly. The question would have to be answered, for he had to be an avowed member of the Republican party before his name could be entered on the ballot. Sherm decided to find out just what Ike's party affiliations had been. He instructed his attorney general to write to the county clerk of Dickinson County in Abilene, Kansas, to inquire about the politics of one Dwight David Eisenhower. The answer that the Attorney General received five days later was typed on the bottom of his original letter:

Mr. Eisenhower has never voted in this county as far as I know, the Primary laws were first put into operation in the year 1928 and he has never voted since then, I have been county clerk since January 14th, 1927, Dwight has never voted in the city as far as I know of until after war No. 2. at least he has never voted or I would have known it as the party filiation books are still here ever since the primary or branding law was passed in the spring of 1927 and never went into effect until the Primary Election in 1928.

Dwight's father was a republican and always voted the republican ticket up until his death, however that has nothing to do with the son as many differ with their fathers of which I am sorry to see, the multitude believes in going into debt and see how much they can spend, it has become a habit & will sink this nation into bankrupsy.

I don't think he has any politics.

Your truly

C. F. MOORE. COUNTY CLERK

The message from the County Clerk in Abilene proved nothing. And to add to the growing uncertainty were the persuasive overtures being made to Ike by some Democrats, including President Truman. Another was an upstate New Hampshire man who obtained petition papers and other information from the Secretary of State's office in Concord and was sure he could get the required number of signatures to put Ike's name on the Democratic ballot, where it would stay unless the General had it withdrawn. The Littleton man was taking a great deal for granted in being so sure Eisenhower was a Democrat.

Senator James Duff of Pennsylvania, who had come to New Hampshire about the middle of December for an Eisenhower-for-President kick-off dinner in Keene, told his audience, "I know of my own personal knowledge that he's a Republican." He went on to say, "We can't afford to miss this time. It may be our last call to dinner."

At a news conference following his speech the Senator said he was "completely confident" that the General would be a candidate. The Senator also reminded his questioners that Eisenhower had definitely asked that his name be omitted from the ballot in 1948 and asked, "You haven't seen him doing anything like that this time, have you?"

My husband decided that the situation would have to be clarified, and "laid the dilemma squarely in the lap" of Senator Henry Cabot Lodge, who was the National Chairman of the Ike forces. The Governor told the Senator he "would have to get a statement from the General before a single nomination paper could be signed in his behalf." Senator Lodge obtained a statement from Eisenhower in Paris to the effect that:

1. Lodge was correct in calling him a Republican.
2. He had no intention of asking to be relieved of his duties.
3. He would not engage in pre-Convention political activities.
4. He recognized the rights of others to place his name before the Convention.

His New Hampshire supporters were elated. Now if they could roll up an impressive vote for the General in the March primary there was every reason to believe that he would be the next Republican candidate for the Presidency. The Taft forces thought differently.

On the 11th of January my husband entered the office of the Secretary of State as soon as the doors opened. He was the first candidate to file for delegate to the Republican Convention the following July. He stated that he was a Republican as was his proposed candidate and that he was "favorable to the election of Dwight D. Eisenhower for President." Later in the month he presented a petition with the necessary number of signatures to ensure that Eisenhower's name would be placed on the preferential ballot. The General would have ten days, according to the law, in which to remove his name if he desired to do so.

Informed of these facts by cable, Eisenhower acknowledged the message within seven minutes. The ten days that followed were undoubtedly tense ones for the General. They were tense for his supporters in New Hampshire too. Though they were pretty sure he would allow his name to remain, still they were a relieved lot when the tenth day finally passed and no notice was received to withdraw his name. Officially, and apparently with the General's consent, he was now a candidate for President of the United States.

During following days candidates for the post of delegate continued to file, not only those favorable to Eisenhower but those interested in Taft and MacArthur as well. There were more candidates than posts to fill, since New Hampshire was allotted only fourteen delegates. My husband, as chairman of the delegation, had to decide how best to fill the fourteen delegate posts. Some of the contenders would have to drop out and that difficult decision was made considerably easier for the Governor by the co-operation of two of his former councilors. Others contributed much to the unity and purpose of the delegation.

By the time the filing period had ended, both the other presidential candidates had full slates of backers. General MacArthur finally withdrew his name. Senator Taft entered the New Hampshire campaign with some misgivings; in the latter part of January he had announced from Washington that, in spite of the factors that were unfavorable to him, he would permit his name to appear on the ballot. His supporters, he said, had entered his name without being asked by him.

Mr. Stassen had already made up his mind to enter the popularity contest with Eisenhower and Taft—without bidding for the support of delegates. The different camps were now ready to go to work in earnest. Those behind Eisenhower knew there was much work to be done. Approximately eight weeks was all the time left in which to make the effort one of victory or one of defeat. The Governor was one of the group who had no doubts. That he and other New England supporters of the General were considered rank amateurs by many people around the country who considered themselves professionals did not bother him the slightest bit.

Along with the Eisenhower interest the Governor had other things on his mind besides the usual state fiscal worries and the always full days of appointments, staff, council, and committee meetings. He would have to decide before long what course he was going to pursue regarding his own political career. Would he try for a third term as governor? The idea had little appeal for him. It had been a tempting but unusual procedure at times in the past history of the state to seek a third term as governor. Would he consider running for a seat in the Senate or would he return to private life? If he ever made a decision of any kind, it was thoroughly drowned in the flood of interest aroused by his patient and painstaking groundwork for the Eisenhower candidacy. As the days went by he became more and more the backbone of the General's slowly but constantly moving political army. He was the drummer boy up front sounding the call—he was the center of the force as it gathered momentum—and he was the man at the end of the procession ready to urge on any who faltered.

There were some sore spots at first. The early admirers of the General back in 1948, and earlier, couldn't help resenting to some degree the arrival on their side of the lines of such men as my husband who, they thought, were rather late in joining up. They nevertheless insisted that all was unity in the Eisenhower State Committee and that was indeed the impression the average voter got. And, as many people know, the Governor had a way of helping people to work together and to forget, or at least put aside, their personal differences in favor of the urgent work to be done. That the Governor's patience was short on occasions also was true. He had little tolerance for anyone, then or later, who had a personal ax to grind. There were many who expected him to go further up the political ladder because of his wealth of political knowledge and his ability to get things done. Also there were many who preferred to remember his brusqueness and to forget that good men are hard to find for the field of politics.

By the middle of February Ike's forces were leaving no stone unturned in their efforts to spread the Eisenhower appeal into every corner of the state. The women were well organized under the leadership of Mary Senior Brown of Sandwich, who was co-chairman of the New Hampshire Eisenhower-for-President Committee.

How best to go about interesting people in campaign speeches in the middle of winter gave the Ike workers considerable food for thought and they spent many hours considering ways and means of encouraging voters to leave their firesides for a cold ride to and from an evening of political eloquence. Finally my husband had to make a difficult decision. Although he had never before seen any need to turn a campaign rally into a show, he now realized, along with the rest of Ike's supporters, that something extra would have to be done in order to fill the halls.

The help of well-known radio, TV, and stage performers was solicited to assist with the rallies around the state. The Governor was criticized by those favorable to other candidates and by some in his own group for insisting that the rallies needed the know-how of professional entertainers to help draw the crowds. Perhaps the crowds would have appeared in any case, but since the General couldn't be present himself, the Governor and others felt there had to be all the come-on interest possible to fill the halls and acquaint the public with the Eisenhower story, the reasons why he would make a good President, and the great need for getting behind a man who could undoubtedly win.

The Governor found that Fred Waring wanted to bring his Pennsylvanians into the state to help with the rallies. Tex McCrary and his wife, Jinx Falkenberg, and Carl de Suze were among many others of exceptional talent who wanted to do all they could for Eisenhower. Tex McCrary quit his job on a television program in order to be free to campaign. Bernard Baruch, when he learned about it, said, "Fine. You can't fight with your hands in your pocket." The attraction of such people, in addition to the top-notch oratory of men like Senators Lodge, Duff, Saltonstall, and Carlson, Congressmen Walter Judd and Christian Herter, was irresistible to countless Granite Staters— even when the mercury was low and the snow deep.

Fred Waring said, "We are advised that people in show business shouldn't get mixed up in politics. Well, I just want to say we *aren't* mixed up—we're for *Eisenhower*!"

About the time that Ike's New Hampshire bandwagon's gears were shifted from second into high, a politically wise and affable scout was sent posthaste to the New Hampshire scene from the Citizens-for-Eisenhower headquarters in Washington. Apparently the professionals were worried that Governor Adams, the amateur, would be unable to keep the bandwagon from going into the ditch. Tom Stephens was sent to tell the Governor how to do it. The Governor had little patience with the lack of confidence that was apparently permeating the Washington headquarters. However, he and Mr. Stephens struck up a lasting friendship.

Tex McCrary was at least one person who had no qualms about the Governor's qualifications, for he wrote to Eisenhower in Paris: "Adams is the one man I have met so far in this campaign who deserves the title of 'professional,' but even more important than his skill and wisdom and experience is his *heart*." McCrary went on to tell the General about the man he hadn't yet seen but whom he would, eventually, call his "right arm." "Adams is a great man. Never met anybody quite like him. He has many of the qualities of another who worships you—Jim Duff. But he tempers his anger with a sense of fun."

The debates that sprang up throughout the state that year over the respective merits of Eisenhower and Taft produced enough heat to make the winter seem less cold. Things had warmed up so much that New Hampshire even sent representatives to Madison Square Garden for the Ike-for-President Rally.

I missed very few of the many Eisenhower rallies around, up and down, and across the state. Although it certainly wasn't the best time of year for large-scale gatherings, or for driving many miles after late evening speeches, the snowstorms, sleet, and icy roads didn't seem to slow down the Eisenhower enthusiasm. I chauffeured many, many miles during those tense and busy weeks while the Governor talked with campaigners who rode with us, and I listened to the speeches about Ike so many times that I could have recited most of them myself. There was Marty Snyder, who had been the General's mess sergeant during the war, and his stories about the warmheartedness of his boss, of his liking for beef stew—the way Marty made it. He kept hammering away at the audiences with "General Eisenhower is the kind of a man every woman out there would like to have for a husband. He's the kind of a guy I'd like to have for a father. And you know when he would go home he would always call up my mother and say, 'Marty's getting along fine.' How can you help lovin' a guy like that?" And there were the frequent speeches by Senator Lodge, who in response to the oft-repeated question "Where does Ike stand?" would answer "He stands between us and Communism, between us and World War Three!" Senator Saltonstall of Massachusetts and Paul Hoffman of California were among other speakers who came to New Hampshire to do what they could. I wondered at the terrific amount of thought and energy that the Governor poured into the cause. The endless controversies, the planning ahead, the tremendous pressure of his job as governor, along with his work with the Eisenhower Committee seemed to me more than the usual man could take. My participation as a driver when necessary and my comments on how the different rallies went viewed from my seat on the floor were certainly a very small part of the effort, but there were days when I wondered whether I would last through the primary—and then another burst of enthusiasm and excitement would make me forget my fatigue as we dashed off somewhere else flying the "I Like Ike" banners.

The last week of February and the first week in March saw a concentrated effort by senators, congressmen, and other politicians, as well as by the entertainers, to spread the Eisenhower gospel. On Monday evening, the day before election, Cabot Lodge was the principal speaker in Dover for the wind-up rally in the southern part of the state. I drove to Lancaster with my husband and Richard Cooper, the Republican State Chairman, for the last political powwow in the north country. The Governor was the principal speaker, ably buttressed by Clifford Cooper of California, former national president of the Junior Chamber of Commerce, the indefatigable Tex McCrary, the genial and effective Marty Snyder, and Jack Powell, who tirelessly and literally beat the drums in the call to follow Eisenhower. I know my husband felt that all that could be done had been done. It was now up to the voters on the following day.

Before retiring around two o'clock we listened to the first returns, which were recorded shortly after midnight on the 12th. The seven voters of the tiny village of Waterville had journeyed to the polling place in time to make history by being the first town to complete its voting—and every vote cast was for Dwight D. Eisenhower. We went wearily off to bed after hearing the good news, hoping that the Waterville vote was a good omen.

March weather in New England is unpredictable. Almost anything can, and does, happen. The skies, the weather reports, and the almanac are closely watched, especially by those hoping for a good turnout of voters. Since blizzards and floods have been known to keep people from the polls on Primary Day, the weather was now the biggest worry of the Eisenhower supporters. Fortunately it wasn't an unusually bad day, simply typical March weather with a heavy, wet snowfall here and there and cold blustery winds in other areas.

New Hampshire citizens went to the polls in larger numbers than ever before in a presidential primary. Previously the record showed a top count of somewhat less than 80,000, but on that particular March day in 1952 there were 136,536 ballots cast. By evening it was quite clear that the Eisenhower delegates were well out in front and that the General was running strong in the popularity vote also. The following morning the Governor sent a cable to General Eisenhower stating that the delegation favorable to him had been elected and that his margin in the preferential contest would be at least 10,000 over his nearest competitor.

The General lost no time in sending a message to the Governor: "My congratulations to you and your associates. Through you could I please express to the Republican voters of New Hampshire my profound appreciation of the extraordinary compliment they have paid me? This I should like to do, even though I fully realize that the astonishing result was due primarily to the distinguished reputations of the list of delegates, and the efforts of your organization. Dwight D. Eisenhower."

When the Governor released the message to the press on the 13th, he took pains to make it clear that it was Eisenhower the voters had cast their ballots for, and not for any group of Republicans. "Every one of us," he said, in referring to the delegates, "wishes to make it plain that this vote should be taken for what it is—a call to Dwight D. Eisenhower to accept the nomination for the Presidency of the United States. We who have been elected delegates have benefited from a vote of confidence in the man whose candidacy we have endorsed."

Down in Texas, Senator Taft was surprised and disappointed by the showing Eisenhower had made. And over in Frankfurt, Germany, the General "was deeply moved with the outcome."

A letter which Eisenhower wrote to a friend gave his backers added encouragement. He would not, he said, turn his back on those who were working to win for him the presidential nomination.

As the Eisenhower campaign began to catch fire across the country, the Governor was in constant demand as speaker. He was more than willing to help whenever he could and he generally insisted that I go along. In April he accepted invitations to speak at rallies in New Jersey, Vermont, and Massachusetts. From there he was called to Albuquerque, New Mexico, and to Las Vegas and Reno, Nevada—and I went with him. It was thoroughly exciting seeing that part of the country for the first time, and it was exciting to be there in the interest of Dwight D. Eisenhower. Many of the Republicans in the Southwest regarded Eisenhower as an unknown quantity. They were curious about him. At the same time they felt they knew Taft pretty well. Those in the Midwest had a similar attitude. I know the Governor felt that he accomplished very little through his efforts in New Mexico and Nevada at the time, but when the convention rolled around, Eisenhower lacked only one delegate vote in each of those two states to break even with Taft.

While we were out in that part of the country we decided to take some side trips to a few of the historical spots and natural wonders we had heard and read much about. We looked down on the pink rock castles of Bryce Canyon, which had a soft cover of new snow, for it was still cold country in April. Zion National Park, too, we had practically to ourselves. It was like viewing beautiful paintings in a quiet and deserted gallery, except that the beauty of the scene surrounded us and we felt a part of the majesty and quietness.

Our brief vacation over, we returned to New Hampshire, where my husband attended to routine duties at his office in the State House. Then we again packed for a long trip which took us first to Providence, Rhode Island, for an enthusiastic Eisenhower rally. From there we went by train to Portland, Oregon. To a couple of New Englanders, that trip by the northern route through the grazing country and across the continental divide was a constant delight. Our running game of Scrable was often abandoned as we looked out the window at the changing wonder of the continent. In the evenings, when the countryside was dark, the Governor worked on his speeches, or we would have an uninterrupted game of Scrabble. It was always early to bed in order to be up as soon as it was light, for we didn't want to miss any of the scenery.

In Portland we were met at the station by a group of Eisenhower Oregonians. The Governor had a quick huddle with committee members over a cup of coffee in the station restaurant before we started out for the drive to Bend, where he was to speak to a luncheon group. After more huddles there, in the evening he addressed a rally in the school auditorium. The next morning we drove to Prineville where the Oregon Cattlemen's Association was having a Buckaroo breakfast. Those who had charge of the Governor's program thought it would be fine if he could say a few words about Ike to that large gathering of influential Westerners. However, Governor Earl Warren was the guest speaker that morning and my husband was told that Governor Warren's sponsors didn't think it appropriate for him to share the platform. But later in the morning he did receive a summons to appear before the group. He was on hand at the appointed time and made a concise and clear-cut appeal for Eisenhower. But the majority of cattlemen were so amused by his pronunciation of Oregon that I feared at the time the Eisenhower cause wasn't receiving all the attention it should.

The Governor spoke next in Grant's Pass and then in Roseburg, his pronunciation drawing more laughter, and it was fairly well into the evening when we started back to Portland where we would have only a few hours' sleep before taking off by plane for Missoula, Montana.

On the way back to Portland the Governor said he would drive the first hundred miles and, knowing we would have little enough time to sleep, he was no doubt going along at a more than moderate degree of speed. At least a state patrolman thought so, for he signaled the Governor to stop. "Let me see your papers," he said to my husband. The necessary information was produced.

"Where are you from?" asked the officer.

"New Hampshire," answered my husband.

"What are you doing in Oregon?"

"Campaigning for Dwight D. Eisenhower."

"What is your occupation?" continued the officer.

"I work for the government," answered the Governor.

"What kind of work?"

"In the Executive Department," the Governor said.

"What are your duties?"

The Governor decided enough time had been spent in this interesting conversation. "I am the Governor of New Hampshire," he said. The officer's head came right in through the open window. *"What?"* he said with a tinge of disbelief. "I said I was the Governor of New

Hampshire," answered my husband. The officer drew his head out of the window and mustered his dignity and said most politely, "Well, Governor, you came into this state in good condition, and we would like to have you leave it in as good health as when you arrived." Gretchen Cake, the delightful wife of the National Committeeman from Portland, and I, who were sitting in the rear seat, had hard work to control our amusement as the interesting exchange took place. Everyone, however, silently agreed with what the officer had to say and soon we were on our way again, arriving in Portland in time for three hours of sleep before taking the plane for Missoula.

Montana was brand-new country to us. Even the political atmosphere was different. There was courteous attention paid to the Governor's remarks about Eisenhower, but interest in the General as the next President was only lukewarm. However, it was quite evident that the interest was growing, especially in the younger generation.

Great Falls, Lewistown, and Billings were also on the Governor's list of Montana rallies before we returned east. The next two months were busy and anxious ones for my husband. The Eisenhower interest kept mounting but so did the unexpected problems about the voting setup in different parts of the country. Each day brought new issues and perplexities. It was June 1 when Eisenhower was released from his job with NATO. His speech in Abilene, Kansas, was awaited with great interest, for it was the first time he would appear to millions of television viewers as a candidate for the Presidency. But it wasn't until June 9 that my husband was formally introduced to the man in whose interest he had spent many months working.

General Eisenhower invited the New Hampshire delegation to his home at Morningside Heights in New York for a visit. It was the first delegation in the East to confer with him as a group. Everyone came away from the meeting with practically the same feeling: that Eisenhower was a man of personal charm, human interest, and strong convictions. After a question-and-answer period following his brief but adequate acknowledgment to the New Hampshire delegation, and as the group was about to depart, the General said, "I want you to meet my Mamie." In later months, as the campaign train rolled across the country, he repeated those same words many times.

Soon after that first meeting with Eisenhower, my husband and Senator Carlson were invited to luncheon at the General's house. "My own reaction to him on those first brief informal meetings," said the Governor, "was that I had not been wasting my time." Here was a plain, straightforward man, devoid of deviousness or complexities of disposition. He had a healthy regard for his own accomplishments without any braggadocio. There were certain well-defined indications both of his respect for discipline and of the strong self-discipline exercised over his thinking and habits. When at work his mind was applied to important matters. He had no time for trivialities, nor did he like to dwell on the defects of somebody else's personality. He had certain firm convictions. Whatever he got around to being positive about never lacked personal decisiveness. Some of the firm beliefs he held, and which were to weigh heavily in later decisions, were born of his own experience with every phase of military activity. Not only did he know how to lay out a battle plan, but he knew something about a budget and how to convince a Congressional committee. When he expressed an opinion he knew what he was talking about. When confronted with matters outside his knowledge, he asked questions and listened.

After those first two meetings with the General, my husband returned to Concord and put in long days at his desk in the State House. Certain elements of the press, a number of influential Democrats, and even a few of his own party adversely criticized his travels outside the state on behalf of Eisenhower. The Governor was smart enough to know that there was a degree of justification in all the criticism. He also knew that matters had been well taken care of in his absence and, as the president of a large advertising firm had telegraphed him immediately following the primary, ". . . Incidentally, you have had a million dollars' worth of advertising for the State of New Hampshire." The Governor agreed. He had, in fact, good reason to believe that the state was benefiting more than a little from the national and world-wide publicity it had been getting as a result of putting the Eisenhower Show on the road.

As July 7, the date for the annual Governors' Conference in Houston, drew near, so did the date for my maiden speech. I had agreed to fill in for Evelyn Langlie, wife of the Governor of the State of Washington, at the dedication of the fountain at the United Nations Headquarters on June 26. Mrs. Langlie was chairman of the Governors' Wives Committee which had worked with the American Association for the United Nations in sponsoring a campaign by the school children of America to raise money for the fountain which had been placed on the Plaza in front of the Secretariat Building. It would be an impressive occasion and from my faraway home in the quiet hills of New Hampshire I had more courage than judgment—I had accepted Evelyn Langlie's invitation to take her place on the program, since it was impossible for her to get to New York before leaving for Texas and the Governors' Conference. With little knowledge of what I was letting myself in for, I had wired Mrs. Langlie I would be glad to help out. Never having made a speech before a large gathering— and only "a few words" in front of a small group—I began to get a little nervous as soon as the telegram had been sent. It was too late to change my mind, I decided, as I was assailed with more and more misgivings regarding my ability to take the place of Evelyn Langlie, who was an experienced and very able speaker. However, I had little time to think about speeches. Getting ready for the Governors' Conference and the Republican Convention immediately afterward, besides my usual daily round of errands and meetings, left me little time to worry about my part in the dedication of the fountain at United Nations Headquarters.

Our flight out of the Manchester airport on June 25 gave us our first chance to relax in some weeks. After arriving at the Roosevelt Hotel in New York I lost no time in taking the first of three tranquilizers a doctor had prescribed to keep my knees from shaking during my speech on the following day. I was somewhat disturbed about a slight attack of laryngitis which had appeared earlier in the day. It was a warning signal that I was overtired and I hoped my voice wouldn't disappear, as it had sometimes in the past.

When I awoke in the morning my voice was practically gone. I tried everything—hot towels, an aspirin gargle, and another tranquilizer pill, all without any great degree of improvement. I thought if I kept quiet until time to go to the dedication I might have enough voice to get through my short speech. As it happened, when the time came I somehow found the necessary voice, though it was decidedly deep and husky compared to my usual voice. Thanks to the tranquilizers, I was able to get through my small part in the program without the slightest trace of nervousness, but the effort left me literally and figuratively speechless for the next couple of days. To have shared a program with Eleanor Roosevelt and other experienced speakers was a milepost I had never thought possible to reach. I was pleased when Sherm told me afterward, "You did all right, Plum."

After luncheon in the delegates' dining room of the United Nations Headquarters with others who had taken part in the program, including Acting Secretary-General Guillaume Georges-Picot, the Governor and I went back to the hotel to leave for the Governors' Conference in Texas. To break up the trip, we had made plans to stop overnight in New Orleans—a city that the Governor had found exceptionally interesting when he had visited it with other congressmen a few years earlier. I, too, responded to its special appeal, but I was still feeling the effects of many weeks of hurry and tension. The Governor was a little tired too. His mind was full of the problems that would certainly arise and the difficult decisions that would have to be made when the governors from every corner of the country got together. Since it was an election year, there was bound to be considerable political tension, and to top it off, two of the governors, Warren of California and Stevenson of Illinois, were willing and recognized candidates for the Presidency. Furthermore, the conference couldn't have been held in a more exciting part of the country considering the arguments about the selection of delegates in Texas and other parts of the South. To get that situation cleared up was uppermost in the New Hampshire Governor's mind. Other strong-for-Ike Republican governors felt the same way, and at a meeting that my husband and two of his associates called in our suite on the last evening of the conference plans were made for a public statement, aimed directly at Republicans throughout the country, that the nomination of their candidate must be free of the slightest implications of dishonesty. Delegates must be chosen by majority vote and some of the practices in the South could not be tolerated. All the twenty-three Republican governors present at the conference were consulted the following morning by a few volunteers who had been present the evening before, and all agreed to the statement. Two governors not present at the Texas conference promptly gave their approval when notified of the decision by those who were the craftsmen of what became known as the Houston Manifesto. My husband felt it was a tremendous stride in the right direction and hoped that a similar resolution would be adopted at the Republican Convention in Chicago, and that of course is what happened.

I was one of the many governors' wives who accompanied their husbands to Chicago. It was to be my first experience with the excitement, fanfare, and strategy that are a part of all political conventions. I was amazed at my husband's knowledge regarding the workings of a national convention, since he had been to only one other such affair, but he had little trouble carrying out his assignment as Ike's floor leader. He seemed to sense each move that should be made. It was a tremendous responsibility and a tremendous job, but when the roll call was finally over Ike was the Republican nominee for President. Sherm had again done the kind of job he had been picked for.

We had expected to return to New Hampshire with the state delegation but we were in need of a few days' vacation, so when Governor Barrett of Wyoming suggested we go to a guest ranch at the foot of the Grand Tetons, we agreed to accompany him in his plane. We had never before been on a Western ranch that catered to guests; the scenery, hospitality, and food exceeded all our expectations. It was peaceful and quiet, too, but not for long, for the telephone brought a message that would greatly alter our plans for the days to come.

We couldn't have found a better spot to recuperate. My only excuse for needing a vacation was that I had tried to keep up with the

Governor. He, on the other hand, had plenty of reason to need a few days' relaxation. Besides convention fatigue, the duties of the office of governor, added to month's of responsibility in connection with the Eisenhower primary campaign in New Hampshire, had taken much out of him. Then, too, the Governors' Conference in Houston had been packed full of Texas-type hospitality and activity.

It was hard to believe that for four days we would simply sleep, eat, and enjoy the magnificent view of the Grand Teton Range. At the end of those few days we would have to return to New Hampshire.

While we were in Texas all the governors had been showered with gifts from Texas industries, including a complete Western outfit, of the right size, of levis, boots, shirt, tie, and wide-brimmed hat. This was unusual apparel for my husband, but he wore every article the first day of our Wyoming vacation. Lazy 4F Ranch had several guest cabins besides ours, which we were glad to find would be empty during our stay. Being the only guests we had Clay Seton, the caretaker and guide, pretty much to ourselves. He had many exciting stories about the old West which we enjoyed hearing; he knew where the moose liked to stay down in the willows by the river and where the finest trout could be found.

The morning of the 15th of July was sparkling clear. The saw-toothed Tetons pierced the blue sky. The Governor was called to the Seton cottage to take a telephone call. After he left I finished preparing for the ride we were going to take in hopes of scaring up some moose. As time went by and Sherm didn't return, I went in search of him. I found him sitting on the sun-flooded steps of the caretaker's porch. His Western hat was pushed back on his head and the sun accented the newness of his boots. His arms were resting on his levi-clad knees and his hands were clasped tightly together. His head was bent and all was quiet, but I sensed something important had happened from his very attitude. At the sound of my approach he looked up.

"Plum, that call was from Ike out in Denver. He wants me to be his right-hand man during the campaign."

The Governor looked to me as though he hadn't fully recovered from the fireworks in Chicago and wasn't too sure he relished the idea of running any more campaigns for a while. However, I noticed a glint in his eyes and a suggestion of capitulation in his voice. Here we go again, I thought, having not even recovered from the latest battle. The horses were brought up and we went in search of big game armed with cameras and field glasses, though I doubted that my husband's mind was occupied with the moose hunt.

We returned to New Hampshire within a short time. Sherm obtained leave of absence from his gubernatorial duties and went to Denver to help get the Eisenhower national campaign into gear. I, too, went to Denver and it was there I first met the Eisenhowers. A lawn party at the Country Club was the setting for my introduction to the woman who, some months later, would become First Lady. And it was at a dinner at the home of Jessie and Dan Thornton that I was introduced to the man who would be the next President. He and Mamie were the guests of honor. Ike was given the job of broiling the huge steaks that the Thornton Ranch had provided. I watched the process from the terrace and thought the General seemed to be enjoying himself immensely as he talked about the different ways he liked to broil steak.

"Say, aren't those tremendous steaks!" he said. "Dan sure knows how to grow good beef!"

On one of the Sundays while we were in Denver we left the Brown Palace Hotel and went in search of the Episcopal church. Robert Cutler was with us. He had known General Eisenhower for many years and had been asked to leave his business in Boston to help with the campaign. He had a wonderful sense of humor and could be counted on to say whatever came into his head, on any occasion.

The Governor was quite sure he could find the church. The directions were simple and the distance was not great. However, with only a few minutes left before the service, he had to admit he was lost. Mr. Cutler and I suggested that it might be well to ask someone for directions, and my husband reluctantly agreed it was the only thing to do. The first person he asked said he didn't know, he was a stranger in town. The Governor asked another person, and another, receiving from all the same discouraging answer. No one, it seemed, knew there was a church in the vicinity, let alone an Episcopal one. Robert Cutler, with consternation and feeling, remarked, "Well, I certainly hope they are going to vote for Eisenhower—they don't seem to be much interested in Jesus!"

In August the Eisenhower headquarters were transferred to the Hotel Commodore in New York, and on the 14th of September the Eisenhower Special left Pennsylvania Station in New York for the first campaign trip by rail. I was invited to go aboard and very soon found there were reasons for my being included. The mail room needed extra help at times, and Homer Gruenther, who had charge of it, and others, saw to it I was never out of work. Since I knew I should never have such an experience again, I made the most of it.

viii

The Campaign Train

As a member of the working crew I was supposed to be on board when the bell rang. I definitely had no intention of adding to anyone's problems, least of all my husband's; he had all he could handle—and more at times.

I was on my own most of the time and doing pretty well until we visited Fargo, North Dakota. There I had an involuntary leave of absence. The driver of the car I was assigned to for the parade through Fargo was a nice young man. The wife of the Republican State Chairman and another woman from North Dakota rode with me in the car, which was near the end of the motorcade.

After the speeches were over, the line of cars began its escorted trek back to the station. The schedule was tight that day and no time was to be lost. Our driver seemed to have trouble keeping up with the cars ahead, and when we arrived at the station we saw the Eisenhower Special disappearing down the track and into the night. Of course I hadn't entertained the presumption that it would wait three minutes for me, but I did wonder when I would see everybody again.

I didn't know whether there was another stop scheduled for that evening. Perhaps there wouldn't be another one until morning, in Montana. I ran to the station and asked someone whether the train would be stopping anywhere else in North Dakota that night and was greatly relieved to learn that Eisenhower was to make a five-minute speech from the rear platform of the train at Valley City, which was sixty miles away. I asked a policeman whether there was a state trooper who could drive me and my companions to Valley City (and by this time we had been joined by another woman whose driver, like ours, had not been able to keep up). I was told there were no troopers available but that the county sheriff might be able to help us. The sheriff, informed of our predicament, lost not a minute. In seconds we were on our way to Valley City. It was a crisp moonlit night. The highway was straight and the pressure of the sheriff's foot on the accelerator seldom lessened perceptibly. Once a state trooper was a little curious about our hurry; otherwise we had the road pretty much to ourselves.

Arriving at Valley City, we were relieved to see the train. Mr. Eisenhower was still talking to the crowd. Before the sheriff's car had come to a stop I was off across the tracks and clumps of ragweed to the door of our car—which was closed. Moany, Mr. Eisenhower's valet, happened to be looking out the window of the General's car and promptly ran to open the vestibule door. With my companions I climbed aboard the Eisenhower Special just as the General finished his five-minute speech, and I never left it again for an auto ride without first having an earnest conversation with the driver regarding his ability to keep up with the rest of the parade. I have known many sheriffs, but that night in North Dakota they were all relegated to second place. Arthur Narum, the sheriff of Cass County, will forever hold first place in my memory as far as sheriffs are concerned.

Never having been on a whistle-stop tour, I had been a bit unprepared for the excitement that began as soon as we left New York's Pennsylvania Station. It was Sunday, the 14th of September, when we left the Eisenhower headquarters on the sixth floor of the Hotel Commodore for the first trip into the Midwest. The day before, those who were going had been notified to have their luggage at the ramp entrance between twelve noon and two o'clock. At exactly four o'clock we entered our assigned cars and departed for the station. Those who had ridden campaign trains before were like good bloodhounds, straining at the leash and eager to be off. Those of us (and we were in the majority) who were about to be indoctrinated little knew what was in store for us but we were equally eager to get started. The procession to the station was headed, well out in front, by the photographers' truck. Next came the car with security personnel, then the General's car, and following that were cars with staff workers and officials, and lastly a busful of representatives of the press.

When we reached the station we were directed to our train by a large sign—EISENHOWER SPECIAL. It wasn't what I had expected to see for a campaign train—it wasn't all red, white, and blue with EISENHOWER SPECIAL painted on each car. In fact, it looked quite like any other train standing in the station. There was only one outstanding difference that I noticed immediately. Attached to the railing of the rear platform was a large round sign with the words EISENHOWER SPECIAL. LOOK AHEAD, NEIGHBOR!

There were eighteen cars including two diners, a working car and lounge for the press, and a lounge car for state officials and other visitors. The Eisenhower car was at the rear of the train and other cars had accommodations for the large number of staff workers. There were a limited number of compartments reserved for state officials who boarded the train for the journey through their particular state.

The room we were to live in for 20,871 miles of rail travel before the campaign came to an end was rather confining to a couple of Yankees who were used to uncongested territory; and a number of secretaries, upon reaching their assigned rooms at the beginning of the trip, found that they simply could not get inside. Their luggage, typewriters, supplies, and other necessary items were piled bunk-high. It took good nature and patience for several days before they could make space to work in in any kind of comfort. However, Sherm and I quickly became accustomed to the small bit of floor space and were amazed at the number of people who were able to gather there when there was a need, for often it was necessary to have a place for staff workers to iron out the daily problems of running a presidential campaign while traveling by train. When my husband called a meeting in our room, I moved out and into the nearest vacant spot I could find. Sometimes I went into the room that Ann Whitman used for her work. She was personal secretary to the General during the campaign and carried on in the same capacity throughout his eight years as President. Ann could generally find something useful for me to do even if it was only the stamping and sealing of envelopes.

Every morning at about 6:45 the Governor rolled out of his lower berth, got dressed, and bumped and swayed his way through five cars to the diner. I came down from my upper berth after he had left the room, dressed, and also went in search of breakfast. The dining-car menu had a facsimile of the rear platform sign on the cover. The meals were excellent, mediocre, or poor, according to the railway system we were riding on. However, even when the food was poor there was little faultfinding, since everyone had other things to think about and there was generally someone waiting to take your place in the dining car. The only time I voiced a complaint was when I found a sizable chunk of glass in my club sandwich—I thought I was entitled to speak up about that and everyone agreed. As long as no one put glass in my sandwiches I was quite easy to get along with during the whole campaign. Following our breakfast we returned to our room, which the porter would have prepared for its daytime use as office, reception and consultation room.

The Eisenhower car was, of course, the center of much activity. All staff meetings at which the General was present were held in its lounge, as well as many get-togethers with men and women of note across the country. The lounge opened out on the rear platform where Ike made his whistle-stop speeches, after which he would say to the crowd, "And now let me give you my Mamie." That always brought on a renewed burst of cheering. Then the engine would give a little tug, and the cheering would fade into the distance as the Eisenhower Special disappeared from view. The General became better and better at speechmaking. He learned fast. He didn't *have* to be a great orator —all he had to do was meet people and his stock would rise immediately. His personality was infectious, his warmth and genuineness irresistible.

There were bedrooms for Ike, Mamie, Rose (Mamie's personal maid), and Mrs. Doud, Mrs. Eisenhower's mother. She turned out to be a good trouper, too, and earned the respect and love of all connected with that long trek around the country. I have often been asked how it was she happened to be included: "Wasn't it a bit unusual for the mother of a candidate's wife to be along for such a lengthy trip?" I answered that probably Mrs. Doud was included simply because Ike and Mamie wanted her along. As months and years went by it became well known that her son-in-law was very fond of the person almost everyone affectionately called "Mis' Min." It was equally well known that Mamie had found it hard to warm up to the idea of joining her husband as he went about the ordeal of campaigning back and forth across the country. For years she had looked forward to the time when she and her husband could settle down in a home of their own out of the public eye. All their years together had been lived on Army posts. And then there was the war. It hadn't been too great a sacrifice to stay on in Paris when Ike took over as head of NATO, for they could be together, but that would be the end, she had expected, of their public life. And then the Republicans began urging the General to become a candidate for President just when the fulfillment of her dreams seemed only months away. Mamie Eisenhower found herself caught again in another effort for a good cause. That she wanted her mother to share in the campaign train experience was natural—especially as she expected it would be the only chance she would have to see her for many months.

Lovely flower arrangements were delivered to the Eisenhowers nearly every day. Since it was the season for chrysanthemums, they predominated, but there were roses in abundance, and orchids. Mamie was always thoughtful and generous, sharing her boxes of corsages with other women on the train. I was the recipient of many beautiful orchids which were presented to her along the route.

There was fruit in large quantities too. Generally it was specifically intended for the Eisenhower party, but occasionally some more thoughtful apple grower would send a box or more of tree-ripened fruit to the staff and personnel. At times practically everyone on the train could be seen munching a yellow Delicious or a red MacIntosh.

Other gifts poured in at nearly every stop. Keeping track of the long lists of items and the donors was one of the endless daily tasks that kept Mary Jane McCaffrey, Mamie's personal secretary, busy all day long. There were expensive gifts, there were gifts of little material value but full of sentiment and quite often fashioned by craftsmen, and there were gifts from children, good luck charms, among the endless array of cherished items children are insistent upon parting with in order to pay homage to their idol. There were dozens of portraits of the General, ranging from amateur to professional workmanship. Almost every state gave something made from its natural products. There were native precious stones, exotic woods, hand-wrought silver, and copper, and hand-blown glass. In Richmond, Virginia, a reproduction of the Virginia Bill of Rights, among other gifts, was presented to the General and Mrs. Eisenhower. A frozen turkey was delivered to their car in Wilton Junction, Iowa, and in Atlanta a basket of flowers and a slab of bacon. In Columbia, South Carolina, the General accepted a gift of china, and almost always the key to a city was presented with more or less ceremony. And each gift was given out of the respect and love for a man who had done much for his country and the world, and for his wife who had given up much that she loved in order to help him carry out his assignments.

One gift caused considerable amusement on the train. When the Eisenhower Special stopped at Cumberland, Maryland, Governor McKelden presented Ike with an antelope head which had come originally from Wyoming. It was a particularly nice specimen and Ann Whitman and I named it Eunice Horn and thought it was worthy of some special attention. A few evenings passed and the proper time arrived, or so we thought. Robert Cutler was working late on some campaign matter in another part of the train, so Ann and I took Eunice Horn to his room and placed her in his bed with a gorgeous rose at her ear. Then we turned off the light and closed the door. Some time later Mr. Cutler returned to his room, his mind still full of the issues of the past eighteen hours. He worked day after day to the point of physical exhaustion, and when he opened the door without putting on the light and caught a glimpse of something in his bed, he immediately wondered if he was near to a mental collapse also. Then he happened to think of one of the many problems that had come up that day. Kenneth Royal, Mr. Cutler told me later, was expected to board the train that evening, and with every available bed in use, Cutler and others had been wondering where he could sleep. So, when Mr. Cutler saw something in his bed, he thought immediately of Mr. Royal. "They must have put him in my bed," he said to himself as he quietly closed the door on Eunice Horn and went in search of another place to sleep. Kenneth Royal was a devoted friend of Ike's, and although he was a Democrat he was coming aboard the Eisenhower Special to give his friend advice. I believe I am right in remembering that, as it happened, he didn't board the train as planned on that special night.

If, unannounced and unseen, one could have boarded the rear of the Eisenhower train and walked through as it lurched along at fast speed toward the next whistle stop, one probably would first of all have come upon Ike, Adams, Fred Seaton, Tom Stephens, Jim Hagerty, and Gabriel Hauge in the General's lounge car, huddled over the schedule for the day. It is still fairly early in the morning and their particular problem is how to include "just one more" stop in an already tight schedule. Some not-too-large community, represented by eager-beaver Republicans, insists that the train stop "just long enough" for Ike and Mamie to say hello. Even one extra stop of only a few minutes could complicate things and upset the timetable for the whole day, but it was done as often as possible.

One such place was Klamath Falls, Oregon, where the wide-awake Republican committee used every bit of persuasiveness possible to get the train to stop—even if it was in the middle of the night. Finally the staff agreed to find out if the General could be persuaded to say hello to the Klamath Falls folks around midnight. After hearing all the arguments, pro and con, he decided he could be called and he and Mamie would acknowledge the crowd's enthusiasm from the back platform. The resolute Olive Cornett, National Committeewoman, had worked hard for this. I believe it was the only stop on the whole campaign where Ike appeared in pajamas and dressing gown while Mamie demurely shared the spotlight in negligee, with a pink ribbon around her head to hold her curls in place.

Ike once ordered the train to stop without any prearrangement; he couldn't pass the eager and hopeful crowds at one station without "just saying hello." And once the Governor called a halt when the crowds were simply too big to pass by without a word from the candidate.

Fred Seaton was a newspaperman from Hastings, Nebraska. He had been a senator and went to Denver to offer his services in the Eisenhower campaign. The Governor asked him to join the team as his assistant. It proved to be a happy union, for Seaton had a sense of humor that helped to lighten the atmosphere around the Governor when things became too tense. The Governor, for his part, lost no chance to harass the Senator good-naturedly when he became embroiled in one of his numerous "hassles" in connection with campaign issues or the operation of the train. Fred Seaton was one of the many campaigners who, after inauguration, went along into an office in the White House. His stay there was short compared to that of many others, for he was asked to be Secretary of the Interior when Douglas McKay stepped out of the Cabinet to campaign in Oregon. And it was Fred Seaton who gave the Governor the nickname of "the Rock," no doubt because of the immovability of Ike's headman in most instances after he had made up his mind about this or that procedure.

Fred was also involuntarily responsible for my being called "the Pebble." I tried to make myself useful around Eisenhower headquarters in the Commodore Hotel between train trips, and one day the Governor asked me to take a message to the Honorable Mr. Seaton. Fred wasn't in his office so I left a note which I had signed "the Pebble," showing that I clearly understood my position in relation to "the Rock." And ever since then the stream of suggestion has washed each closer to the other, for a mention of "the Rock" brings to mind the lesser "Pebble" which was generally in evidence throughout that swift-running current of events.

Tom Stephens came aboard the campaign train following weeks of effort in lining up convention delegates. He seldom smiled outwardly, but one sensed the underlying humor. His political experience —he had been in Dewey's campaign in 1948—and his perception and affability, together with his sense of humor, were necessary requisites for his particular job on the train as Eisenhower's travel and appointment secretary. The happiness and welfare of all VIP delegations that came aboard for an introduction to the candidate were in Tom's hands. It wasn't all easy by any means but it was part of the political process; and often I saw Tom thankfully wiping the perspiration from his brow as if he were also wiping away the last vestige of a difficult delegation that had just been deposited at a station. He, too, went on to the White House to fill a similar role during most of the Administration.

Senator Frank Carlson, from Kansas, had been in charge of the Eisenhower headquarters in Washington, D.C., earlier in the Eisenhower movement. He was one of those able men who came to New Hampshire in the early days to help by making speeches, and he had been one of the visitors to the General in Paris even earlier. He was not a regular member of the campaign staff, though he did manage the VIP car on one or more swings.

Louis Kelly's good nature was as great as his physical stature. His thoroughness and ability matched both. He had been given a leave of absence from the American Express Company in order to take charge of the train's whereabouts and whenabouts. He had a good tenor voice and a seemingly endless desire to keep in practice, for when everything was running on schedule and there were no smoke signals of distress in the distance, he would corral "the group," of which I was one, and we would practice up on the old songs or invent some new ones. Our favorite was "An Ode to the Road" and if I ever knew who wrote it I have forgotten. But it provided a wonderful way of poking a little good-natured fun at the foibles and tactics of the various members of the staff who, at times, naturally, had their differences. No one escaped. But most of those little differences, queer as it may seem, were the incidents we chose to remember, for they were the happenings that helped to knit men of many temperaments into an unbeatable organization.

There was the night that the train stopped in Peoria, Illinois, and everyone was desperate for a bath, but the water was so hard it did no good at all. There was the conscientious secretary who hunted long and unsuccessfully in the late and cold evening hours in Springfield for an apple to replace one another staff worker had insisted she have earlier in the day, from a box intended for Mrs. Eisenhower.

As everyone became better acquainted, we made up new verses about each other's idiosyncrasies and the vicissitudes of campaign travel by train. They were perhaps exaggerated a bit here and there. But, as the following verses indicate, it was quite a trip, and the men and women who made it work were an exceptional team. (As Ann Whitman said several years later, "I like to think of the spirit that carried a bunch of people from every background through the experience of living tightly packed together for six weeks—without, so far as I know, a single major blow-up.")

AN ODE TO THE ROAD
(tune: "I'm Looking Over a Four-Leaf Clover")

How Ike's train keeps rolling
    With so many men controlling
Will always be a mystery.
    Seaton makes the schedules—
So does Summerfield!
    Adams settles most scraps
But Cutler never yields.
    There's no use complaining,
Kelly's still explaining
    The jolts and bumps we have each day.
With music played by Homer—
    Snyder's patients in a coma—
We've all seen the U.S.A.

WE REALLY MEAN IT!
WE'VE ALL SEEN THE U.S.A.

As Ike's train keeps moving
    Its passengers are proving
A bath is needed every day.
    Sometimes it is three days,
Other times it's four;
    Mum's the word they're saying

When it's a week or more.
　There's no use complaining
It needs no explaining
　We're doing it for dear friend Ike.
Without a bath or shower
　'Twould take atomic power
To scrape off the soot each night.

WITHOUT A SHOWER!
WE'VE ALL SEEN THE U.S.A.

Well, Ike's trip is over
　By plane, trains, and motor.
We've all had a wonderful time.
　Forgotten are the gripings,
Everything that riles.
　Why, even Tommy Stephens
Is wearing a smile!
　There's no use complaining,
Good fellowship is reigning,
　Commander Kelly's troubles are o'er.
With Hauge's written speeches
　And all that Cutler teaches
Ike, our boy, is bound to win.

Further information regarding the duties of Senator Carlson and Lou Kelly is contained in the following "Procedure for Rear Platform Appearances":

　1. Just before the train stops, Senator Carlson will bring to the rear platform on the General's car persons to be introduced from the rear platform.

　2. When the train stops, the local spokesman will introduce one by one those persons to be presented. Each person, after presentation, will retire from rear platform to rear parlor.

　3. (At 15-minute stops, there may next be introduced a campaign leader for a 2-3 minute talk.)

　4. The General will be introduced 5 minutes before the train will leave. He will *first* introduce Mrs. Eisenhower.

5. The General will then speak for four minutes: (1) local reference; (2) recapitulation of principal issues of the crusade; (3) specific instance of the day. Kelly and Cutler will check starting time of his talk.

6. After three minutes (i.e., one minute to go), Kelly will blow his police whistle once. One minute later the train will slowly start and Mrs. Eisenhower will rejoin the General on the platform. They will be alone.

7. No one's but Kelly's order will prolong the train's stay.

To resume the trip through the campaign train, in the Eisenhowers' lounge one would generally find capable and genial Anne Wheaton talking to two or three newcomers who were waiting to be introduced to the Eisenhowers. Mrs. Wheaton was in charge of public relations for women in connection with the campaign train and her ability and personality were qualities that brought her a reward later on as assistant to James Hagerty, presidential press secretary. Upon leaving the Eisenhower lounge car you would pass Mrs. Doud's door and perhaps catch a glimpse of her writing letters to friends back in Denver and to her other daughter, who was called Mike.

The next compartment belonged to Rose, Mamie's maid. She was generally busy getting Mrs. Eisenhower's dresses and accessories ready for the evening rallies in the large cities. Then came Mamie's room and next Ike's quarters, both usually empty during the day.

Next was the dining room, which during the day was converted into an office and sort of waiting room. Here Mary Jane McCaffrey was occupied all day long helping Mamie with her mail and the many other responsibilities of the wife of a presidential candidate. How they could concentrate with the almost constant flow of staff members, visitors, photographers, and members of the press always amazed me. Even the never-ending stack of photographs to be autographed needed a certain amount of concentration and cautiousness at all times as the swaying and jerking train clackety-clacked along, intent only on trying to keep up with the schedule.

Beyond the dining section was the kitchen, where two chefs could generally be seen preparing the next meal. They were always immaculate and had a ready smile for anyone who nodded to them on the way by. Leaving the Eisenhower car one would have to squeeze past the ever-present personal guard who was on constant duty. Mr. Fairly was most genial to all who had a legitimate reason for entering the Eisenhower car. There were one or two instances when over-exuberant persons visiting the train found that Mr. Fairly knew how to carry out his job in the best interests of those he was protecting.

Recording and TV equipment was stored, and used, in the first room of the next car. From here came the strains of "The Sunshine of Your Smile" and "Look Ahead, Neighbor." The first song lasted for about twenty-five playings and then Ike became tired of it. But off and on, now and then, it was heard as we campaigned through the various states. Records were generally played as we slowed down for a whistle stop, but usually the music was lost in the wild cheering of the crowds.

Beyond the "music" room was Moany's room with the door wide open. He was Ike's valet and seemed to be pressing the General's suits much of the time. He gave all passers-by an infectious grin and a word of greeting.

Tom Stephens' door was next and was almost always closed. The next room was headquarters for Katherine Howard of Boston. Some of the women throughout the country who had been especially active in the early Eisenhower venture had got their heads together in time to make sure they had a representative of their sex on the General's staff when it was being set up in Denver. They went to the Governor's office in the Brown Palace Hotel and suggested that Katherine Howard be allowed to represent the women of the country. The Governor discussed their proposal with Eisenhower, who said he was glad to include on his staff a woman who had done distinguished political work in her home state of Massachusetts, and later as secretary of the Republican Convention in Chicago. Aside from her political ability, she had become well known to the TV audience as the woman who stood for many hours with her shoes off at the microphone on the convention platform. There were several reasons ascribed for that unconventional performance: first, it was hot and her feet hurt; second, being tall, she could read the typewritten and penciled notes better without high heels; third, she didn't want to tower over the shorter Honorable Joseph B. Martin. Whatever the reason was, Katherine Howard's shoeless feet were indicative of the way she worked with people. There was never any pretension or affectedness; she was always herself, a delightful and conscientious member. Aboard the train, you would probably have found her entertaining a couple of Republican women from the state we happened to be going through at the time. Listening to their problems pertaining to the Eisenhower campaign and helping them with plans was one of her many jobs. She was a good speaker, too, and sometimes left the train to take part in rallies not included in the train schedule.

Our room was just beyond that of Mrs. Howard. Here the Governor dictated to his secretary and held countless strategy and staff meetings. I seldom used it except to sleep in—it was too much in demand. After a few late evening hassles had become rather excited and noisy, I pasted a sign on the door leading to Katherine Howard's room: "Remember, Katherine Howard would *like* to sleep here."

There were other staff members' rooms beyond ours which were usually empty. The occupants generally worked elsewhere on the train. The visitors' or VIP, car was next, containing the lounge which was likely to be overflowing throughout the day with representatives from whatever state we were passing through. It would be hard to make one's way, for the aisle would be packed solid with enthusiastic Republicans getting acquainted or renewing old friendships, and all eager to meet the General.

In the rest of the train up front you would find men and women busy with their particular jobs. Charlie Brown had charge of the telegraph setup and he took on an extracurricular job, that of keeping track of the people who got left behind, placing silver stars on the map to mark the towns where those mischances occurred. The men and women to whom this happened considered themselves a somewhat special group. A meeting was called and steps taken to form an organization with an honorary degree to be presented to each of the wayward (or perhaps "backward" would be better) members. The wording on each diploma was as follows:

THE HONORABLE DEGREE

OF

L.B.

Is CONFERRED, this the .... day of November, in the Presidential Election Year of One Thousand Nine Hundred and Fifty-two, upon ....

> By this inscription be it known
> (It's not a thing for laughter)
> The flight had flown; with grunt and groan
> Then I came running after.
>
> Be known to all in this campaign
> (for this, dear friends, don't flout me)
> With sweat and strain I sought the train
> Which, dammit, went without me.
>
> This makes me one of the elect
> (your scoffing no one minds)
> A minor sect, yet how select,
> We of the *left behind*.

The verse was the work of the late Stanley High, an editor for the *Reader's Digest* and one of Eisenhower's chief speech writers. His poetical abilities were in frequent demand as birthdays, anniversaries, and other occasions supplied an excuse to relax from the ever-increasing tension of the campaign train schedule.

There were twenty people, including myself, who at one point or another got left behind as the campaign train tried to keep on schedule. Only four of that select group were staff members: Dr. Gabriel Hauge, who later became administrative assistant to the President, Bernard Shanley, whose future role would be that of special counsel to the President and who, by the way, missed the train twice (that made him eligible for the presidency of the "Order of the Left-Behinds"); Mary Jane McCaffrey, who continued on in her job as personal secretary to the First Lady throughout the Eisenhower

Administration; and Mary Burns, one of the secretaries on the Eisenhower Special and later a hard-working and devoted secretary to my husband. Henry Griffin, Frank Cancellare and Frank Jurkowski (the three photographers) and Fred Collins of the Providence *Journal* were among the press people who had a star placed on the map where their involuntary leave-taking took place.

Besides Charlie Brown's interesting corner on the train, there were many other places of fascinating activity. A whole car was given over to the press. It was always untidy—especially the morning following a big evening rally where Ike had made a particularly vigorous speech. The members of the press would have worked late into the previous night to beat the deadline, and as one walked through in the morning all would be quiet and deserted, but the littered floor, the full wastebaskets, and the nervously crumpled cigarette butts gave evidence of the battle that had taken place in the early morning hours.

The photographers had headquarters in a fairly small room not too far from our car. They had transformed their darkroom into a gallery—the kind of gallery that might better have been in constant darkness. It brought many grins to the faces of passers-by as they parted the curtains and peeked inside.

Those three photographers are high on the list of my special acquaintances. I first came to know them at the Eisenhower headquarters in Denver. We became better acquainted at the Hotel Commodore, and as soon as the campaign train started rolling they frequently helped me in some predicament or project. They were always ready for a bit of fun, and I liked a little fun myself; during those days and days of speeches, schedules, and statistics, it was necessary for everyone to sandwich in some diversion now and then.

One day, when Helen Knowland, the wife of the California Senator, was aboard while we were traveling through her state, I decided to do something about the gallery in the photographers' darkroom. They had left the train for an assignment, so the coast was clear. I suggested to Mrs. Knowland that I needed a little help. Her first impulse was to find something else to busy herself with, but she finally warmed up to my suggestion about how the photographers' room could be changed in a way that would surprise them when they returned from their hard day's work.

So, for an hour or so, Helen and I thumbed through all the old magazines we could find. We were looking for a particular type of picture: Girl Scouts, Boy Scouts, nationally known men and women, men in uniform, babies—in fact, anything as far removed as possible from the beauties in bikinis or fans, or less, that now covered the walls. After a neat pile had been gathered, we placed each chaste picture over one of those blondes, brunettes, or redheads. The difference was astonishing.

And astonished was what the photographers were when they wearily returned to their darkroom, heavily laden with cameras, equipment, and films to be processed. Even in the subdued light the change was immediately noticeable. Rumors spread through the train as fast as a prairie fire; it was said the boys knew who had altered the scene in their darkroom and retaliation could be expected. I worried more than a little for a few days—photographers can be so quick with a camera. But there was no reprisal—at least none that I was aware of—and "the boys in the darkroom" continued to be helpful when I needed advice about my own picture taking. They even let me climb onto the truck with them during the General's tour of Bronxville near the end of the campaign. I shall always remember them with a great deal of admiration, for aside from being good-natured they were extremely good photographers. I should know, for they gave me a stack of photographs taken during the entire campaign circuit—a pile of pictures that are memory provoking and that remind me especially of the three photographers without whom the campaign train wouldn't have been so much fun.

If you succeeded in shuffling and lurching your way through all the eighteen cars you would come finally to the locomotive and the engineer. How many alert and dependable engineers took part in piloting what was probably the last campaign train to go across the country and back, I have no idea. I do know that because of their constant vigilance a number of tragedies were averted. Once eager children skipped across the tracks as the train rounded a corner. The engineer braked quickly and the children fortunately were unharmed, though many of the people on the train were badly shaken up and bruised. Flowers, gifts, luggage, and writing equipment flew in every direction in all the eighteen cars. There were other times when it was necessary to stop or slow down suddenly. People joked about their bumps, scattered papers, and spilt coffee, and suggested that the engineer that day must be a Democrat.

Walking through a train that is going eighty miles an hour needs practice if it is to be accomplished with any degree of dignity and progress. There was no one who didn't bruise an elbow or a hip bumping from side to side in an attempt to negotiate passageways.

For me, at least, every trip was hazardous. In Providence, Rhode Island, I went out into the dense crowd to get some pictures while Ike was speaking. It was a foolish move which I never attempted again, for, despite my badge of identification, a policeman grabbed me to prevent me from going back to the train. The gates were closing and I was caught in a mass of surging, yelling, laughing Ike enthusiasts. I couldn't explain to the policeman because he was behind me and wouldn't relax his hold on me. It took the emphatic language of an alert fellow campaigner on the other side of the now closed gate to make him let go of my arm. It got so that every time I alighted from the train to attend a rally in a city or simply to walk along the station platform I did so with some uneasiness.

When we pulled into the station of one of the cities where we were to have a big evening rally, everyone had to be ready to get off the train as soon as it stopped. In fact, that was the usual procedure whenever we were to ride in a motorcade. If it was to be an overnight stay, I had to be sure that I had the necessary equipment. It wasn't long before I was able to pack in less than five minutes—one of the most necessary accomplishments of the traveling campaigner.

Some of those stations were enormous! We would walk and walk before we finally found the motorcade. The Governor was always ahead with the Eisenhowers and other members of the staff. I, loaded down with camera equipment, hatbox, and handbag, generally found myself not too far behind. Many kindhearted staff members would offer to keep me company, or try to help me by carrying my camera bag. They thought they ought to look after me, since my husband was occupied elsewhere, but I insisted on being on my own.

Sometimes when we reached the station we found a line of new cars, all of the same make. Other times the motorcade was made up of all kinds of privately owned autos. But the procedure was always the same. Members of the staff and their wives would have been given a number that corresponded to one on a car in the waiting motorcade. In the car to which I was usually assigned there would be Republican committee members of that particular city or state and sometimes one or two staff workers from the train. Within minutes, while still introducing ourselves to each other, we were off through the city's main streets to the hotel. Ike and top members of his staff, plus the Republican leaders of that locality, would be several cars ahead, but we could get glimpses of Eisenhower as he stood up in the open car waving to the crowds that lined the streets.

On reaching our hotel we would find one or two of the elevators making express runs to the floor allotted to the Eisenhower party. I would ask the first person who looked knowledgeable which way I should go to find my room. The hotel corridors were always teeming with security personnel, staff workers, local Republicans, and others like me just looking for their rooms. There was always a feeling of great suspense and high excitement. What kind of rally would the evening produce? Would there be a good crowd? Already in the General's room a meeting would be in progress. My husband would be there—or he would be in our room on one of the several telephones —or perhaps on two of them. It was simply incredible how some on-the-ball Republican up in New England, or down in Texas, or back in Chicago, would know just when we were arriving at that particular hotel somewhere in the West—or wherever it was. The difference in time didn't discourage them either—the telephones kept ringing constantly, while we were trying to get baths or eat or sleep. I expect they kept ringing after we left for the rally. One of the most active telephone callers was Jerry Lambert. The Governor could always count on a call from him as soon as he reached a hotel.

Gerard B. Lambert, a man of personal charm and unlimited interests (as a boy he could even play a harmonica backwards), had been head of the 90-million-dollar Listerine Corporation. Not the least of his interests was politics, and he entered the Eisenhower campaign in time to make a public-opinion survey in New Hampshire just before our primary election. As a result of his poll, he found that the Taft followers were in the minority and he thought from his past experience in Dewey's first primary that it would be best to keep silent about the figures. As he put it, "It was best to underestimate the situation." But Jerry found it wasn't easy to keep such figures secret. Somehow certain Eisenhower followers got wind of the good news that Mr. Lambert's poll showed Ike to be far ahead. My husband tried unsuccessfully to get the figures himself, but Jerry's assistant who had run the poll had orders not to let anyone see them. It wasn't until Tom Stephens came to New Hampshire to see what the "amateurs" were doing that the Governor had his first look at the results of the poll. I should imagine that he, or anyone else in his position as governor, titular head of the Republican party in the state, and without any question the New Hampshire man most responsible for the Eisenhower effort would have felt a little piqued at having to ask a New Yorker for a look at a poll taken in New Hampshire indicating the public's interest in Eisenhower and Taft. He knew the poll had been taken, and he knew he had been unable to see it; what he didn't know was that Jerry had shown it to others, from whom Tom got it. But if the Governor was in the least exasperated, he never let on.

Jerry had his own good reasons for wanting to keep the figures as secret as he could. Too much optimism in the Eisenhower camp might ruin everything, he thought. He was elated to hear that Taft's own poll had put the Senator far ahead of the General. And he was equally jubilant when he heard that the Eisenhower interest in New Hampshire was thought to be lessening. He *knew* differently. Things were working out just as he had hoped. Now the Taft men would get complacent and overconfident, and the Eisenhower men would buckle down to fight even harder. Perhaps Jerry's reasoning was right. It certainly could have been. Although Lambert thus had considerable to do with the New Hampshire primary behind the scenes, he and my husband met for the first time the following August in Denver and became good friends. That fall when the Eisenhower bandwagon began to move across the nation Jerry Lambert continued with his survey. When information was assembled, he made some personal observations and sent it along to the Governor and other Ike men.

Later, in the Eisenhower headquarters at New York's Hotel Commodore, Jerry had advised Eisenhower not to waste any time in states like Mississippi and Texas. At dinner with the Governor that same evening, he urged him to keep Ike from making the mistake that Willkie had made—that of spending too much time trying to win over the Southern states. To impress the Governor with the vigor of his conviction he had offered to bet him $1,000 to $1 that Ike couldn't carry Texas. The Governor, never one to refuse a challenge, said something about not having much to lose and accepted the bet.

As soon as the big evening rallies were over I immediately hurried to the car to which I had been assigned for the ride back to the hotel. If we weren't spending the night, it was my duty to be sure that all our belongings were gathered up, including, of course, anything that had been thoughtfully left in our room by some generous person or group. There was one kind of gift that always added greatly to my uneasiness as I made my precarious way back to the train, through the long, long waiting rooms out to the long, long platforms, laden with camera bag, handbag, and hatbox—the last heavier than on the incoming trip by a bottle of Scotch or bourbon that had been left in our room. I never enjoyed trips less, worrying lest the hatbox break and the contents land on the marble floor of the waiting room. I had been told by the Governor to look after everything—the key, all our belongings, messages, etc.—and get back to the train on time. It was little enough to do, but how I dreaded those seemingly endless marble floors!

One of the busiest and liveliest times was when the Nixon telegrams flooded the train as a result of the furor whipped up by many newspapers, commentators, and politicians following the disclosure of the so-called Nixon Fund. As the 11,000 telgrams piled up, Mrs. Hugh

Scott (wife of the Congressman from Pennsylvania), Ann Whitman, and I, along with other staff members, opened, counted, and sorted the many messages. There were all kinds, from all sorts of people, from every corner of the country. One that I opened and read touched me deeply. It was from Nixon's mother and it was a simple statement of her faith in her son. There were brilliantly worded telegrams, and there were straightforward short messages; 90 per cent of them were favorable to Nixon. From the smaller percentage group there was one we couldn't help smiling at. It read: "Send Hagerty, Adams, Clay, Seaton, Carlson, Stephens to the boxcar for the duration of the trip."

Somewhere along the way I started collecting clippings from the papers that came aboard at each stop. Occasionally I found it difficult to keep up to date with my project and stored the pile of papers in our drawing room until one day the Governor asked if I was collecting for a paper drive. He suggested that there might be some other place for them if I had to keep them. So, when no one was looking, I cached them under a couple of chairs in the little room that the railroad officials used when it wasn't engaged for conferences. I checked frequently as I added to the pile, to see that none was missing. Then one evening I decided it was time to do some clipping and filing. Upon entering the room I found three railroad men, sitting quiet, watching the passing scene beyond the window, but my papers were gone. I said nonchalantly, as if talking to myself, "Wonder where my papers are." There was no explanation from my friends. In fact, they seemed all the more interested in the country we were passing through as they leaned closer to the window—even though it was pitch-black outside!

Understandably, the strain on Ike and those immediately responsible for the efficient handling of the campaign was tremendous. I think everyone on the train had, at one time or another, an attack of some form of cold. Ike had several bothersome bouts which were subdued with shots of penicillin. And sooner or later most of the staff was uncomfortable, if not miserable, with stomach upsets and respiratory infections. The General's physician, General Howard Snyder, kept close watch over his charge and staff members who were under the weather.

Besides Dr. Snyder, there was another man who worked at keeping Ike and the people immediately under him in the best of physical condition. For tired nerves, bruises, and that cramped-up feeling which came from sitting hour after hour poring over schedules or working on speeches, there was Bob Lipoff. His first assignment at the end of a long hard day was Ike. Then he would come in search of my husband. He knew how to roll, knead, pound, and stretch the knots and aches into oblivion. My husband nicknamed him "the Masher," for his administrations often made his subject feel he was being worked into a pulp. Bob Lipoff was a familiar sight late in the evenings, going to or coming from his work, carrying an electric vibrator, a bottle of rubbing alcohol, astringents, and towels. "Here comes the Masher," someone in the lounge car was sure to sing out as the grinning Lipoff swayed along toward his evening's job.

Because of Bob Lipoff and his nightly workout on my husband, I was always the last of the Adams family to climb into bed. I sought a chair in the lounge while the Masher took the kinks out of Sherm's muscles and nerves. There were generally other members of the staff or personnel relaxing with a highball, Coke, or nothing at all. My favorite drink was Seven-Up—about which I was teased considerably. There were seldom any deep discussions at that time of night. Everyone was usually joking about the events of the day or speculating about what the morrow would bring. I was generally so tired that I could hardly keep my eyes open and as soon as the Masher came through the vestibule door, I lost no time in saying good night to those who still lingered.

It was on a Sunday during the long ride across Montana that a stop was made in Livingston for fifteen minutes in order to have the train serviced. Some state officials came aboard, and also a minister whom the Governor, after conferring with Ike and other staff members, had made arrangements with to conduct a short service as the train traveled to Whitehall.

The Eisenhowers gathered with members of the staff in the lounge car. It was a gorgeous day and there was no feeling of tension or hurry. The minister's words and prayers added to the already tranquil atmosphere, while stamped forever on our memory was that unforgettable Montana landscape and the welcome pause in the usual rush and worry.

As the service ended and the train slowed down for the Whitehall stop, where the minister and visitors were to get off, we were treated to another scene on that already memorable Sunday. From the windows we could see the flat grazing lands stretching for miles into the distance until they caught up with the foothills of the Tobacco Root Mountains; with the clear blue sky they made a breath-taking backdrop for the group of riders that were lined up waiting as the train came to a stop. The men and women in colorful and authentic Western regalia carried large American flags and were mounted on beautiful horses, also outfitted with the finest equipment. It was a scene that we were loath to leave, and perhaps the riders and their mounts sensed our reluctance, for they followed the train for some distance at top speed, flags waving, horses' manes and tails flying in the clear, crisp air.

It wasn't long before we were weaving up through the continental divide, passing old landmarks and trails used long ago by Lewis and Clark, early trail blazers, and immigrants and Indians. There were numerous hairpin turns and breath-stopping vistas, and presently we were over the pass and rounding the last mountain before getting our first view of Butte, where the train paused just long enough for a new set of excited visitors to climb aboard.

As the train crisscrossed the country in a frenzied attempt to keep up with the daily schedule, the sound of the wheels on the rails seemed to be saying Ei-sen-hower, Ei-sen-hower. And at the same time the end of the whistle-stop tour was nearing, as was the whole Eisenhower effort. The last train ride was to Boston on the night before election. The Garden quickly filled for the final engagement of the Republican campaign. That enormous crowd of humanity which had gathered to listen to the last speeches was a mélange of excited, worried, or confident individuals. But those of us who had followed the Eisenhower bandwagon from the very beginning were filled with a mixture of sadness and hope. No one spoke of his feelings, but I am sure everyone felt the same in his heart: the battle had been a good one, it had been fought cleanly and in the best American tradition. Surely the outcome the next day would prove to the world that there was more than one political party in America. Surely the tireless effort of all who had worked so devotedly for Eisenhower would pay off as voters began to flock to the polls in a mater of a few hours. Groups of staff workers and personnel stood around in little clusters, but here and there a lone member of "the team" watched the scene from a shadowy corner near the stage. When so many have worked together so long for so good a cause emotion runs high, and even with all the heartaches and headaches which no day had been devoid of it had been a wonderful experience which none of us would probably ever know again. We hated to see the end of the Eisenhower campaign and we couldn't bear to think of anything but a decisive victory for Ike.

After the speechmaking, the vaudeville acts, the singing, and the cheering, we boarded the Eisenhower Special for the last time.

On the way back to New York the Eisenhowers joined the staff in the VIP lounge car for a party. The Governor took part in the fun for a short time and then disappeared toward his room. I knew he was very tired. The General seemed completely relaxed and in a jovial mood. He enjoyed the gaiety and joined in the singing led by Fred Waring and his Pennsylvanians. There were songs from the North, East, South, and West which brought back pleasant memories of our brief stay in each section. And as a change from the usual "I Like Ike" buttons, there were posters and huge buttons with the lettering "I Like Mamie," which greatly amused the General's wife.

There was a feeling of closeness, for most of those present had campaigned together for months, through discouraging days and less trying ones, for long hours, and for thousands of miles. There was a feeling of sadness too as we all realized the end of a wonderful campaign was near.

We were still singing as the train brought us into Pennsylvania

Station in New York—the Eisenhower Special had come to the last stop.

Possibly there will be other Republican trains, but there most certainly will never be another blessed with such glorious weather, for all across the country and back we had but one rainy day. America never looked more beautiful—the cornfields of the Midwest through which we rode for a day and a half, with the stalks waving and nodding as the train passed, and the seemingly endless wheatlands rippling in the wind, the fields in the South bursting with cotton. In the Northwest apple trees hung heavy with fruit, and in the West beef cattle could be seen on the grazing lands in uncountable numbers. All across the land were farms where plantings and plowings made a picture comparable to grandma's "crazy quilt." Lakes and rivers shimmered in the sun or moonlight; the aspens, dressed in brilliant gold, paraded up and down the foothills of the snow-capped Rockies. And when we finally reached New England we found still more of the beauty that is part of America. The skies were deep blue, the air pure and crisp, and the maple trees in gorgeous color.

Forever, I believe, when fall arrives I shall experience a restlessness —a feeling that I should be on my way—a hope or an uncontrolled desire to see a big sign with the words: EISENHOWER SPECIAL—ALL ABOARD!

ix

We Settle In

It was queer to wake up on Election Day and know it was all over. There was nothing that had to be done all day long. No hurried packing to be on time for the departure of the train. No rush for breakfast so that the Governor could be in his office for an hour or so to work before the surge of appointments, discussions, strategy and organization meetings began. We hardly knew what to do with ourselves. One thing was certain, we didn't want to sit around discussing with this person and that the probable or possible outcome of the voting which had already started.

Following a leisurely breakfast, the Governor went to the office to go through the morning's mail. The corridor of the Commodore's sixth floor was almost deserted. There were no groups of photographers, newsmen, or VIPs waiting in front of the elevators or the clearance desk; no staff workers hurrying hither and yon. Eisenhower's campaigners had listened, queried, argued, consoled, demanded and concurred through months of intense campaigning—now it was up to the voters.

Later in the morning the Governor returned to our room where in a leisurely way I was packing things that would be mailed to New Hampshire. "Let's get outdoors, Plum," he said, "there's nothing to do around here." On the way to the elevator we picked up Bobby Cutler and were soon riding in the direction of the Bronx Zoo. How we happened to choose that particular place to get away from the strain and anxiety of waiting for the day to pass I can't tell, except that we wanted to be where we could walk, and far away from countless persons who could only ask, "Well, how are you betting?"

or "It's all over but the shouting, isn't it?" or "How much of a lead do you think Ike will have over Stevenson?" But even at the Zoo the tenseness prevailed. The elephants reminded us of countless others we had seen during months of hectic and happy campaigning. As we looked at the monkeys, giraffes, bears, lions, and numerous other quiet, noisy, beautiful, obnoxious, or simply interesting specimens of the animal world, still hammering away in our minds were the words "Will Ike win?"

We returned to the hotel for lunch and I knew the Governor was hoping there would be some indication already coming over the wires that the voting was heavy and in favor of Eisenhower. In the elevator riding up to the sixth floor were other staff members. One of them asked where we had been all morning. "Out to the Zoo," I replied. "Ha, ha, ha, that must have been quite a change from the campaign," he laughed. "Not very much," I answered, thinking of the numerous species of humanity I had encountered on the campaign trail: the dependable, the dauntless, and the difficult.

After a leisurely lunch and several errands, we returned to the hotel to find that the first waves of returns had started to come in. As the flood increased, little by little, so did the lead of Eisenhower over Stevenson. Up and down and across the country the Republicans were showing enormous strength. By early evening people had started to sift into the ballroom of the Commodore where official tabulators kept the huge scoreboard supplied with the latest figures to the very end. Soon there was little standing space and no empty seats, except the ones that were being saved down front for the Governor and me. We wandered around speaking to old and new friends and ignored the insistent requests of those in charge of the seating arrangements that we claim our seats for the exciting hours that were to come. My husband had no intention of being a part of the scramble he expected would take place. If, as he believed in his heart, Ike came out well ahead, everybody would be trying to elbow his way to that large, but not adequate, stage where he would be accepting the ovation. Already poised for the flight to the stage were excited GOP leaders, old friends of the Eisenhowers, and campaigners. The Governor looked for a less congested spot and found it in the gallery among photographic equipment and television cameras. There we sat and looked down on the crowded ballroom where between two to three thousand Ike supporters shouted, laughed, and sang. Groups here and there held their own with a lusty, "*I Like Ike*" while other clusters of equally vociferous enthusiasm managed to the finish "The Sunshine of Your Smile" or other campaign songs with the help of Fred Waring. From our adequate, if not too comfortable, seats in the gallery we watched the figures on the bulletin board grow. We watched the distance between Eisenhower and Stevenson widen and we heard the wild cheering below us become even more deafening as Ike and Mamie appeared on the stage after receiving Stevenson's telegram of congratulations. My husband silently watched as Eisenhower acknowledged the cheers. I wondered what was in his thoughts. I wondered at his preferring to be in the gallery when all the rest of "the team" was crowding the stage. I wondered even while I knew the answer. To have had a part in such an overwhelming triumph—to have been one of those who helped it come about was enough in itself. He had no desire to be among those swarming around the platform where the Eisenhowers stood. Just before the Eisenhowers left to return to their rooms and the gathering of friends, my husband said, "Come, Plum, let's go down and congratulate Ike and Mamie." We found our way to the back hall which led from the stage, arriving just as the jubilant couple appeared. Ike and Mamie were all smiles. Sighting the Governor as we moved toward him, Ike reached out to grab his hand. "Oh! *There* you are! Where have you been? I thought you had been avoiding me!" The future President of the United States then turned and put his hands on my shoulders and gave me a kiss on my cheek. The hallway was in semi-darkness compared with the brilliance of the floodlights on the stage, and that was the way my husband liked it. He always preferred to be in the background. That was where he thought he belonged. When holding public office he often had to be out front to pacify the photographers, but in his work for Eisenhower he always sought out the back row if possible—there were always plenty of people eager to get up front, if not already there.

The Eisenhowers had a reception in their rooms for members of their family, friends, and members of Ike's staff on the train. We obediently appeared, knowing it would be another jam-packed session. Since we had just congratulated the Eisenhowers, after one look at the exuberant milling crowd, we left for the less congested but no less excited staff party, where we joyfully and with deep sincerity drank a toast to the President-elect.

At 1:30 the Governor and I decided some sleep was in order even as the jubilant celebration continued, and we returned to our room. But before the Governor turned out the light, he sat down on the edge of the bed and thumbed through a notebook for a telephone number. By the time the operator succeeded in getting the call through, it was two o'clock. When a voice on the other end of the line said, rather sleepily, "Hello," my husband asked, "How about that Texas bet, Jerry?"

We woke early and rushed to the door to get the morning papers. We could hardly wait to read it in print: IKE WINS BY LANDSLIDE!

The border states of Oklahoma and Kentucky had shown a preference for Ike and even Ohio, which had gone Democratic in the previous election—and which was also Taft's state—rolled up an impressive tally for the General. And down in the South some of the Democrat strongholds showed an almost unbelievable Eisenhower lead over Stevenson. Texas was one of those states, as the Governor had reminded Jerry Lambert in the early-morning hours. (Later Jerry told someone he figured it was less expensive to make the bet with the Governor than to poll the state.)

During the days that followed there were continuous lines of visitors at the Eisenhower headquarters in the Hotel Commodore. The General consulted with this one and that one about a thousand problems, including selections for Cabinet posts and other top jobs in the new administration. Late in November he announced he had chosen my husband to be the Assistant to the President—a position hitherto nonexistent.

While the conferences, appointments, and planning kept up at a steady pace for the remainder of the year, the sixth floor of the Commodore began to return to normal. Republican reservations on planes and trains going to Washington mounted every day. The hotels filled up and there was a decided increase in the number of parties and receptions. One was the Victory Luncheon in the Presidential Room of the Statler, a most thrilling occasion for hundreds of jubilant Republican women. Other events which seemed to mushroom up overnight had a distinct Republican flavor also. It had been a long time since the GOP had been in power. Of course, it wasn't only dyed-in-the-wool Republicans who were responsible for the new regime in Washington; Democrats-for-Eisenhower gave a great deal of assistance as did Independents and the Young Republican groups. Naturally the preponderance of Democratic residents didn't feel much like celebrating. The Washington deck of cards was being reshuffled.

On January 5 I had driven from New York to New Hampshire for three days to pack the things we would need in our new home in Washington. After the truck left with its full load, I hurried off to Manchester to get a view of a very new granddaughter. It was too short a visit, for I had to drive to Washington in order to have our house ready for the arrival of our furniture.

I stopped overnight in New York and awoke with a bad case of laryngitis. To make matters worse, it was snowing hard. I had little enthusiasm for the trip ahead of me but was glad that I was going to be alone—I wouldn't have to talk. For most of the way I battled with heavy sleet and snow. The turnpike speed was thirty-five miles an hour and I began to wonder if I would ever reach Washington, let alone arrive in time to unlock the doors so that the movers could unload. As it happened, they were waiting for me.

With a few items from our home in New Hampshire, the Governor and I settled down in the old federal house on C Street across from the House Office Building. He had asked the real estate agent to find us "a place to sleep" so that we wouldn't have to stay in a hotel. And that, literally speaking, is exactly what it turned out to be. The long days in the White House office plus numerous social and political engagements left almost no time for just living. "Settling down" with a husband who is a conscientious, hard-working politician in the upper brackets of a new administration was, I found, akin to settling down for a picnic in a nest of yellow jackets!

Before going to Washington we had received a number of communications from real estate agencies there. The turnover of real estate in Washington is greater than in any other city in the country. Service personnel come and go continually and, especially when there is a change in the administration, so do government workers. Then the men and women in the realty business have a wonderful time.

The types and conditions of property vary widely, as widely as the individual real estate people, who may be retired Army personnel, widows, heads of families, or wives helping out with the family income. In some cases, women take on the job of selling real estate not so much for the financial returns as for the chance it gives them to be busy, or to do something besides housework. There are women whose names appear in Who's Who and the Social Register who have hung out their shingle sans gène. Whatever their walk in life, all are assiduous in their quest for clients. I was told that every morning, over the coffee cups, they eagerly search the columns of the morning paper hoping to find that a government official has retired, returned, or resigned, opening up a possible turnover of real estate. Undoubtedly, the newspaper is the best way of finding out who is leaving, or coming to, Washington. But there are other channels, one of which is the cocktail circuit. A real estate operator can often pick up a choice piece of information that will give him, or her, a head start in the race.

As soon as the news got around that we would be going to Washington, the letters and telephone calls from real estate people began to arrive. I made tentative appointments with one or two "reliable persons" who had been suggested to me or to the Governor. Finally, when I had a chance to spend a few days in Washington looking for a place to live, I found that ardent real estate agents can be most congenial companions. The ones with whom I spent many hours certainly were. They were agreeable to anything from taking me to lunch to dropping me off downtown "any place at all" to do some shopping. They would even go without lunch in order to show me "the most desirable areas in which to live."

There were several stock phrases that carried little weight as far as the Governor and I were concerned. We merely smiled when someone said, "A person of your importance should have the right kind of house." We were adamant in our desire to find something we could afford in the area we wanted it in. Our insistence pigeonholed us—apparently there were others who felt the same way—much to the exasperation of at least one agent who said, "Oh! You Republicans! You all insist on living within your incomes!"

The Governor was generally too busy to accompany me on the house-hunting trips. Only once was I able to get him inside one of the "packing boxes" in quaint and "*so* much atmosphere!" Georgetown. Those old, old dwellings standing cheek to cheek did not interest him at all. As a rule the narrowness of the buildings and the garden patch—charming as they certainly are—in no way match the colossal rent or sales figures. At least that is how it seemed to us. We were interested only in renting, and in one or two instances, when informed of the monthly rent, the Governor, with a twinkle in his eye, asked if a deed would be forthcoming at that time.

There was one conscientious, hard-working young woman who tried desperately to find a house for us. She had other good qualities, not the least of which was her luscious Southern accent and blonde beauty. The Governor found time to go along on one trip, naturally, but it was again a waste of time. He made fun of the places with "atmosphere" which our attractive guide showed us and said he couldn't afford that kind of atmosphere. We crossed and recrossed trails from Capitol Hill to Montgomery County in Maryland. And finally, when only a short time was left before Inauguration Day and the need to get settled was urgent, a retired Army officer showed us the place on C Street, almost in the middle of Capitol Hill where the capricious breezes sweep refuse into the dooryards and the solons have difficulty finding places to park.

The charming old federal house on Capitol Hill, which we eventually found, wasn't exactly what we were looking for but there wasn't time for any more house hunting. Closing up Eisenhower's headquarters on the sixth floor of the Hotel Commodore in New York and at the same time clearing his own desk in the State House in Concord, and delivering his Exaugural Address, together with getting the machinery of a new administration off to a good start, took up all the Governor's time. We decided on the C Street house because it was fairly close to the West Wing of the White House where his office would be.

As the change of administration affected the real estate business, so also vibrations were being felt in other circles on the Washington scene. Hostesses were busy replacing the old names, high on the precedence lists, with new ones. It was astonishing how quickly some of those hospitable souls could accommodate themselves to the new political order of things. Of course, many of them had a preference for Republicans and were overjoyed at the change that was finally taking place. A number were intent on making up for lost time. Then there were other hostesses who carried on pretty much as before, inviting an assortment from both political parties which, especially in Washington, makes for anything but a dull evening.

Washington hostesses found out quite early that some of the new faces in the government were not going to be seen too often at late-evening affairs. Most of the men felt as my husband did: they had come to Washington determined to do a good job, and they thought one of the best ways to accomplish their purpose was to use the nights for rest in preparation for the next day's duties. All of them enjoyed an occasional evening out, especially with old friends, but it was extremely hard at times to convince Washington hostesses that after a day such as the Eisenhower staff put in, the energy and will for a long evening out were sometimes lacking.

Soon after moving into the C Street house we decided to do no more redecorating than was necessary. I'd had considerable experience with paper hangers and painters back in New England, but combining them with an Inaugural in Washington was something quite different, I found. They arrived simultaneously with an abundance of invitations to luncheons, teas, dinners, and cocktail parties. The Washington hostesses were losing no time. For all the newcomers it was the same. Messages and invitations continued to pour in before and during the Inaugural season.

The sun shone on Inauguration Day, January 20; the warmth of its rays must have felt good to the thousands who were waiting along the parade route and standing or sitting in every available spot around the Capitol Plaza. Earlier in the morning, about nine o'clock, our official car-with-driver arrived to take us to the National Presbyterian Church, where the President would worship in years to come. I was taken aback by the color of the car and asked the Colonel (our escort for the day) to please swap it for something less obnoxious in color —obsolete if necessary—while we were in church. He grinned and said he guessed there wasn't a chance. We didn't need any police escort to be sure we arrived at the church on time. The always busy Washington streets and avenues seemed to open up as we appeared. The fiery tomato-red color of our car apparently suggested fire engines, for we didn't have to slow down anywhere. At least, I thought, if someone throws tomatoes along the parade route they will blend!

After the church service we joined the motorcade for the trip to the Capitol. We gathered with other members of the official family in the Senate Chambers until time to be ushered to our special seats. Mine was on the sixth row of steps behind the inaugural platform. Wives of Cabinet members then appeared to claim their seats in the row in front of me. When all the national and foreign dignitaries, inaugural officials, the Eisenhower and Truman families were in their places, I craned my neck and could just barely see my husband whose seat was close to one of the great columns of the Capitol Building. As I watched him I thought it must be giving him a great deal of satisfaction to know that his efforts had helped so greatly to bring about this particular inauguration.

For a few days, during the height of the inaugural week festivities, the workmen were at the top of the scaffolding on the stairs of our house—the only stairs. Here and there their dropcloths conformed to the stair treads; on other steps anyone going up or down had to navigate by guesswork. Somehow we got through the hectic inaugural period. It hadn't been easy on the days when several changes of attire were necessary, all the way from breakfast-in-a-tweed-suit to dinner-in-white-tie, to negotiate the cluttered stairs, to scramble under and around the ladders and scaffolding, to keep one's full skirts from hitting the painted door-casings.

The day finally arrived when the work, according to the contract, was supposed to be finished. I opened the door for the two white-overalled gentlemen at the usual time that morning—or perhaps it was just a few moments earlier than usual. Anyway, when I returned to the kitchen several minutes later those two Southern workmen, one short and one tall, were sitting on the floor, their backs to the wall. I was nonplused.

"Weren't you supposed to be through today?"

"Wa-ll, ah dunno," said the tall one.

"Well, *I* know! The contract says all is to be finished today!"

"Reckon we-all waon't be gitten don toda-a-ay," said the short man. They continued to sit.

"*Why* don't you get to work? Maybe you *could* finish if you got a move on!" The tall one did some deep thinking, then he looked at his pal with a noticeable degree of animation and drawled, "Yo-all know? She mus' be from de Nawth!"

It took us awhile to get used to the slower pace of work in Washington, just as it took time to accustom ourselves to the fast-moving social whirl. I'll never forget the TV workman who said he would "get around fust thing in the morning."

"What time will that be?" I asked disbelievingly.

"Oh, somewhere round ten or so."

To a couple of early risers like us, the day was considered pretty well gone by ten o'clock.

I had returned to Washington with one well-defined, insatiable desire. It had been growing on me for many years but had become almost an obsession during my first Washington sojourn when Sherm was a member of Congress. At that time I had promised myself I would take art lessons if ever I came back to Washington. It was

Mrs. Sherman Adams
in the living room of their Tilden Street house in Washington

Mary Sheehan White and
Edward Everett White,
the author's mother and father

The house in Belmont where Rachel Adams (sitting on porch at left) grew up

The author, aged seven

erman Adams, about five years old

Rachel White and Sherman Adams
shortly before their wedding in 1923

The Adams family at home in the early 1940's, when Sherman Adams was in the State Legislature. Left to right, Marian, Sarah, Jean, Samuel, Rachel and Sherman Adams.

The Adams house in Lincoln, N.H., taken several years ago (*Photo by E. B. Conant*)

Snowshoeing on Cannon Mountain.
Mt. Lafayette in the background.
(Photo by Reg Keniston)

Rachel and Sherman Adams with
their son Sam on a fishing trip
during the early governorship
years
*(New Hampshire Fish and Game
Photo)*

Ann Whitman and the
author sorting the flood
of telegrams that followed
Richard Nixon's
"Checkers" speech

General Eisenhower and the three press photographers,
Frank E. Cancellare, Henry L. Griffin and Frank Jurkowski

A party in the lounge
car on the way back to
New York after the final
campaign rally in Boston

Portrait of Mrs. Eisenhower by
Thomas Stephens.
While artist began work
on the portrait the author
and First Lady chatted.

For Rachel Adams with affection.
Mamie Doud Eisenhower

Arriving at the White House
for the first state dinner
of the season
(*Photo by Abbie Rowe,
Courtesy Nat'l Park Service*)

The President visits Lincoln, New Hampshire. Leaving the Adams house, left to right, Governor Dwinnell, Sherman Adams, the President and Mrs. Adams.
(*Photo by Reg Keniston*)

Outside the Tilden Street house. The lambs were a present from Sinclair Weeks. (*Washington Star photo by Paul Schmick*)

The First Lady poses with the Cabinet wives after a White House luncheon. Left to right, first row: Mrs. Martin Durkin, Mrs. Douglas McKay, Mrs. Richard Nixon, Mrs. Eisenhower, Mrs. Charles E. Wilson, Mrs. Herbert Brownell, Jr., Mrs. Harold Stassen. Back row: Mrs. Sinclair Weeks, Mrs. George M. Humphrey, Mrs. Oveta Culp Hobby, Mrs. Sherman Adams, Mrs. Arthur E. Summerfield, Mrs. Henry Cabot Lodge, Jr., Mrs. Joseph M. Dodge. (*Associated Press Photo*)

The Lincoln sewing club comes to Washington. Left to right, Marian Stewart, Faith Herrick, Emma Crump, Nora Parent and Bertha Audley.

Above: Some of the Monday group of White House staff wives who met to do needle work for the Washington Cathedral. Left to right, the author, Mrs. John Hamlin, Mrs. Jack Z. Andersen, Mrs. Rocco Siciliano, Mrs. Arthur Larsen. (*Photo by Abbie Rowe. Courtesy Nat'l Park Service*)   *Below:* The ball gowns of former First Ladies. The models are, left to right: Mrs. Leonard Hall (Mary Todd Lincoln); Mrs. Thomas P. Pike (Martha Washington); Mrs. Gordon Allott (Jane Findlay, hostess for President Harrison); Mrs. Ralph Becker (Harriet Lane, hostess for President Buchanan); Mrs. Maurice H. Stans (Grace Coolidge); Mrs. Sherman Adams (Angelica Van Buren, hostess for President Van Buren); Mrs. Donald Lewis (Abigail Adams). (*Washington Post Photo*)

Above: In the President's box during a concert in Constitution Hall. Left to right, Rachel Adams, Mrs. and Mr. Gerald Morgan, Robert Cutler, Sherman Adams.

(*Washington Post Photo*)

Below: The author with grandchildren Christina, Karin and Billy Hallager.

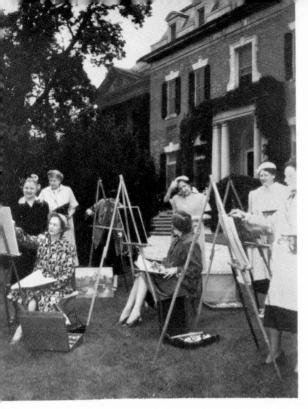

Painting class in Georgetown. Left to right, Marion Adams, the author's sister-in-law; Rachel Adams; Mrs. A. Lyle Prather; Rosamond Gaydash, art instructor (partly hidden by easel); Señora de Castro, wife of the Ambassador from El Salvador; Mrs. C. M. S. Skene; Mrs. C. Raymond Wire; Mrs. Bradley C. Hodgkins.

Easter egg roll at the Tilden Street house for children of the White House staff. (*Photo by Abbie Rowe. Courtesy Nat'l Park Service*)

Sherman Adams with grand-
children and neighborhood
children about to climb
Mt. Osceola, 1960

A Washington sleigh ride. The author with Mrs. Jack Z. Andersen, Washington, D. C.

Off for the ski slopes
of Cannon Mountain

The Adams family in the living room of "Fieldhouse," the author's converted barn in Lincoln. Left to right, Sarah Adams (daughter); William Hallager (son-in-law); Marian Freese (daughter); Bill Hallager (grandson); Jean Hallager (daughter); Martha Freese (granddaughter); Karin Hallager (granddaughter); Dana Freese (grandson) on end of bench; Nancy Adams (daughter-in-law) holding her daughter Melinda; Samuel S. Adams (son) standing by fireplace; Christina Hallager (in front of Sam); Thomas and Timothy Freese (grandsons) backs to camera; Sherman and Rachel Adams.

On Artist's Bluff, Franconia Notch, N.H. (Gordon Parks, Courtesy *Life* © 1959, Time, Inc.)

Mary Hanes, one of the agents who had tried desperately and un-availingly to find the type of house we were looking for, who showed me the way. While we were driving about one day in search of a place to live, she told me about herself and her interest in painting. I confided in her that, next to a house, I was most anxious to find an art instructor, and I went on to tell her about the promise to myself, which I had hardly expected would ever come true. She had high praise for her teacher, Rosamond Gaydash, who had a studio in Georgetown. I decided I would get in touch with Mrs. Gaydash about the possibility of joining her classes.

A few weeks later I was admitted to Rosamond's already bulging art class in the basement of her charming house. Her generous spirit found it impossible to say "no" even to a neophyte such as I. No one's talent was too poor, or too evident. Rosamond gave to all the same amount of encouragement, praise, and assistance. She could make a beginner feel like a Renoir—just as she could take the dullest of scenes and make a picture of enchantment. She shared all her secrets, all the skills that she had acquired over years of close asso-ciation with colors and canvas.

As I sat before my easel waiting for my first lesson in oil painting, I felt powerless to lift my brush. That stark-naked canvas seemed to glare at me and dare me to touch it with paint. As I tried to get up courage to invade that white expanse, I realized it was much easier to think of painting than to do it. Months later I would wholly agree with Degas, who said, "Painting is not very difficult when you don't know how—but when you know—ah! Then it is a different matter."

As I continued to gaze at my clean canvas, my neat pallette of colors, and my new brushes, the feeling of paralysis became even more intense. At last Rosamond finished instructing one of the other pupils and came over to me. She showed me how to sketch in the scene that I was going to work on. And then with a few strokes the clean canvas had been conquered. I relaxed and lost myself in a New England scene of mountains, farmlands, and squash blossoms. I had learned to arrange color on canvas with a not too discouraging result.

I would never be the same again. My world would never be the same again either. For the rest of my life I would be watching more intently the cloud formations and the constant changing of color— how could I transfer what I saw to canvas? Mountaintops with a skirt of mist, waves hurrying across a pond before a sudden breeze, children knee-deep in a field of wildflowers—my fingers longed to reach for a brush and start painting with each new scene. I noticed shadows, the effect of "warm against cool," the changes of light— in short, all that I could see, anywhere, everywhere, became more interesting.

In that crowded basement studio I worked closely with a group of interesting women, some of whom had been painting for years, others who, like me, had just recently taken up the avocation that can banish all thoughts of time, fatigue, tension, and, as happened in my case, worry over an illness.

Throughout the first few weeks after we arrived in Washington I had been having a series of chest X rays. An earlier physical checkup had indicated that all was not well. I submitted to what seemed at the time unnecessary interruptions of my busy and exciting days. I couldn't believe that there was anything wrong with me—or could there be? I began to feel uneasy. Undoubtedly the doctors had reasons, which they hadn't told me about, for continuing the X rays. Anyway, the days were so full of things I had to do, and wanted to do, that there was little time to worry.

On February 17 I was admitted to the hospital for further observation. Having been told I might be there indefinitely, I reluctantly canceled all my engagements.

As days went by, with weeks, then months, dragging past, I was informed the X rays continued to show improvement. An early, light case of tuberculosis was being arrested. Through those six months that I was in the hospital the Governor was beginning the most grueling job he had ever had. He thoroughly understood the needs of the President, and he worked from early morning until long after many offices in the city were closed. Then, after stopping at a restaurant for a quick dinner, he would drive the several miles to the hospital to visit me every evening, unless he had to be out of town. Often, to vary my hospital fare, he brought with him a freshly boiled lobster that he had ordered prepared while he ate his dinner.

The Governor found living in the house on C Street without a wife a dreary business. Except for his companionable Siamese cat and the daily visits of the old cleaning woman, he was alone with his hi-fi and his work. Generally he didn't feel like talking much when he arrived at the hospital; he would hand me the mail and a special thoughtful remembrance he had brought along, and ask, "What have they done to you today, Plum?"

If there had been any new medication I would tell him about it. Then, after a few moments during which I glanced through my mail, he would rise wearily from the chair, saying, "Well, guess I'll go along and get to bed. This has been a hard day, Plum."

After I had been in the hospital two months I was allowed to start painting for a short interval each day. The corner behind the door of my room had been well stocked with paints, brushes, and canvas boards for sometime. It was necessary to shorten the legs of my easel, for I would have to paint in bed. In that first reunion with my painting equipment I knew the height of contentment.

It was a long ride out to that hospital, but it wasn't too far for Rosamond Gaydash to travel, even on those hot and sticky Washington summer days, to give me encouragement and instruction.

Camille Pissarro, the oldest in the Impressionist group of painters, would have wholly appreciated Rosamond Gaydash, for in his *Letters to Lucien* he put into words the feeling that so many of us had about her. "When you put all your soul into your work," said Pissarro, "all that is noble in you, you cannot fail to find a kindred soul who understands you, and you do not need a host of such spirits. Is that not all an artist should wish for?" While looking for a house to live in, I had been led to Rosamond Gaydash, a part of the Washington experience without whom it wouldn't have been nearly so much fun.

The almost daily arrival of flowers and gifts and messages from friends across the country helped immeasurably to pass those slowly moving days. That the President of the United States should find time to write a message in longhand touched me deeply.

Thursday Morning

Dear Rachel:

These flowers looked so pretty on my desk this morning that the thought came to me that you might like them!

Anyway, sending them gives me a chance to tell you again that we all miss you; we pray you will soon be well.

Mamie doesn't know I'm sending these, but when I tell her, she will say, "I hope you sent along my love to her"—which I do—

Devotedly,

D.E.

Mrs. Sherman Adams

By Easter Sunday my sojourn at Walter Reed Hospital was about half over. Knowing that I would enjoy listening to the Sunrise Service, my nurse moved my bed nearer the window from which I could look down on the early-morning gathering of visitors, patients, and personnel. With the window open it was a little cool, so the nurse placed a hot-water bottle at my feet. I suggested she hand me the hatbox in the closet. Opening it, I took out a hat that Sally Victor (the designer of Mamie's hats) and Maggie de Mille Kaplan (sister of Agnes de Mille, creator and choreographer of many well-known ballets) had sent me. They hoped it would lift my spirits on that particular Easter Day.

I placed the arrangement of pink flowers on my head and settled back against the pillows, enjoying the comfortable warmth of the hot-water bottle, and waited for the singing to begin. With my pale face and my tired permanent I didn't imagine I was a thing of beauty on that glorious Easter morning but I took considerable satisfaction in being able to indulge in a little frivolity.

On August 4 Sherm brought me home from the hospital. He arrived after work and as we drove slowly through Rock Creek Park in the early evening I experienced a great feeling of liberation. It was almost too good to be true. I was keenly aware of a multitude of sounds and smells, of colors and textures. I was fervently thankful to be a part of the out-of-doors again—and I was profoundly grateful to be with my husband once more.

It didn't take long for us to realize that the house we had rented wasn't going to work out very well for a couple of New Englanders. All available parking space in our immediate neighborhood was sought with determination by members of Congress whose offices were across the street. When I dared ask the Metropolitan Police for a "reserved" parking area in front of our house, a Democratic congressman, looking down from his office window, became highly indignant when he saw the restricted space for the car belonging to the Assistant to the President. Later we finally relinquished the privilege in order to stop the criticism in the papers, which was the result of remarks made on the floor of the House by Congressman Bass of Tennessee. But it wasn't only the dearth of parking space that made us long for a house in a less congested area. Our tiny bit of lawn, next to the sidewalk, had to be gone over every morning to remove the several whiskey bottles that had been tossed there during the night. There was always a collection of debris which blew in from the not-too-neat neighborhood. We had little, if any, privacy. We were surrounded by office buildings and close to other houses. It was a way of life we were not accustomed to.

Our Siamese cat Sylvia had been used to the freedom of the fields and forest back home and she seemed quite bewildered by the noise and confusion of traffic the few times we dared let her out on the upper sun deck. She early found the magnolia tree a means of getting to the ground, and she barely missed the wheels of fast-moving vehicles before I could catch her. After one night when I spent considerable time trying to get her to come down from the rooftop of a neighboring house (meanwhile hoping her penetrating and constant Siamese yowling wouldn't get me a summons for disturbing the peace of Washington) I decided she would simply have to remain indoors until we could find a place more like the kind that we, including the cat, were used to. In any case, the owners of the house were returning from England and wanted it for themselves.

X

The First Lady at Home

As the days went by and my strength returned, I spent more and more time house hunting. Near the end of 1953 luck was with us. The Minister from Australia was recalled and our realtor immediately thought of us, for she was sure the place that the Minister was relinquishing on Tilden Street was exactly what we were looking for. I had become quite discouraged, and when the Tilden Street place was suggested, I expected it would be more wasted time to go to look at it. However, the agent was so insistent that I agreed to an inspection trip.

I went through an old wooden gate in a high cedar fence and looked around the corner of a beautiful old stone building to a spacious lawn with many trees of several species. Then I went through the door to the front hall. Even in the soft glow of the lights my eyes immediately traveled to the far wall where a fine likeness of Sir Winston Churchill hung. He, like the hall, had a comfortable and friendly appearance.

I walked down the two steps into the large living room and said to myself, This is it, I think. From the living room, with its barrel-back chairs, slip-covered in yellow, rust-colored draperies and huge fireplace, I took the two steps up and into the dining room. A long tavern-type table and a fireplace even larger than the one in the living room left little to be desired as far as I was concerned. Sherm would like it, I knew. It was our kind of house—as relaxing as the slow tick-tock of the grandfather's clock by the living-room door; as warm and friendly as the smile on Sir Winston's face in the front hall; as dignified as only hand-hewn timbers and carefully selected stone could be; and as secluded as the brown thrasher's nest in the brambles by the fence. I could hardly wait for Sherm to see it.

The next evening he agreed to go with me to Tilden Street, although he expected, as I had, that it would be wasted time. I encouraged him through the gate and to a look around the corner of the house. Then we entered the hall, and the living room, and the dining room. He had taken it all in without a word from either of us. As he glanced about the dining room he said, "Plum, I guess you've found your house."

So it was that we settled down next to Rock Creek Park for the duration of our stay. We were only a 15-minute drive from the White House. We were in the midst of Washington yet we seemed miles away.

After the hi-fi was installed we began a regular routine. The alarm, unless intercepted, pierced the dark winter mornings at 6:15. While I prepared breakfast, Sherm turned on the Washington Good Music station, then went in search of the morning paper. Sometimes it would be in the mailbox, sometimes in the driveway, and on occasions, at first, it wasn't there at all. We sat down to breakfast about ten minutes of seven. Traces of morning light would begin to appear in the sky above the mimosa tree on the hill. As the light increased, so did the flock of crows which slowly circled above the zoo down the creek, where it was feeding time for the birds and animals. After a second cup of coffee Sherm would finish reading the paper, then he would turn off the hi-fi and, going out to the garage, drive to his office, arriving there at 7:30 or soon after. I would not see him again until dinnertime.

Returning home after a busy day he would immediately turn on the hi-fi and listen to WGMS if a good program was scheduled; if not, he would play some of his favorite records. As long as he was in the house there was music. We seldom watched television unless the President or someone else in the official family was making a speech, or when sports programs were particularly interesting. Evenings at home were often spent playing scrabble or rummy.

There were other women during those early days of the new administration who were having difficulties similar to mine, not the least of whom was the First Lady. She, too, had redecorating and rearranging problems, along with all the hundred-and-one responsibilities that a President's wife falls heir to. Mrs. Eisenhower's ambition was to run the White House in the best interests of tradition, dignity, and good housekeeping. Having been the wife of a general, she had had extensive training in diplomatic etiquette, which would prove most helpful to her as the new hostess of the White House.

Contrary to the expectations of many of my friends, Mrs. Eisenhower and I did not become intimate. Many of the men whom the President had gathered around him during the campaign were old friends from Army days. And when the staff was being set up in the White House a number of younger Army men were added. Many of their wives were long-time friends of Mamie Eisenhower, and naturally they had many things in common. I presume that the First Lady felt more at ease with them also. Politics was a new venture for her.

If I had been an avid canasta player I might have been called to the White House more often, for Mrs. Eisenhower never tires of a game of cards. But my spasmodic, lukewarm association with bridge or canasta in previous years had brought me little joy—and my partners much pain. A few of Mrs. Eisenhower's close Army friends, as well as a few of the Cabinet ladies, liked a rousing game of bolivia now and then but not so well as the First Lady. She could have played hour after hour and day after day if her heavy schedule had not interfered. After the lengthy sessions with her morning mail, the autographing, and the many details connected with running the White House, there was little time for her favorite diversion. The daily official schedule, as well as her participation in an endless array of worthwhile causes in the name of charity, gave her scant time to indulge in a few hours of fun with friends.

Undoubtedly Mrs. Eisenhower yearned at times for the freedom to which she had always been accustomed, to come and go without causing a curious crowd to congregate. The thought of just wandering along Connecticut Avenue for some window shopping or of visiting the intriguing shops in old Georgetown must have, many times, made her wish a little wistfully to be a private citizen again.

Eleanor Roosevelt, on the other hand, had found her days were more exciting with her numerous projects outside the White House. Politics she was well accustomed to. And she had an insatiable interest in the world around her. It is doubtful that she ever had a feeling of being oppressed by public life. Her good health was most certainly a great asset for one so active. Mrs. Eisenhower, however, had since her youth favored a heart condition. Nevertheless, in their own individual and dedicated ways, each First Lady carried on the treasured traditions and the tremendous tasks of hostess of the White House.

On one or two occasions when I stopped in for a morning chat during the early part of the administration I found Mamie, though still in bed, looking very chic in a pink bed jacket, and a wide pink ribbon around her hair. Her bedroom faced the south, and during the years that were to follow she became well acquainted with the view from her windows. She was particularly interested in the well-being of the little scarlet oak that her husband had set out with the usual ceremony that accompanies the planting of a tree by each President. From here, too, she could get an occasional glimpse of him as he practiced his golf shots, and of Moany, his valet, as he darted for the balls.

By the time I arrived for those informal morning visits the First Lady would have finished her breakfast and discussed the schedule for the day with the housekeeper and Mr. Crim, the head usher. After I left, she would have a lengthy session with her personal secretary, Mary Jane McCaffrey, as they went through the stack of morning mail. Later she would sign her name in her free and flowing style on countless messages and photographs. Undoubtedly there are thousands of women who would welcome a chance to spend a morning in this way, but there are few who could continue the practice year after year with the diligence and sincerity of Mrs. Eisenhower. Her faithful maid, Rose, was always close by. Now and then, as we talked, Mrs. Eisenhower would call to her regarding some item of dress which she would need later in the day. One morning she also asked her to show me the new evening gowns which had just arrived and were hanging in her dressing room.

There were other occasions at the beginning of the new administration when I enjoyed Mamie Eisenhower's hospitality. One that I remember in particular was the luncheon she gave in honor of Cabinet wives and high-ranking officials. Naturally I was delighted to be included in that group of fourteen women, most of whom I knew fairly well, having met them earlier during the campaign or at Governors' Conferences.

I wondered how it was I had received an invitation, for a First Lady has to be very careful about how she handles her lists of guests. My husband's position, according to the Office of Protocol, was twenty-sixth, which was well down the ladder whose rungs started with the President and continued down through all the high-ranking officials, and on to the senators who squeezed in a rung just ahead of Sherman Adams. Whatever the reason for my being included, I thought little about it.

It was our first luncheon with Mamie Eisenhower in the White House. A variety of fur coats were in evidence as the ladies stepped from their chauffeur-driven sedans, taxis, or, like me, from behind the wheel of their own cars. Pat Nixon was not alone in her "Republican cloth coat"—as it was described during the campaign to emphasize her unpretentiousness and modest means. Doris Brownell and Esther Stassen were similarly outfitted. My squirrel jacket was just beginning a number of years' service.

Of course all wore hats but none became so well known as mine. It was comfortable, it went well with almost any dress, and while it didn't "do very much" for me, still the whole effect wasn't at all bad. So, as the days and weeks swiftly passed, I wore it and wore it. To luncheons, teas, cocktail parties went the little black velvet pillbox with the rows of pearl trimming. And then came the day when I wore it to a concert at the Lisner Auditorium. As I walked through the foyer, a woman with red hair and determination in her demeanor descended upon me.

"Aren't you Mrs. Adams?" she called out.

"Yes" was all I had time to reply.

"I *thought* so! I'd know you by your hat!" she exclaimed in a voice that seemed, to me at least, to resound through the auditorium.

That night I left a note pinned to my husband's pillow, "TOMOR- ROW I AM GOING TO BUY A NEW HAT!" His reply scrawled on the bottom of the note was, "I should think you would!"

Some years ago I had found that leaving a note for Sherm worked out very well as a rule. If I spoke to him about some problem when his mind was busy with other matters I often wished I hadn't. So, after a couple of trial runs which worked out even better than I ex- pected, I began making a practice of the penciled note. He enjoyed it even when the reminder had to do with financial situations. To make the message emphatic, I would place an elephant statue beside it—to remind him not to forget. If nothing happened as time went by, I placed a silver-handled dagger across the note. That encouraged him. If necessary, I chose places to leave the memos where I knew he couldn't miss them—on the steering wheel, at his dinner plate, on the turntable of his record player, in the bathroom, and on the stairs. Whatever the psychological reason is, I have never known the device to fail. Once, for instance, some of us decided that the Presi- dent looked too old on TV with his rimless glasses, so I left a note for the Governor. The next time, the President had on horn-rimmed glasses—a great improvement, we thought.

Mamie Eisenhower had told me on the campaign train why she was always picking up a new hat here and there. "I won't be caught having my picture taken over and over in the same hat," she had said.

Some of the women at that first White House luncheon were as hat conscious as the First Lady. Others seldom wore anything on their heads. And on one or two like myself, a hat that we liked would probably be seen for some time.

After leaving our coats to be taken care of, we were shown a diagram by White House aides which explained where we would be seated at the luncheon table in the State Dining Room. We were then escorted to the door of the Red Room to await the appearance of Mrs. Eisenhower and Mrs. Nixon.

We chatted for a few moments and then the aides gently urged us into position according to our husbands' rank. Emily Lodge, whose husband was Ambassador to the United Nations, was at one end and I was at the other. Mrs. Nixon arrived and greeted each of us, returning to the head of the line. Almost immediately the First Lady appeared and, after shaking hands with everyone, led the way to the state dining room.

The lunch was simple and delicious. The conversation was most polite and in a decidedly light vein. All the women were still anxiously feeling their way in the new positions in which they found themselves. All of us were experiencing the same problems of moving, getting settled, trying to keep up with social demands, and wondering which invitations to accept and which to refuse.

When the time came to leave, Mrs. Eisenhower put on a velvet wrap and led the way to the veranda where photographers were waiting to take our picture. It was the first time in many years that the wife of a newly inaugurated Republican President had entertained at luncheon.

I remember how amused Mamie was when some months later two other women and I went to the White House to be photographed with her to publicize some fund-raising affair for the Salvation Army. The picture that finally appeared in the newspapers showed the President's wife laughing and the rest of us determinedly sober-faced. The photographer had grouped us the way he wanted us and then, giving the usual nod as he aimed his camera, had said, "Just be talking together." This was a sentence that always made me and other Capitol wives wary: seldom is a woman flattered by a photograph showing her with her mouth wide open, so we usually tried to let someone else do the talking. Mamie, of course, didn't have to worry about this since she or her secretary could always see the proofs and choose the picture to be used. This particular day, in response to the photographer's instruction, she had been asking us questions and getting no answers, and as he repeated his plea that we look non-chalant and fall into conversation, one of the women muttered firmly between almost closed lips, "I'm not going to have my picture taken with my mouth open!" That was when Mamie laughed and the shutter clicked.

The women at that first luncheon, despite their different back-grounds, had one thing in common—a desire to assist their husbands in the difficult positions they would hold during all or part of the Eisenhower Administration. All of them, that is, except Oveta Culp Hobby, the Administrator of the Federal Security Agency, who later became Secretary of Health, Education, and Welfare in the President's Cabinet. Outside of being a devoted wife she was an able and charm-ing politician.

Close association with politics was a new venture for Pam Humphrey, Jessie Wilson, Flora Benson, Anna Durkin, and Julia Dodge. The first four were wives of Cabinet members and Julia Dodge's husband was Director of the Budget. The remainder of the luncheon group included Pat Nixon, wife of the Vice-President; Doris Brownell, wife of the Attorney General; Jane Weeks, wife of the Secretary of Commerce; Emily Lodge; Miriam Summerfield, wife of the Postmaster General; Mabel McKay, wife of the Secretary of the Interior; and Esther Stassen, wife of the Director of the Mutual Security Agency, all of whom had been associated to one degree or another with politics.

There was another visit with Mamie that I remember very well. Knowing of my interest in painting, she suggested I come down and watch the start of her official portrait by Thomas Stevens, the artist who had already executed several Eisenhower portraits. It would be a somewhat tedious engagement for her, as first this pose, then another, and another were considered, and someone to talk with during the sitting would help to pass the time. Feeling somewhat like a court jester, I endeavored to keep our conversation on the light side. My efforts were not wasted. At one of my flippant remarks, she turned and looked at me with an expression at once regal and amused. It was this expression that the artist captured and that in time became well known when the painting was reproduced for the jacket of the book, *Mamie Eisenhower.*

One particularly thoughtful act of Mamie's I shall not readily forget, for the pleasure it gave to a group of women who little expected it. My sewing club from Lincoln was to visit Washington. Ever since our children were small we had met for the purpose of keeping up with historical events relating to our home town and dispensing with mounds of mending while enjoying each other's company. When Mrs. Eisenhower heard about their plans to visit me, she said, "Rachel, why don't you bring your group down to the White House for tea?"

The only date that was still open on her calendar was March 10, the day the women were arriving. They expected to reach Tilden Street the latter part of the morning, which would give them plenty of time to rest and be ready for tea with Mrs. Eisenhower. However, it was three o'clock when their car turned into our driveway. They were obviously tired. With everyone talking at the same time, it was hard for me to get their attention to make my announcement.

"Listen carefully," I told them, as they stopped for the moment to gather up numerous bags, packages, and plants. "It is now three o'clock. At four o'clock Mrs. Eisenhower is expecting you for tea." I went on to suggest that they be ready at exactly 3:30. One or two of them looked as though they didn't quite know whether to believe me or not.

Women never unpacked so fast, nor forgot their weariness so quickly. Everyone appeared shining and resplendent, complete with white gloves, at precisely 3:30. None of us had ever imagined in those earlier years, as we lengthened growing girls' dresses or patched our boys' overtaxed blue jeans, that we would someday be having tea with a President's wife in the White House.

Incidentally, another famous lady who that same spring helped me turn what might have been a routine affair into a special occasion was Lady Astor. Trying my best to think of a person who would add zest to a tea I was giving for a group of Republican women who were in Washington for a conference, I suddenly remembered that Lady Astor was visiting friends in the city. Having met her several times, I decided to call and ask whether she would like to help me with my tea for the New Hampshire women, most of whom seldom got to Washington. I knew they would enjoy meeting her. She was most understanding and said she would be there. If that tiny, sprightly, spontaneous Virginia-born Democrat had been born in Vermont she quite likely would have been a Republican—anyway, I had no qualms about inviting her to a Republican tea, for she was a wonderful sport and my guests couldn't have been more excited and appreciative.

Each year when the President was to deliver his State of the Union message I was invited by Mrs. Eisenhower to sit in the front row of the Executive Gallery with her and members of her private and official family. On one of these occasions it was suggested that I go to the White House and ride to the Capitol Building in the car with the Eisenhowers' daughter-in-law, Barbara Eisenhower, and George Moore, the husband of the First Lady's sister. Upon reaching the gallery, I was ushered to the farther seat in the front row.

On my right, in the Diplomatic Gallery was Madame Koo, wife of the Ambassador from China, diminutive and exotic in her gown of Oriental design. We exchanged greetings and she offered me a Life-Saver. I never saw Madame Koo without thinking of the story a senator had told me about her. He claimed she had come out "second best" one evening in a little exchange with a colleague of his who happened to be her dinner partner.

When the cigars were passed, Madame Koo told her escort she would like one. The Senator, gallant and accommodating as all senators try to be, complied with her request, but after he had taken the extra cigar for his partner she began to demur. The Senator, however, apparently wasn't one to be trifled with, for he said firmly to Madame Koo, "You asked for this cigar. I have lighted it for you. And now, by God, you are going to smoke it!"

If I remember the story correctly, Madame Koo took a puff or two.

As I looked down on the floor of the House, which was full to capacity, I noticed the preponderance of navy blue and gray suits

worn by the gentlemen. The quiet tones of most of the women members' clothing was relieved by a brilliant burnt-orange dress on the far
side of the aisle, and even those in the gallery could note with what
enthusiasm the wearer was chewing gum. The only other spot of
vivid color below us was a dress of royal purple. Both Clare Boothe
Luce, who was later to become American Ambassador to Italy, and
the late Congresswoman Edith Nourse Rogers were conservatively
dressed and were sitting together.

As the President came to the bottom of each typewritten page of his
message, hundreds of pages of copy turned simultaneously. The
sound reminded me of the great flock of pigeons which now and then
soar into the air from the plaza in front of the Milan Cathedral in
Italy.

My glimpses into the routine of Mamie Eisenhower's days aroused
no wishfulness in me. After a visit to the White House my own
housekeeping duties, in comparison, suddenly seemed less burdensome and confining. I, like many other wives in the new administration, was unused to having domestic help except on special occasions.
Other women who had followed their husbands to Washington either
brought their servants with them or found adequate help there.

Being willing and able to do my own housework didn't, however,
get it all done. There were too many other demands on my time.
So I floundered around in the pitfalls of employment agencies. Returning home from a concert one afternoon near the beginning of
1953, I was riding with a group of wives who were new to the
Washington scene. They were talking about their maids, the concert
having apparently been forgotten as soon as the music stopped. Not
having any maids of my own to talk about, I listened.

"Do our girls know each other?"

"I don't think so. Mine are Irish."

"Oh, well! I guess not. Ours are Scotch, and you know how the
Irish and the Scotch get along together!"

Well, I thought from my corner in the limousine, I might not
have the benefit of regular domestic help, but neither did I have to
worry about an international crisis with the maids next door. Later I

did have my troubles with domestic help, but the activating ingredient wasn't Scotch or Irish—it was gin.

As we drove along through the saturated Washington climate we talked of other things that are on women's minds at moving time. Everyone still had boxes to unpack. All the closets in all the houses were too small—and too few. We poured out our earnest and heart-felt sympathy to each other as, one by one, we lamented this or that piece of furniture, the draperies, or something else in the way of furnishings that we were going to have to put up with as long as we were tenants in someone's house. My chief worry in the house we were renting was the beautiful dining table said to have been made by Thomas Jefferson.

Good old colored Dora was my standby; she would do anything. She especially enjoyed changing furniture around to suit herself, saying, as she stood off to reflect on what she thought a big improvement, "Mis' Adams, does that-all look better! Yes, ma'am!"

Dora was honest. I never had to worry about leaving jewelry or money around. I could count on her not to touch anything—that is, anything but gin. I had been cautioned by another devoted employer of Dora's that it would be necessary to keep alcoholic beverages locked up—especially gin. I forgot the admonition only once. That was when my husband and I were getting ready to go abroad and I had put an assortment of medicinal supplies, clothing, and other necessary items on one of the guest-room beds. In another bedroom was a collection of our son's belongings which I was going to send to him. I sent Dora upstairs to get Sam's things and bring them to the kitchen where I would get them ready for mailing.

All was quiet as I proceeded with other chores; then all at once a great clamor, crash, and clatter echoed from the top of the stairs to the bottom—and then an awful silence. I didn't dare go into the hall. I called out with what courage I could muster, "Dora! Are you all right?"

"Yes'm, yes'm, I's all right!" More quietness while I waited.

"Dora!" I called, still dreading to learn the worst, "*What happened?*"

"I's *all right,* Mis' Adams, I's *all right!*"

My curiosity conquered my dread and I went reluctantly to the front hall. The immediate area was littered with a wreck of medicinal and first-aid supplies. There were no signs of Sam's belongings.

I was greatly relieved to find Dora was able to move. In fact, she was moving fast, trying to clean the tincture of merthiolate off several steps of green carpet before I saw it.

"Ev'thin's going to be *all right,* Mis' Adams. It's all acomin' off!" she volunteered before I had a chance to say anything.

"It had better come off, Dora—" and then I got a whiff. It wasn't tincture of methiolate, it wasn't bismuth-and-paregoric. What I smelled was gin. Too late, I went to the dining-room closet with the lock on it—yes, Dora had been there. I had forgotten to snap the lock. As I went upstairs to get Sam's things, Dora was still scrubbing.

I had one other similar experience before I learned my lesson. A most agreeable colored girl had on numerous occasions given me expert help when I had invited a large group for tea. One day I had used a few drops of rum for flavoring in cooking. I left the kitchen to answer the telephone and was gone for several minutes. When I returned, my helper looked as if a great inspiration had come to her in my absence.

"Mis' Adams, how 'bout me making a rose out of grapefruit for decorating the plates of sandwiches? Ah can make 'em look real purty!"

"Fine," I answered unsuspectingly, as I went about my several duties and left her to hers. I locked the rum bottle in the closet, arranged the flowers, placed the silverware on the table, and saw to numerous other necessary details.

My helper had the kitchen much to herself and her imagination. She did things to *all* the grapefruit in the refrigerator and then she attacked the oranges. My ivy was stripped of some of its best leaves which were placed around the fruit flowers. I thought the effect quite artistic and charming and it was all done before I could believe it.

With the decorations complete, the tiny sandwiches were tackled next. All kinds of fillings and decorations complemented all kinds of shapes and sizes, and the happy humming which accompanied the whirlwind of movement never let up. The tempo kept up even later when guests were milling around the tea table. The coffee urn was whisked into the kitchen for refilling every few minutes. The teapot disappeared from under the surprised eyes of the distinguished pourer long before it was empty. The guests were relieved of cups that were still half full. Never had one domestic kept a party going so diligently. On getting close to her to suggest a slightly slower pace, I caught a faint odor—so *that* was what was keeping things on the move. I had locked the door on the rum too late. Still, it had been a pretty good party—I thought—even as I wondered what we would have for fruit in the morning.

There were other occasions that added to my fast-growing knowledge of the help problem. One or two girls whom I tried out would have carried off everything that wasn't nailed down had I not terminated our relationship almost as soon as it began. One was a white girl. I had never before had any experience with someone like her. It was only intuition on my part that saved two of the Governor's shirts as they were going out the door.

Then there was the time I called up an agency that advertised "Dependable and experienced help by the hour." I had found some of their domestics unusually dependable and experienced—in the art of doing exactly as much as and what they wanted to. A brand-new "dependable and experienced" domestic with dark skin arrived to do "general" work. After she had done the dishes, I told her to watch the cookies in the oven and to take them out when they were done— I had to go up to the Avenue on a quick errand. I added that when this batch was done she could put more cookies in the oven if I hadn't returned.

Her reply wasn't at all what I expected. She put her hands on her hips and announced that I had asked for someone to do general work and if she was going to have to cook she would have to get $2 an hour. Perhaps my reaction surprised her, for I told her that when I hired someone for general work I didn't expect them to tell me what they would or wouldn't do, that I never asked help to do something I couldn't do myself. As I opened the door of the oven to see how the cookies were progressing I said, while taking off my coat, "You can leave right now."

"Wal, ah spose ah c'n call the agency an' see what she saays—but ah jes' don' think it's right." I became interested and glad to have a chance to learn more about the operation of employment agencies. I showed her where the telephone was and continued to look after my cookies. After listening to the weighty problem, as presented by the representative of dependability and experience, I was told that the manager of the bureau said she had better stay. I went out to do my errands.

Eventually we found James—or, rather, he found us. He came to our house one summer looking for work. He said he hoped to enter Howard University in the fall. Having a healthy appetite for education, he wanted to put himself through college as he had worked his way through a colored boys' school in Pennsylvania. He needed a home and a job. Finding he was a conscientious boy, we took him in. He learned to wait on table and was helpful in many ways. During the school year he would assist with breakfast, then the Governor would drop him off at the university on his way to the White House.

Once when we were returning from a concert in Constitution Hall with Murray Snyder and his wife, Murray asked the Governor whether he used the park route to go to the White House in the mornings.

"No," answered the Governor, "I go down Fourteenth Street, then Fifteenth Street."

"I should think that would be out of your way," Murray said.

"It is, but I have to take my butler to school!" explained the Governor with a grin.

James had a healthy respect for the Governor. One day, after investigating a couple of clocks the Governor had said needed attention, he reported to me.

"You can tell the Gov'nor those clocks are all okay," said James, with a grin on his very expressive features. Then he added, "All they need is windin' to keep 'em goin'."

"You go and tell him, James," I suggested.

James looked more amused as he replied hesitatingly, "Er—I guess I like my job too well!"

There were other wives new to the Washington scene who had their troubles with the domestic situation. Mrs. Franklin Floete, the wife of a government official, invited me to a luncheon, along with other friends, in her apartment. As she greeted us she could hardly suppress her amusement.

"This is the first time I have hired that maid. I told her the dining table didn't look very good and would she please keep a plate in front of each guest at all times. She considered my request for a moment, very seriously, and then said, 'Miz Floete, yo-all is new here, an' ah would lak to be able to do as yo asks, but ah got my reputation to consider!' "

Small informal luncheons were numerous in Washington, as were more formal ones. There were one or two instances when I forgot to record engagements in my book; and twice I accepted invitations to two luncheons on the same day. It was painfully embarrassing, but I gained some degree of comfort upon learning that the same thing happened quite often to other people in the endless flutter of invitations and acceptances which kept the Washington whirlpool rotating at a dizzy pace.

Bess Gruenther, wife of a White House staff member, was one of the many who told regretfully of an omission in her date book. Under a certain day appeared the notation "luncheon." The place, time, and even the hostess's name were lacking. Bess checked with one or two friends but no help was forthcoming. As the luncheon hour drew near she could have been seen—only she preferred not to be—sitting by the telephone. She was all ready for a luncheon, she knew not where, but she was quite sure when the time came to sit down at the table her hostess would call and say, "Bess, *where are you?*" And Bess was all ready to say, "I'll be right there!"

But Bess sat and sat, complete with hat and white gloves, and nobody called. Telling me about it later, she confided, "I never did find out whose luncheon I was supposed to attend!"

One day I gave what I considered a very special luncheon indeed.

On our fishing trip to New Brunswick that spring I had landed a good-sized Atlantic salmon and the Governor also had been well rewarded for many hours of casting in the high spring waters of the Miramichi and Renous rivers. My catch, I had immediately decided, would be saved for a special occasion, and after some thought I elected to serve it to the First Lady and the Cabinet wives. So I mailed the invitations, and sent the salmon to a caterer's to be properly prepared. No Atlantic salmon was ever laid out in finer frills and adornments. It had looked majestic in the river as it fought to free it-self from my line, but after the caterer finished with the decorations it looked regal. However, I had a feeling that Mrs. Eisenhower and the Cabinet wives failed to grasp the importance of the occasion. To them it was just another fish course. Except for Jessie Wilson, who was unable to be present, there were no fishing enthusiasts who could appreciate what lay behind my announcement that I had caught the salmon myself.

I often think, too, of a luncheon in Anderson House in honor of Secretary of Agriculture and Mrs. Benson's married daughter, at a time when Alaska, soon to become the forty-ninth state, was much in the news. I was sitting next to Mrs. Anderson, the very attractive, Texas-born wife of the Secretary of the Treasury. She wanted to know what our son was going to do when he finished his college work. I told her he was interested in geology and hoped sometime to go to Alaska, adding that there must be all kinds of opportunities there in his field. The Secretary's wife looked alarmed and concerned at my even considering anything so unheard of.

"But," she earnestly replied, "*Texas still* has many opportunities!"

xi

The Washington Whirlpool

I had been out of the hospital only a few days when a formal invitation from the Eisenhowers arrived in the mail. A state dinner at the White House is a memorable experience—especially when it is your first. We attended many affairs there during our six years in Washington but none held for me the excitement of that first official gathering.

It was the evening of September 28 and unusually warm. The benches in Lafayette Park were all full and couples or solitary walkers strolled along the paths, most of them hoping to find someone ready to relinquish his seat. There was still enough light for some of the more experienced squirrels to be scurrying around but the pigeons were already settling for the night, with considerable cooing and visiting, up by the eaves on Dolly Madison's old house and the other old buildings that surround Lafayette Park.

Beyond the park to the south and across Pennsylvania Avenue one caught glimpses of the White House. The stately elms stood in front of that magnificently simple Presidents' house, like immovable but courteous guards, intent on protecting but at the same time letting everyone see the home of America's Presidents. On that particular night, all the portico lights were on, signaling that the President and Mrs. Eisenhower were entertaining.

The invitations had been received about two weeks earlier. White cards, measuring about six inches by four and a half, were embossed with the United States seal in gold at the top. The black handwritten script of six lines said that the President and the First Lady requested the pleasure of our company at a dinner on Monday, September 28, 1953, at eight o'clock. In the envelope with the invitation were three smaller cards which gave the necessary information regarding dress, the gate to use in entering the White House grounds, and whom to inform of our acceptance or regret.

An invitation from the President or the First Lady is always accepted unless there are good and substantial reasons for regretting. Nothing short of illness could have kept me from accepting that first formal invitation to dinner at the President's house and I am sure the Governor felt the same way. We had accepted several invitations to small informal gatherings soon after the Eisenhowers moved into their new home but an invitation to a state dinner was something else again.

The printing on the smallest card said only WHITE TIE, which of course meant formal dress. The remaining two cards were equal in size. One, stark white with engraved script, notified the recipient to send a response to the social secretary in the White House at his earliest convenience. The last card was very important also. It was to be used as identification, if necessary, as the guests passed through the northwest gate. In the upper left-hand corner was a hand-printed symbol of particular interest to members of the Secret Service. Underneath the engraving and handwriting on that particular card was a two-toned engraving of the White House.

The guests of honor at this first state dinner were José A. Remon, the President of Panama, and his young, attractive wife. They had arrived at the White House earlier in the day for a state visit and would spend the night there. The following day they would move across Pennsylvania Avenue to Blair House, the official guest house of the President and Mrs. Eisenhower.

At a few minutes before eight o'clock sleek black cars began to turn in at the northwest gate. Every once in a while a taxi would politely try to join the distinguished procession; ignored, it would insist, and add a cosmopolitan sprightliness to the somber, dignified, and slow parade of limousines.

There was at least one private car without chauffeur. The driver was my husband. He found it hard to accept the black-limousine-with-chauffeur type of transportation. He could have had the use of one of the many small White House cars, with driver, which were reserved for the staff, but he insisted on driving his own car. I tried on several occasions to get him to make arrangements for a car with driver to pick us up when we were going to official functions but it wasn't until we had been in Washington nearly two years that he began to see the wisdom of my insistence. Many downpours and the absence of parking places helped my argument and by the time we left my husband was able, on occasion, to relax on the way to a reception or some other form of official entertainment. The times when he couldn't relax were when the driver who had been assigned to us was unable to make any progress through the heavy traffic or, worse yet, couldn't find the place we were going to. Then it was that the Governor wished he were driving his own car.

As we entered the proper gate the night of that first state dinner, the guards noticed the white-tie-clad gentleman at the wheel and without more inspection ushered us on. They needed only one guess as to which of the guests would be driving his own car. I could have been more than a little out of sorts at the Governor's insistence as I tucked my voluminous skirts under the dashboard of that convertible —I would have preferred the roominess of a larger car; but the evening was one of entrancement as far as I was concerned and I didn't intend it to be spoiled, and anyway probably my husband was right.

The limousine in front of us stopped expertly; the doorman hardly had to move as he reached to open the car door, out of which emerged Vice-President and Mrs. Nixon, the latter radiant in a gown of pink net well sprinkled with sequins. But it took concentrated effort for the doorman to extricate me and my many skirts. The line back of us had to wait.

Once beyond the large glass doors, protocol and custom took over. Almost our every move for the rest of the evening was planned. Here again the Governor found it hard to conform. Anything suggesting pompousness irritated him.

After entering the foyer we were guided to a small table near one of the pillars fashioned from Vermont marble where the Governor was shown a chart indicating the seating arrangement for the dinner. An aide pointed out just where he would be sitting and then handed him an envelope containing a card with a smaller diagram and with the name of the woman he would escort in to dinner. On the reverse side of the card was the same information about my escort and our position at the table.

While the Governor was talking with the aide, I looked around the foyer. Over at the right of the entrance sat nineteen members of the Marine orchestra—their leader standing ready to raise his baton. Their scarlet tunics with the gold braid contrasted spectacularly with the white marble hall. One or two of the men were turning pages of the music but most of the musicians were watching the arrival of the dinner guests.

On the opposite side of the foyer was the grand stairway which led to the second floor where the President and Mrs. Eisenhower lived. It was in a comparatively new place, for during the renovation of the White House in the Truman Administration, it had been changed from its old location near the door of the great East Room.

A young lieutenant who was one of the White House aides, offered his right arm to me and we walked along the hall to the entrance of the East Room. The Governor followed behind. At the doorway another aide announced to those already gathered, "The Assistant to the President and Mrs. Adams."

Across the room, and at each end, were ladies and gentlemen grouped according to rank. Most of them were looking our way and in the assemblage on our left were familiar faces among the members of the Supreme Court, Diplomatic Corps, and the Cabinet. In the center directly across were members of Congress, most of whom we were acquainted with, and to our right at the south end of the ballroom were many old friends of the Eisenhowers and of the new Administration. The aide guided us to our place according to rank and went back to take charge of the later arrivals.

In the remaining few minutes before eight o'clock, those in each group mingled and renewed acquaintance or were introduced to other guests. Gowns were of particular interest; many women like myself were wearing their inaugural finery but here and there were new creations in honor of the special occasion. The men looked pretty much the same so far as apparel was concerned. Undoubtedly there were a few who had rented the necessary formal outfit and there were still others who looked a bit uncomfortable in suits that they hadn't worn for many years. Time had altered their figures but not the dress suits. Others wore suits in the latest style. Of all the men in that glittering ballroom I expect my husband was having the best time. His special delight was in asking someone he knew fairly well, and who he expected would enjoy the story, how old they thought his suit was. He would say, "Just feel of that! Ever see anything like that nowadays?" and a friend would dutifully finger the end of the sleeve, while chancing a guess. All were curious and the Governor was ready with an explanation.

"Well, I'll tell you. This suit used to belong to a fellow named Charles Henry. It was his father who started the logging operations up in my home town in New Hampshire. I needed something like this once or twice when I was Governor, so I had it fixed up. Mr. Henry last wore it about forty years ago! I wonder what the old boy would say if he knew his suit was going to White House functions!"

It wasn't that the Governor couldn't afford a new dress suit. He simply delighted in being able to make something else do. As the evening progressed, he became more and more relaxed. He turned on his charm, of which he was ever capable, and added much to the enjoyment of the evening for others. Earlier in the evening, while dressing, his predominantly good nature had deteriorated somewhat as he discovered two moth holes in the tails of his dress suit and, worse still, someone had starched his white tie! I had forgotten to remind the laundry about NO STARCH in the white tie. As for the moth holes, certainly anyone should *expect* to find them in a suit as old as that one was.

At eight o'clock a blare of trumpets announced the arrival of the President and First Lady. They walked toward the East Room as the band played "Hail to the Chief." A few paces behind them were the guests of honor. As the party reached the doorway they stopped.

"The President of the United States and Mrs. Eisenhower," announced the aide.

The Eisenhowers moved slightly to the left to make room for their guests.

"The President of Panama and Señora Remon," proclaimed the aide.

The two couples stood together facing the line that was forming around the room. Suddenly the President shifted to Mrs. Eisenhower's left side. Apparently there had been a little mix-up somewhere but it made anyone who had been feeling a bit nervous less tense.

An aide suggested to the Vice-President that it was time to start the line moving. Everyone was to be received by the Eisenhowers and introduced to the Remons. As the band played softly, the line moved briskly along, husbands or escorts preceding their ladies as is the custom at such functions. Aides were prompt and articulate as they announced the name of each guest to the President and Mrs. Eisenhower and to the Remons. Sometimes the introduction was lost as the President welcomed an old friend. His words of greeting to me were an informal, "Hello there, Rachel. Haven't seen you for a long time!" Later, at other White House functions, he would add, "How's the painting?"

After the guests had passed the receiving line there was a regrouping as each of the gentlemen went in search of his dinner partner—the lady whose name was on the little white card. Some were definitely baffled, being unacquainted with the ladies they were looking for, and would sidle up to a friend and ask advice. A guarded glance here and there would be followed by a look of relief as the sought-after woman was located.

There were times when a man, on learning the name of his partner, turned just a bit pale, for—infrequently to be sure—women were included in the White House gatherings who could very easily have tempted an escort to take out his sword and test the edge—if he had had one. But all the gentlemen could do under the circumstances was to give the white ties another tug and hope for the best. Such a situation was unusual—fortunately everyone was generally passively content or really pleased with his or her partner.

As soon as the last couple had been introduced, the President, escorting Señora Remon, moved down the hall toward the state dining room. They were followed by President Remon and Mrs. Eisenhower, and the other guests. It was a moment in my life that I would have liked to prolong. The prisms of the three glittering chandeliers above threw back and forth the thousands of iridescent reflections caught from the movement of brilliant gowns along the red carpet. The Strauss waltzes played by the scarlet-clad orchestra seemed to suggest how many times before other beautifully gowned women and their escorts had followed their President along this same hall. The gentleman on whose arm my white-gloved hand rested was the brother of the President of Panama. He informed me that he didn't speak much English and wanted to know if I was familiar with the Spanish language. I was genuinely sorry that I had to admit I was not. However, we managed, and on entering the dining room everyone found his place with little trouble. If directions had been forgotten, there were butlers and waiters ready to help. Holding my evening bag in one hand, with the other I managed to arrange the many folds of my full-skirted gown, as I answered a nod from across the table and acknowledged an introduction to the gentleman on my right.

The U-shaped table set for fifty-three guests was a symphony of green and gold above the white damask cloth. The gold-plated flatware from the Madison Administration, with the pearl-handled fish knives, glittered; the gilt epergnes from the Monroe Administration were overflowing with clusters of deep-purple grapes and other varieties of fresh fruit. The tall gilt candelabra held long white candles whose flickering flames added to the sparkle of the crystal goblets, the place settings, and the reflections in the plateau mirror, which also dated back to the Monroe Administration. The white Lenox service plates which the Trumans first used had a border of green, and in the center was the United States seal in gold. Between the candelabra and the epergnes were low arrangements of yellow roses, yellow single chrysanthemums, and yellow snapdragons. Garlands of feathery light-green smilax trailed the length of the table framing the gorgeous centerpieces. The decorations of the table blended with the gold draperies and the green-painted paneling of that historic room. The colorful gowns, interspersed with the exclamation points of the black dress suits, made the whole picture as richly vibrant as a Renoir painting and, with the tinkle of glass and crystal mingling with mellow voices and soft laughter, I thought of the music of Mozart.

My place at the table was on the inside of the U facing the south wall of the room. It was difficult to glance backward to my left to catch a glimpse of the Eisenhowers and the Remons. The two Presidents sat beside each other on the outer part of the center of the table while their wives sat directly opposite.

I took the monogrammed napkin from the service plate and laid it in my lap. The sherry glass was filled and the shrimp cocktail was placed before me. The first state dinner in the White House during the Eisenhower regime had begun.

After the several courses were disposed of, champagne was poured and President Eisenhower arose and smiled as he changed the position of a piece of flatware; then, with his fingers barely touching the top of the table, he made a few graceful welcoming remarks, and closed by proposing a toast to the Republic of Panama.

Everyone joined in the toast though the champagne was ignored by a few in favor of water! President Remon replied briefly in Spanish but his remarks were not interpreted.

At the end of dinner President Eisenhower spoke to his guest and they rose from the table and led the way to the Green Room where the gentlemen would gather for liqueurs and coffee. The ladies were served in the Red Room. During the fifteen minutes or so that we spent together, Mrs. Eisenhower passed from one group to another. She never was at a loss for some special, intimate greeting. Complete strangers were surprised and delighted with her natural way of putting them at ease.

I was a little surprised that there was no powder room on that floor of the White House. One of the Cabinet ladies asked me to show her where it was. I had to admit I didn't know, hoping she would forget the matter, but when she insisted, I suggested she had better ask one of the aides. Her informant gave her directions for finding the room she was looking for down on the lower floor.

When it was time to join the gentlemen in the large oval Blue Room, Mrs. Eisenhower and Señora Remon led the way. There the men found their dinner companions again and escorted them back to the Great East Room where the Eisenhowers and the Remons were already settling themselves in comfortable front row chairs for the concert.

Too soon, it seemed, the evening was over. As the last car left the grounds the guards closed the great iron gates. My husband guided our car along Pennsylvania Avenue toward Capitol Hill and our house on C Street.

After we had entered the house the Governor looked at my Trifari necklace and laughed.

"What is the big joke?" I wanted to know.

"Well," answered my amused husband, "I was talking with the President of Panama and he wanted to know which of the ladies was my wife. One of his aides quickly spoke up and said, 'You know, the one with the beautiful necklace!' "

Like other newcomers I had a lot to learn about the Washington whirlpool. There were the insistent invitations to cocktail parties and dinners from a number of would-be aspirants to the role of leading Washington hostess. They were interested primarily in having their parties well sprinkled with persons in the higher echelons of government. Sometimes the name seems to be all that matters, since for many people a party falls flat when there are no high-ranking guests.

Protocol "is the code of international politeness," and when we arrived in Washington the gentleman who knew most about social pitfalls and how to avoid them was the affable John F. Simmons. For a number of years, as Chief of Protocol, he had been responsible for interpreting the rules and dispensing wisdom in the business of being polite to people, particularly our foreign friends. But even Mr. Simmons was fallible.

There was that time during the early part of the Eisenhower Administration when the President traveled to Canada for an official visit. The Governor was invited to go along because of his knowledge of Canadian affairs and because of his friendship with numerous Canadian officials. I was also invited, and, as on most of the President's official trips, John Simmons went along to look after everybody's social behavior.

Before leaving Washington the official party had been issued instructions regarding correct dress for all occasions, black coats and striped trousers for the men being prescribed for the official ceremony of welcome at the Ottawa station. We were still some distance from Ottawa when word of a major disaster spread through the train. "Mr. Protocol" couldn't find his striped trousers! He took the laughter at his expense good-naturedly, and appeared in trousers without any stripes.

Precedence, "the act of going before in time, rank, etc.," is a necessary part of all formal social functions that include high-ranking officials. Alice Roosevelt Longworth makes quite clear in her book, *Crowded Hours,* how ridiculous the practice can be at times, and often we agreed wholeheartedly with her. On arriving at a less formal party on several occasions, it was a relief to have our hostess say, "Everyone is of the same rank tonight!"

At a formal party the ranking guest of the evening enjoyed all prerogatives of his position unless, as happened once or twice, my husband decided he had had a long enough day; then the ranking guest lost his privilege of departing first.

I remember one evening when we were invited to a dinner at the British Embassy in honor of the Queen Mother. Following dinner, coffee was served in the living room. Later there was a small reception as more guests arrived to be introduced. After the reception everyone moved into the music room and settled in the rows of chairs for an informal program of old musical favorites. President and Mrs. Eisenhower sat up front with the Queen Mother and Lady Makins. The Governor and I took seats near the back of the room. As the evening wore on and as additional nostalgic numbers were asked for,

I surmised he was thinking seriously that it was time to go home. Finally he nudged me and we crept out into the hall as unobtrusively as possible—and there was the Ambassador. The Governor said something to him about it being almost time for him to get up and go to work, and that he was sorry but he would have to be getting home. The Ambassador replied very softly, "I say, Governor, I wish I could join you!" He was a very genial and considerate host, and of course would have said almost anything to make us feel better about leaving.

The Governor didn't object to protocol and precedence . . . as long as neither kept him from the rest he should be getting. Once or twice when the ranking guest at a late affair seemed to be unmindful of his duty to depart first—and if he were someone the Governor knew well —he would be gently persuaded to consider how much better he would feel in the morning if he got to bed fairly soon.

Usually the Governor wasn't the only one who was ready to leave. Often there were suggestive glances in the direction of the ranking guest of the evening—glances which meant: "don't you think it is about time to conclude this delightful evening—so we can go home? Once or twice when my husband was ranking guest everyone got to bed early.

During the years in the nation's capital we received many invitations to dinner, most of which we had to refuse. As invitations were repeated, and also our regrets, many hostesses began to realize the Assistant to the President seldom spent his evenings away from home. Because of his reputation as a genial and entertaining dinner partner, some of the more eager hostesses were considerably frustrated by their inability to snare him.

I could never understand why some of them were so insistent. Perhaps, after having failed once or twice in their attempts, they had been told, "You'll never be able to get hold of Sherman Adams," and had simply made a firm resolution to keep on trying. We wanted to do what was necessary and right and after a couple of experiences we learned fairly well what to accept and what not to. If we were ever in doubt, the Office of Protocol in the State Department would offer advice. I remember in particular one woman who never gave up trying. One December day she got in touch with me by telephone: "Oh, we do so want you and your husband to come to dinner on the eleventh of April." Luckily for us, that date had been reserved for salmon fishing in New Brunswick, Canada. I could, with honesty, politely refuse the early invitation.

It was hard for me to understand how so many people could, apparently, live only for the time when the lights came on. To have a really successful affair, I was told, one must choose a room too small for the number of guests invited so that it looks and sounds as if *everybody* was there—making it a *very* important affair. Of course, there must be distinguished people present—or at least people whose names were newsworthy.

One of my friends was pretty well fed up with what was considered a good party and she planned a nice affair when the moon would be full. Her garden would be enchanting. She overlooked no small detail. The next day I saw her and she wailed, "You know how I planned that party—so everyone could move from the bar on into the garden where it was simply heavenly in that moonlight! Well! Did they go out into the garden where it was beautiful and cool? They did not! They used up every inch of that little drawing room, looking to see who was or wasn't there, and what everyone else was wearing. I couldn't have gotten them outside if there had been a fire—they were so afraid of missing someone they should be talking to!" Near to tears, she exploded, "I'll be so glad to get back home where people are better mannered, and not always looking around to see if there's someone more important they should be talking to."

One popular clergyman had a name for this acute eye condition: "the Washington eye," he called it. Long practice had made experts of many.

Some people made a habit of crowding in every party they were asked to. I was more than a little amused when told of the following conversation which was heard during one of the many busy evenings which Washington can produce with seemingly little effort: "Goodness, do you go to *everything* you are invited to?"

"Oh, yes! And when there are a number of parties in the evening, like tonight, we at least drop in at each one long enough to be *seen*."

And then there was the Washington wife who, when asked at a big party where her husband was, said in all seriousness, "My dear, there is so much going on, he covers one party while I cover another."

It is often said that cocktail parties serve a useful purpose, affording a chance to meet new friends, to exchange ideas, and to gather information about what is going on in social and political Washington.

To me, however, many of the parties and dinners seemed superfluous. Now that I have the benefit of long-distance perspective and retrospect, I am even more sure that they were.

On the infrequent occasions when the Governor and I attended receptions or cocktail parties the procedure was likely to be the same. After going through the receiving line, the Governor would whisper in my ear, "Plum, do you know where the back door is to this place?" (Which meant, "Let's not stay too long.")

After twenty minutes or so we were off to the next place we had promised to stop—or returned home. We were not antisocial, as some people believed. We were simply among those who crowded every hour throughout the day with work and, if lucky, a bit of outdoor exercise.

I am not by any means suggesting that Washington was not full of charming hostesses who gave delightful parties. Mrs. Herbert May could well head the list of unpretentious large-party givers. We especially enjoyed her square dances, a type of entertainment and fun we had not expected to find flourishing among Washington socialites. Mrs. May has more vitality and vigor than many women half her age. Her capacity for making friends and for giving pleasant parties, and for ceaseless work connected with charitable causes, is well known. All this she does in a quiet, dignified way. She loves to dance, and is a most attractive figure on the floor, whether executing the rumba or following the calls for a square dance.

When she found out we liked square dancing she immediately invited us to her next "Square Off" party at the Army-Navy Club near Alexandria, Virginia, about fifteen minutes from Washington's

14th Street bridge. The hundred-plus guests were augmented by both male and female instructors from the Arthur Murray Dance Studio. Their job was to see that the square-dance formations didn't get mixed up, as they certainly do when those uneducated in "allemande left" and "dos-à-dos" take off in the wrong direction. A set that everyone hops and twirls through without losing their bearings is an accomplishment, but when one or two bold and fearless newcomers to the square dance set just stand and wonder what to do next and in what direction all the fun and rhythm disappear for the rest of the people in that set. So the Murray group installed themselves where they thought they were most needed and tried to keep all wandering feet within the line of march and obedient to the caller's commands. They also gave instruction and encouragement in the latest round dances, if there were those who wanted them.

We were a diversified group that evening. Members of the press were included, and found this a somewhat different gathering from those they were in the habit of covering. They seemed to be really enjoying themselves as they listened to conversation on all sides, hoping to weed out of the roomful a gem for their columns. There were representatives from Congress, the Supreme Court and the federal agencies. There were old and new Washington residents and members of the foreign Diplomatic Corps—I remember especially the Austrian Ambassador and his wife and the vivacious members of the South American embassies.

Mrs. May was having one of her parties on the night when the President gave his "Don't Worry" speech, in connection with all the sputniks. Many of the men adjourned to the TV room, leaving their partly eaten supper. Some of the women joined them but I was one, along with my hostess, who waited for the gentlemen to come back. I was most anxious to learn how the speech came over TV and listened intently when the news came to the table.

Colonel Robert Guggenheim, former ambassador to Portugal, was the first to return to the table after the broadcast. He was sitting on Mrs. May's right and he leaned over to her and said, "That was a good speech—yes, very good." Mrs. May was glad to hear that. Congressman Fulton then returned to his seat, which was next to the Colonel's. As he picked up his napkin he turned to the Colonel and said, "You know, that speech left me cold—absolutely cold!"

"It did me too! Absolutely cold," agreed the Colonel.

Mrs. Guggenheim (since remarried) was another very popular hostess. Mrs. Robert Low Bacon gathered relatively small groups of interesting people from the Diplomatic Corps, government circles, and members of old Washington families. Whenever Arthur Rubinstein came to Washington for a concert at Constitution Hall, she gave a party in his honor, and these we seldom missed, for however the Governor felt about parties, he seldom turned down a chance to attend a concert anywhere. We went to Philadelphia twice for outstanding entertainments, at one of which—the centennial celebration—it was his duty to represent the President; and we frequently made a quick trip to New York for the opera. No matter how crowded the day had been he would gladly change into black tie if we were to go to a concert, though when a reception, cocktail party, or a dinner was in the offing, he had a hard time getting into that black tie and leaving his comfortable chair and his hi-fi. A good concert relaxed him and made him forget for the time being the worries of the day just ending and the day to come. His candid and informed remarks regarding the relative merit of this or that part of the program were beyond the comprehension of some of our concert companions. Many were astonished at the scope of his knowledge. He always had the right answer to anyone's question about scores, composers, great singers or conductors, and a number of devotees of good music who knew of his years in the woods as a boss of lumber camps were surprised by his easy and accurate answers and his unsolicited and intelligent comments. Werner Jensen, when in Washington the latter part of 1957, was "amazed at Sherman's grasp of musical knowledge." He had known my husband when they were students at Dartmouth College. Mr. Jensen composed the musical score for *Oh! Doctor!* which the Dartmouth Players had put on with the help of members of the Glee Club. The Governor had been leader of the Glee Club during his senior year.

The night we went to the symphony concert at Constitution Hall, as guests of President Eisenhower and the First Lady, probably made my husband as happy as any other single invitation we received in Washington. It was the first time since the Inauguration that the Eisenhowers had attended a concert there.

The Governor and I arrived at the south entrance of the White House at eight o'clock and were ushered into the Oval Room on the ground floor. On our right was the fireplace made famous during President Roosevelt's "Fireside Chats." Above the divan on our left hung the appealing portraits of two former First Ladies, Mrs. Theodore Roosevelt and Mrs. Herbert Hoover. In a few moments we were told the Eisenhowers were on their way downstairs. Chief Justice Warren, whom they had also invited, arrived simultaneously with the appearance of the President and Mrs. Eisenhower. The latter was radiant in a short gold-printed sea-green silk evening gown.

We left immediately, the President laughingly saying he didn't pretend to know much about the program we were to hear, but he was sure it would be a most interesting concert. He reminded us that we would be hearing the choir of the National Presbyterian Church, which he and his wife often enjoyed, and he insisted we were in for a treat. "They do a fine job," he said, as we all entered the White House limousine.

Upon arriving at Constitution Hall we were escorted to the reception room, where we met Dr. Mitchell, conductor of the National Symphony Orchestra, and George London, the soloist of the evening. There was little time for conversation, but what time there was gave the President and Mr. London a chance to discuss Ike's favorite pastime. Not music, golf!

It was a memorable evening in which talented musicians executed, with something akin to perfection, Beethoven's Fourth Symphony, two works by Samuel Barber, and, after the intermission, excerpts from the opera *Boris Godounov,* that great and demanding work by Moussorgsky. It was to this music that Mr. London brought his extraordinary voice. The Presbyterian Choir, excellently trained, performed admirably. It was an evening of superb music. Even Paul

Hume, music critic for the Washington *Post,* rhapsodized in his column the next morning.

Following that "first night," Box No. 13, the presidential box, was usually empty or, at the Eisenhower's suggestion, was made available to servicemen. Though any unused seats throughout the hall were available to interested service personnel, being able to sit in the presidential box was an event to write home about. Some of the members of the National Symphony Orchestra Committee thought otherwise. The presidential box, they reasoned, should be used by the President or, if he was unable to be present, by someone in his official family who could represent him. There must have been concentrated effort on this score for, after a year or so, Mrs. Eisenhower sent the tickets over to the Governor, asking that he use them if possible. Thereafter the presidential box was filled for every concert. We tried to find staff members and others who enjoyed the orchestra and its guest musicians as we did.

A few years later we were again invited to be guests of the Eisenhowers for a symphony concert. It was on the Governor's birthday, and we were asked to a small dinner party at the White House beforehand. Other guests included the Nixons, former Secretary of the Interior and Mrs. McKay, the President's physician, General Snyder and Mrs. Snyder, and Mrs. Doud, Mamie's mother. When the dessert was served, a birthday cake was placed in front of the Governor and the walls of the family dining room echoed, as they no doubt had many times in the past, to the singing of "Happy Birthday to You." Following the dinner everyone went to Constitution Hall. It was the second appearance of the President and Mrs. Eisenhower at a symphony concert there.

Of especial interest to the President and the First Lady on this occasion was the world première of a new composition. Robert Rogers had set to music "The President's Prayer," which was the first number played following intermission. The Governor and I were greatly interested in this but we were especially excited about the prospect of hearing Arthur Rubinstein, the guest soloist for the evening. He played the Beethoven Concerto No. Four in G Major, and as was usual when he performed in Constitution Hall, he completely enthralled his audience. The final number on the program was Tchaikovsky's Fourth Symphony, which the President said he especially enjoyed.

The following evening the Governor and I again went to Constitution Hall for another Rubinstein evening and after the concert went on to the home of Mrs. Robert Low Bacon, along with many other music lovers, for a late supper. Virginia Bacon had not forgotten the Governor's birthday either. A large beautifully decorated cake, aglow with candles, was placed before him and again everyone sang "Happy Birthday."

Another musical interlude we enjoy recalling was when the Governor and I were easily lured to New York for Maria Callas' appearance in *Tosca* at the Metropolitan Opera House. It was an exciting performance. We were part of a group that had been invited by friends to share their box for that unforgettable evening. Following each act we went to Sherry's Metropolitan Opera Restaurant on the grand tier for refreshments, which produced a comment from my husband.

"This is quite a procedure, isn't it, Plum? A brandy after every aria!"

The Governor was the only one wearing a Homburg that evening; the rest had tall silk hats. He had changed in many ways since leaving his timberland job in the hills of New England, but the wearing of a top hat was one change he would never consider. Earlier in the evening we had been concerned about the rusty condition of the buttons on his white vest, which had just come back from the dry cleaner's. He had had the vest since his Dartmouth Glee Club days, and it was about time it began to show a little age. Whatever we were going to do to rectify the situation had to be done quickly—our hostess expected us to be ready within a few moments. I thought rapidly of all the white mixtures and ingredients I could use—if I had them—all possible kinds of whiteners. My brain in a whirl of improvisations, I put my hand to my forehead—and then I thought of aspirin! With a little moistening, a fairly large dose did the the trick. We were a bit late—but we didn't look rusty!

Aside from the big occasions, there were many small informal "black tie" dinners and parties. There was the time Henry Cabot Lodge and his wife Emily were to be in Washington for a few weeks. They found a charming tiny house in old Georgetown which they rented furnished. On the evening we were invited for dinner, Emily Lodge had draped white cotton bedspreads over several pieces of tired-looking overstuffed furniture. The effect was somehow quite regal. Mrs. Rowan Shevlin, now the wife of Senator Cooper of Kentucky, was wearing a brilliant red gown which, with her dark hair, furnished an exquisite contrast to the white-draped furniture. Alice Roosevelt Longworth was another guest at that particular party, which in itself ensured an interesting evening. The décor is of little importance when the guest list includes such colorful and delightful people.

At one of Lorraine Shevlin's famous luncheons a week later Alice Longworth—Princess Alice, as she was called during her father's term in office as the twenty-fifth President—had gleeful praise for the Governor. He had recently upset the Democratic camp by a few words in a speech he had delivered in the early part of 1954. As I sat beside her, she said, "Oh, your husband is so, so wonderful! So delicious, what he said about the Democrats being sadists—I loved it!" But the Democrats didn't.

Especially pleasant to recall was the dinner the David Finleys gave in honor of Lady Astor. That diminutive, sometimes saucy, always entertaining little lady took quite a liking to my husband. She was appreciative of the load he was carrying and she scolded him for working so hard and seldom taking a rest. After she returned to England she sent us many telegrams and letters inviting us to visit her, insisting that the Governor needed a rest and would be little thanked for his tremendous efforts in the political field. We wish we could have accepted.

I remember too a dinner at the home of Secretary of Commerce Weeks and Mrs. Weeks honoring General Robert Cutler, Special Assistant for National Affairs, when the presence of the Eisenhowers added both pleasure and luster to the occasion. The Governor was driving our car that evening and we arrived in the vicinity of our host's residence fifteen minutes early. The time of arrival on the invitation was 7:45 and in Washington it is quite necessary to be punctual, neither early nor late, especially when the President and his wife are among the guests.

With considerable time to spare, we drove around Georgetown and returned to the Weeks' a couple of minutes before the appointed hour. Even if we hadn't known the house we would have had no trouble finding it for there were numerous policemen about, as is the custom when the President is expected.

Mamie's mother, Mrs. Doud, was one of the guests. The others were Cabinet members and Congressman Wigglesworth of Massachusetts and his wife. My hostess suggested that I sit on the President's left during the dinner, while insisting protocol was not being observed for the evening. Everything "was absolutely informal," she announced. We reminisced about our campaign train experiences, some involving the three photographers who managed to keep themselves in good humor—and everyone else too. Recalling them, the President laughed. "Say, they were a lot of fun!" he said heartily. We also talked about our common interest in painting.

"I don't have very much time to paint, actually," the President remarked. "By golly, it seems as though I just get started sometimes and then I have to leave." He told me that the first painting he ever tried was of Mamie and that she still had it. He enjoyed doing portrait work more than landscapes and probably had more fun painting his grandchildren than anything else he ever attempted.

Some time later, knowing of his admiration and affection for Sir Winston Churchill, I sent to the White House the framed print of the grand old gentleman that hung in the hall of our Tilden Street house with a note saying I thought the President might like to copy the best likeness of Sir Winston I had ever seen. The President lost no time in copying the picture and sending it to Sir Winston, and he was most appreciative as he thanked me for sending him the print to work from.

Dear Rachel:

I understand that . . . with your characteristic thoughtfulness . . . you brought down to the White House the study of Sir Winston Churchill. It is truly striking.

We had several photographs made of it, from which I can work at my leisure and without fear of damaging your picture, which I am returning today.

I can't tell you how much I appreciate all the trouble you took to bring this to my attention.

With warm regard,

Sincerely,

DWIGHT EISENHOWER

The President had a very small room in the family quarters of the White House where he retired to paint when his duties would permit. His brushes, paints, and other equipment were always ready for immediate use. If he was called away after becoming absorbed in a painting, Moany, his valet, would carefully clean the brushes and leave everything in readiness for the next painting session.

Several evenings we dined with former President Herbert Hoover, and I never ceased to marvel at his wisdom and extraordinary memory. There was nothing wrong with his sense of humor either. We particularly enjoyed hearing him talk about his fishing experiences. On one occasion he was on the Rapidan River with former President Calvin Coolidge. "Cal wanted me to teach him how to cast a fly for trout," Hoover recalled. "He wasn't much good at learning. In fact, his efforts scared the Indian guide so much he lay flat in the middle of the canoe to keep from being hooked."

A dinner party at the home of the Nelson Rockefellers, honoring the Dillon Andersons, is also pleasant to recall. I think I expected a Rockefeller to be different somehow, but he was a thoroughly likable person, one of the most unpretentious, genuine, and affable men it was my pleasure to meet on the Washington scene. He was easy to talk with and always ready to help others with their projects, no matter how large or how small. That evening he told me about his interest in the works of certain contemporary artists whose paintings I found hard to understand; and he seemed genuinely to want to learn more about our state of New Hampshire.

The embassies also add a great deal to the gaiety of Washington. Of course, it is part of their job—dispensing hospitality and good will. It is an endless one, too. The huge receptions given in honor of their national holidays are enjoyable and interesting occasions, and the buffet tables are laden with delicious and exotic native dishes. Wives of ambassadors are almost without exception extremely conscientious and charming. They made an indelible impression on me. I often wondered if the countries that sent them to Washington fully appreciated the painstaking care with which they carried on the unusually busy life they led, and the grace with which they fulfilled all obligations. The embassy wives with whom I became really acquainted deserve, to my way of thinking, credit for efforts far "beyond the line of duty," and I am sure those whom I did not know so well were just as deserving.

Madame de Kauffmann, wife of the Ambassador from Denmark, and I had one thing in common. We used to laugh together about the work our husbands made of helping us with the long back zippers to our formal gowns.

"The Ambassador makes such work of a little zipper," Madame de Kauffmann said. "You must have put on weight!" he says. "And when a zipper gets stuck, then you are really in a fix! For that is just what often happens, the men are so much in a hurry—so excitable!"

Mrs. Hatfield Chilson, wife of the Under Secretary of the Interior, who was listening to us, was in perfect agreement while I smiled at how similar the Ambassador's remarks were to those of my husband under like strain. For, on the occasions when I finally broke down and asked him to assist in zipping up my gown, he would tug and emit soft groans. Then he would ask me to move nearer to the light. Then he would have to go and get his glasses. If, and when, the zipper finally co-operated to the very top, there was a sigh of relief on my part and the usual insinuation from my husband that I must have put on more weight.

One fall Kathy Bass, wife of Congressman Bass from New

Hampshire, and I called at a number of embassies representing countries that Kathy and her husband were about to visit. We were cordially received by each of the ambassadors' wives who seemed genuinely delighted by Kathy's interest in learning about their particular countries, and they made arrangements with their governments for her to have special tours and opportunities to meet various women's groups.

Our first call was made on the Begum Ali of the Pakistani Embassy. She was a stately person with beautiful black eyes and a very soft voice. Her black hair with a natural wave was caught in a loose chignon. She spoke excellent English, which she had started learning at the time Pakistani women were allowed to remove their veils. Her pointed shoes of beige leather peeked out from under the hem of the misty gray-blue silk sari. Her blouse was of ice-blue brocade. On her left arm were four narrow red-and-gold bracelets, on her right was a beautiful red-gold wrist watch. The tea tray was full of Pakistani delicacies and the cups and saucers were pink and white with gold trim.

Hanging on the walls throughout the embassy were paintings from all over the world, including Switzerland, Canada, Turkey, Italy, and Australia. In one of the smaller rooms adjoining the reception room glass shelves across a mirrored wall, reaching to the ceiling, held a collection of jade, antique glass, and other objets d'art. On one wall hung a lovely Persian rug and scattered around the rooms were numerous tables inlaid with mother-of-pearl, gold and silver, on which were set out exquisite ivory carvings. The Begum Ali gave Kathy the names of several of her friends to see when she arrived in Pakistan, who would make sure that she met other women from whom she could learn much about the home life of that country.

The Indian Embassy was next on our list. As we drove up the winding road we saw Mrs. Mehta looking over the awnings. When she saw us arriving, she quickly disappeared inside the building. When we entered the drawing room, she was serenely waiting for us. She wore a sand-colored sari with a white short-sleeved blouse. Her lovely gray hair was pulled tightly into a chignon, and on her feet were sandals with toe and instep straps. The tea tray was heavy with a service of Indian silver. We enjoyed our Indian tea served in white china cups with a gold edge, accompanied by many different kinds of Indian pastries. A sandalwood chest covered with designs worked in silver depicting scenes of India rested on one of the coffee tables. It had been presented to the Ambassador by the people in his village.

The following day we called at the Burmese Embassy. Mrs. Win could speak but little English, so she kept an interpreter close by. The room we were entertained in had large paintings of Burmese temples. Our hostess wore a brilliantly flowered straight wrap-around skirt with a white blouse, and her hair, too, was worn in a chignon. Her three boys and one girl were in school in this country. According to Burmese custom, she had been named Mya Mya, after the day (Thursday) on which she was born, and she wore a gold ring set with an emerald, her birthstone. The tea service was of English design and instead of Burmese delicacies we were offered caterer's cakes and cookies. A very old harp, "perhaps a thousand years old," shaped like a gondola, stood in one corner of the room. It was a pleasant visit, as were the others.

That same afternoon we also visited the Indonesian Embassy. Madame Notowidigdo wore a long sarong of red batik with a green blouse, a large bone comb in her low brown chignon, and green and gold earrings hung from her small ears. Her feet, seemingly long for so small a woman, were encased in sandals similar to Mrs. Mehta's. She was a friendly and vivacious person and she served crisp and good Indonesian food, and tea in brilliant blue-bordered cups. A heavy ornate tea service in silver dominated the large silver tray.

Throughout the first floor of the embassy were a number of interesting native paintings. One in particular, which was quite modern, was pointed out to us; a nearly life-size stuffed tiger seemed to be snarling at it, which amused the Ambassadress. She seemed always to be on the verge of laughter.

Our third call that afternoon was at the Thai Embassy, where we were greeted by the friendly and plump little Madame Sarasin and her companions. Later the Ambassador joined us for tea. He was delighted to hear of the plans for the Basses' trip to his country. Here again we were served tea and a beautifully decorated cake. We also sampled some tiny ribbon sandwiches. As we were leaving, Madame Sarasin presented me with a beautiful scarf with a design worked in gold thread.

The Thai Embassy had better luck with their "ribbon sandwiches" than one of the Service clubs in the city. Once when a party was being planned by the wife of a government official, she ordered "ribbon sandwiches" as part of the list of delicacies. She, as well as her guests, were surprised to be served small sandwiches rolled up neatly and tied with little ribbons. I was told it was a bit frustrating to have to untie the ribbons while trying to balance a cup of tea!

On the evening of the same day that I went with Kathy Bass to three embassies for tea, the Governor and I stopped by at the Panamanian Embassy for a reception. Former Ambassador Joseph E. Davies was there and was insistent that I allow Salisbury of London to do my portrait: "He is the world's best portraitist; I know he would deem it an honor." The Ambassador had seen a picture of me in one of the papers and "thought it was beautiful." I enjoyed his remarks while at the same time I was sure I would never be painted by that illustrious portraitist. After arriving home that evening I had no appetite for dinner. Three teas and a reception had provided adequate sustenance as well as food for thought.

xii

The Outer Rim

Perhaps because of the painting classes I was able to stay on the outer rim of the Washington whirlpool. In the beginning, after six months in the hospital, the continual merry-go-round was not what I desired. Though I loved parties I wanted to make the most of my Washington experience in my own way. There were so many enticements, so many time-consuming ways to fill up the pages of an appointment book. Washington was full of fascinating people, interesting social gatherings, and of course one always had the feeling of being close to history in the making. But the city was also full of groping, tireless crowds of people who wanted to be seen at the biggest parties or associating with those in top government positions —people who worked hard at being "among those present." It was difficult to sort the wheat from the chaff at times, the momentum carried us along with such speed. It took a little doing to put on the brakes and be sensible about the whirl of events. What helped me most were Rosamond Gaydash's classes. In the one that I entered there were three ambassadors' wives whom I became very fond of. Polly Yang, the wife of the Ambassador from Korea, was a diminutive fashion plate and very popular and attractive. Madame Barrington, the wife of the Burmese Ambassador, was a warm and friendly young woman, and Señora de Castro, the wife of the Ambassador from El Salvador, was one of those always-the-same sort of people, unaffected and natural, with seemingly no favorites and with a smile for everyone. Then there was Dorothy LeCompte, the wife of the Congressman from Iowa, Penny Ridgway, General Matthew Ridgway's wife, and Esther Stassen. A number of other

Washington women added greatly to the interest and pleasure of those art classes in Rosamond's studio on 18th Street. I am sure that in no other basement in Georgetown was there such warmth of hospitality and sense of fellowship. Every available inch of that studio floor was covered with the sprawling legs of easels, boxes of paints, stools covered with paint-daubed palettes, boxes of facial tissues, and brightly smocked students. Three of the walls were hung with paintings and swatches of brilliant material, and on the wall facing the class was a large blackboard with a chalked outline of the art lesson for that particular day. It always seemed as though we had just got settled with our paints out, our eyes focused on the still-life problem for the morning, our brushes poised for that not-too-sure first stroke, when Rosamond would stand in front of the class and say: "If you will stop painting for just a few minutes—you are getting too tense—and I simply must teach you these things about perspective before we can go outdoors and paint a landscape." After a glance in my direction to see if I had put down my brush, she would turn to the blackboard. I wasn't the only one to put down her brush unwillingly. It wasn't that what Rosamond had to say was uninteresting; quite the opposite was true. She was able to imbue us with the belief that even we could learn to paint. She believed wholeheartedly in us and it delighted her to see the results of her faith and effort. But there was something about covering up that white canvas with color that was infinitely more exciting than listening to a talk about foreground color, values, relationship, composition, etc.

We returned home from Rosamond's classes exhausted. And after working with us for nearly four hours Rosamond would be worn and seemingly drained of the spirit that had been so apparent at the beginning of the class. Why did she give so much of herself to make us happy? It was as if she willed, with great strength of concentration, that we should absorb her love for and her knowledge of the art of painting.

Esther Stassen and I were not strangers when we went to Washington at the beginning of the new Administration, for we had met several times at various Governors' Conferences, but we became better acquainted through our common interest in painting. We both wanted to copy certain paintings that hung in the National Gallery. So, with a great deal of courage and little painting experience, at least on my part, we obtained permits to set up our easels in front of our favorite masterpieces. Throughout the gallery were other copyists, many of whom were considerably more experienced than we but no more enthusiastic. The crowds of visitors to the gallery during the winter months were small compared to the steady flow as soon as spring got under way. I thought I would mind being watched as I floundered around with a palette full of Renoir or Monet colors, but I found I was generally unmindful of those who peered over my shoulder. Sometimes I was amused by snatches of overheard conversation. I remember the nice elderly couple who were looking for a certain painting they especially wanted to see.

"Now," asked the husband, "where is Dali's last meal?"

"No, no!" exclaimed his spouse. "You mean Dali's last supper!" What they were really looking for was Dali's painting of "The Sacrament of the Last Supper." It was one of the most popular works of art in the gallery.

Many people were puzzled about our reason for wanting to copy a painting. Sometimes they would ask, and my answer was that I was trying to learn to paint. If I had told them that I considered the painting an old friend and wanted a replica to take back to New Hampshire, they would quite likely have been still more puzzled.

Sometimes they stood off at a distance and whispered loudly enough to be heard, thinking, I suppose, that they could get me straightened out. My colors weren't the same, they said, or something else bothered them. And there were those memorable occasions when some warm-hearted soul would earnestly say, "Yours is better than the original!" Perhaps they were painters too and knew of the struggle I was going through.

Esther Stassen was no less glad than I to get her mind on painting and off politics. Her husband, like mine, came under considerable fire now and then and, although Esther never said anything, I knew it bothered her. I felt that if I could get her off on a painting spree she would forget about the unpleasantness and have a number of enjoyable hours.

When Rosamond went to Paris for three years with her husband, we acquired Professor Elfinger, who had recently arrived from Germany. The Professor could speak little English but we managed very well most of the time, though during one of his classes he succeeded in thoroughly startling the dignified and quiet Esther Stassen. Like most artists, he would get excited now and then when something bothered him. One day he looked over Mrs. Stassen's shoulder at the canvas she was intent on.

"Est iss so hell, so hell, so hell!" he exclaimed.

Poor Esther Stassen was speechless. Could it be *that* bad? she wondered. At the same time she thought the Professor was going a little too far in speaking about her painting in such strong language! After inquiring about the English words he should have used, he explained it was "too bright, too bright!" and Esther felt better.

Not all our work was indoors. Spring comes early in Washington and with it rare beauty as the cherry blossoms, dogwood, and azaleas burst into color. Eager painters appear on the scene with the blossoms. Easels are set up at Haynes Point, where there is an array of double-blossomed cherry trees, and the reflecting pool near the Lincoln Memorial always has its quota of art enthusiasts. When I was in Washington the most popular place in the spring was the old Pierce Mill in Rock Creek Park. The brown waters of the creek flow past, dotted here and there with bobbing white ducks. In the summertime the mill hides from the hot sun and the tourist's eye in a tangle of vines and a luxuriant growth of shrubs and trees. The green moss on the roof blends with the leafy branches hanging overhead to camouflage one of the most interesting old buildings in Washington. Here Rosamond Gaydash had often brought our painting class. In our enthusiasm to capture the surrounding beauty on our canvases— fearful that it would suddenly disappear—we set up our easels along the bridle path or on the little bridge of the mill brook, or wherever there was a comparatively flat place. One particular morning there was a capricious and energetic breeze and sooner or later everyone's canvas and easel went flying into the gravel of the bridle path. We laughed and set them up again, wiped the hair from our eyes with paint-daubed fingers, and continued, oblivious even of the cameras of *Life* magazine, which had asked permission to photograph our class that day. We had just settled down when a rider came along the path on a prancing bay. I thought he seemed a bit disturbed as he tried to guide his horse among the array of brightly smocked would-be artists, the unpredictable canvases, and the sprawling feet of the easels. Some of us moved, a bit grudgingly, I have to admit, to give him room to pass, and then replaced our equipment in the middle of the path.

We had just resettled ourselves and were concentrating on "cool colors against warm colors" and "find your darkest darks and your lightest lights," when we were interrupted again by the clatter of horses' hoofs. This time it wasn't another well-dressed, disgruntled rider out for a morning canter—it was two park policemen. Again we moved our paraphernalia from the path, with considerably more alacrity than before, and waited for our latest visitors to pass. But they stopped, smiled down at us in an understanding way, and explained that if we wanted to paint we would have to move to areas that were off the bridle path. The previous rider had apparently put in a complaint. So, once again we gathered our stools, boxes of paint, brushes, canvases, and easels and moved from the path to the bank of the creek. As Rosamond went from student to student, reassuring and suggesting, a gust of wind followed the creek down from the northwest and sent the canvases flying again. Rosamond's landed in the creek and went floating along under the bridge, to be finally caught in a tangle of branches at the water's edge. We decided to give up the struggle for that day. An early lunch was agreed upon, the active morning in the fresh air having produced a healthy appetite if not a finished canvas.

All during those first few months of painting lessons the Governor was an interested bystander. He wasn't ready to commit himself regarding my progress. He had that "wait and see" attitude which had been so apparent on the campaign train during the Nixon crisis. He didn't, however, want to wait too long for me to become a painter of note, so after a certain length of time passed and he decided that I had no intention of giving it up, he became more interested and sometimes quite outspoken when he thought I was straying from the path of representational painting.

I well remember his reaction to one of the canvases I worked on while I was in the hospital. It was a Western scene and my inspiration had come from a Kodachrome slide which we had taken in Wyoming. I had the painting propped up in a conspicuous spot where the Governor couldn't help seeing it when he came to visit me that evening.

"What is that a picture of?" he asked when he entered the room.

"It's a place we visited in Wyoming," I answered, unable to believe that he didn't recognize it.

"I certainly don't remember anything that looked like that," he said flatly.

"You are standing too close," I told him. "A painting looks better when you stand at a distance."

"Well," my husband said, with a trace of a smile, "I'd have to get way down in Georgia to make *that* look good!"

The Governor didn't think much of the frames I was using on some of my pictures either. In fact, he was quite upset about one which had an unmistakably antiquated appearance.

"Where did you buy *that* frame?" he wanted to know.

"Same place I bought the others," I said.

"It's all full of worm holes," was his disgusted reply.

"Or termites," I said unconcernedly.

"Yes," he said with more emotion. "And that's a good way to get them in the house, buying frames like that!"

I decided that I'd better not encourage his displeasure to any greater extent. I told him the frame maker would be pleased to learn he had done such a good job at imitating old wormy wood. The Governor felt better.

Some months later, when we were packing the car to leave for a few days of Christmas vacation in New Hampshire, the Governor brought out several packages from a hiding place, suggesting I might like to see his Christmas gifts for me before we left; perhaps I would prefer to leave them in Washington.

For some reason or other I imagined the parcels contained a rotisserie and the equipment that goes with it. I was completely overwhelmed to discover one of the packages was a fully equipped painting box; the other contained frames, brushes, and easel. Not only had he given me the tools necessary for my newly found hobby, but what was even more gratifying to me, he showed thereby that he had finally capitulated. Anyway, he wanted especially to surprise and please me that Christmas. I was so surprised and pleased that I wept.

It was the same with skiing, golfing, apple pie, or pancake making; in fact, anything I did he encouraged and at times insisted that I do better. It hasn't been easy living with a perfectionist—but living with the type of perfectionist that the Governor is has meant many years of fun and excitement, all of which in retrospect rises to the top of the memory pool like oil on troubled waters.

Aside from my painting class, there were other groups of women I enjoyed being with—women who liked to feel they were accomplishing something, however unimportant that something might be. If the accomplishment wasn't anything more than refraining from idle chatter, it was considered worthwhile.

It is hard to say which I enjoyed most, for each was interesting in its own way. The smallest group, and one which I was surprised to find myself associated with, was made up of professional writers. I never did completely recover from finding myself an accepted member of such erudite company. However, because of my earlier acquaintance with one of the women I was asked to take the place of a charter member who had left Washington temporarily. Dorothy McCardle was a member of the press, submitting her columns about politics, parties, and personalities to the Washington *Post* and it was she who, hearing that I was thinking of doing some writing, suggested I come to one of the meetings.

"The Group," as those productive writers called themselves, had been getting together spasmodically for four years for a luncheon and then an afternoon of listening to one or more members read from their latest manuscripts. Marjorie Holmes (Mrs. Lynn Mighell) was the author of several novels and many short stories. Carley Dawson of Georgetown had at least three children's books to her credit plus numerous articles. Then there was Cecily Crow, whose *Miss Spring* had been well received and who had sold many short stories. Undoubtedly the best known of that illustrious group was Catherine Marshall (now Mrs. Leonard LeSourd), author of the Peter Marshall books. As one of the other members of the group said of her, "Catherine's freshness, frankness, and goodness set her apart." And while we listened to her read each chapter from the book she was writing, *To Live Again,* we felt the presence of something greatly worthwhile. I felt privileged to be accepted by them, for not only were they gifted writers but they were also filled with a desire to make the most of their talents.

The writer whose place I was allowed to take was the talented Jane McIlvaine (now Mrs. Nelson McClary), the author of several juveniles; and many will remember her book entitled *It Happens Every Thursday.* They were all generous in their criticism of my attempts at writing, not only generous but understanding and forbearing, and gave me the courage to continue.

The members of another writers' group I was associated with were no less scholarly and interesting, though out of the five members there was only one, Grace Jordan, who had the distinction of having had a book published. She was working on another book, *Canyon Boy,* which has since been published, and everyone looked forward to the meetings at which she would read her latest chapters. Margaret Holmes really started the group. She had many qualifications for being a writer of note but seemed to get more enjoyment out of writing light verse. Only recently I received a little book of her poetry. Helen Lowell and Jacqueline Broadbent were Washingtonians, excellent and long-suffering listeners to the rest of us. They were good critics, and their well-developed sense of humor helped to keep the rest of us from getting too serious about ourselves. They were a wonderful group of women.

The largest group of women with which I met regularly during my last few years in Washington were a diversified assemblage whose husbands were on the White House staff. There were generally about ten who came to our house on Tilden Street to spend the morning together working on individual projects. Luncheon consisted of sandwiches, which they brought, and dessert and coffee, which I furnished. For the most part they were younger than I. There were Army wives, professors' wives, career wives, and politicians' wives, and one or two were wives of retired businessmen who had come to work for the Eisenhower Administration. Their talents were as diversified as their backgrounds.

I felt it would be good for us to get to know each other better. Our husbands worked together day by day and I knew many of the women had small children, which made it necessary for them to be at home much of the time. Then, too, I missed my sewing club. I wanted to continue work on the hooked stair runner I had started some years before, depicting the life of my husband, step by step. Early in my married life I had found that mounds of mending for a large family disappeared fast and painlessly when one worked in the company of a lively group all doing the same thing. I hoped to finish my stair runner while in Washington and thought the best way would be to gather the White House wives at my house and get them interested in similar projects. Many of them already had a piece of needlework under way, but to a few it was a challenge, so I made an appointment with an instructor. I had the answer too for those who did not care to hook.

As a member of the Needlepoint Committee of the National Cathedral I was enthusiastic about the work that was being done throughout the country and in other parts of the world which would result in hundreds of pieces of beautiful needlepoint for eight chapels, the Great Choir, and the High Altar of the National Cathedral. I suggested to the White House staff wives that this was a wonderful chance for them to leave behind them something tangible and beautiful and useful. Under my high-pressure salesmanship most of the women decided to work on stamped kneelers which would be placed, when finished, in the Bethlehem Chapel. Some had never attempted needlepoint before. Some were experts. There were those who finished two or three pieces while others were still struggling with the first one. One of the first places I will go when I again return to Washington will be the Bethlehem Chapel where I will look among the hundreds of kneelers—all of a different design—to find those worked by the White House staff wives. My only tangible contribution toward the kneelers was a couple of designs which others worked. Later, following a dedication and Communion service I, with other members of the Needlepoint Committee, placed the first 332 pieces in the Cathedral. As I carried to the Bethlehem Chapel one of the kneelers I had designed I thought of the little juggler of Notre Dame and knew how he must have felt—my effort was so small in comparison with many, but it was wonderfully satisfying to have had any part in adding beauty and comfort to the already beautiful Cathedral.

One January Monday I decided to give the women gathered in my living room a special treat for dessert. The previous night there had been a heavy snowfall, and by morning the house and lawns and every leaf and twig had a thick white topping. The surprise I had in mind was maple-sugar-on-snow. After making some inquiries, I found that not one of my guests had ever tasted what to most New Englanders is part of the process of growing up. So I interspersed my hooking with frequent trips to the kitchen to watch the boiling of the maple syrup. Somehow on one of my many trips to the kitchen a pot holder was left too near the burner and slowly but odorously scorched away. The smell wafted in through the dining room and on into the living room, where the Monday group was working away. Some of them later told me they considered leaving early—that dessert I was making "didn't smell very good!"

While the syrup was boiling I had suggested to Mrs. Toner and Mrs. Asakai, the Japanese Ambassador's wife, who was our special guest that day, that they go out and fill up dishes with the new snow. They were gone a long time. The syrup cooked to the right consistency and still they hadn't come back. I went to investigate the cause of their absence—snow gathering, especially with so much available, ordinarily takes only a few minutes.

I found the lawn covered with crisscrossing footprints going in every direction, and finally I saw the women. They were, oh, so carefully lifting selected spoonfuls of snow from this or that evergreen branch as high as they could reach. They looked half frozen and the dishes were only about half-full.

I asked what was taking them so long and they answered, "We were trying to find *clean* snow!"

I showed them how to scoop away any lightly grayed snow and find the pure whiteness underneath—and there were acres of it in the vicinity!

There was another group of women with whom I became acquainted. They were members of the Montgomery County Farmwomen's Cooperative Market, and a more versatile, more hardworking, and congenial group would be hard to find. Furthermore, they were excellent cooks. I often went to their market on the outskirts of Washington to buy the farm produce and home-cooked foods, and I was so interested by the story of the organization that I asked if I might visit some of their homes and learn more about the women who had kept such a profitable enterprise going over a number of years. In fact, for twenty-five years they had been supplying the market with food, flowers, fruits, vegetables, and farm-raised beef, pork, lamb, and poultry.

Lillian Matson, manager of the market, was only too glad to accompany me to a number of the homes where kitchen shelves displayed an assortment of freshly baked items, ready for the early trip to the city in the morning. The women were so friendly and cordial that I decided to invite them to my home in Rock Creek Park for tea, and to see the pictures I had taken of them in their houses and at the market. I was a little nervous about baking for such an experienced group, but everything turned out quite well. I made two of my favorite recipes—Sour Cream Cookies and Meringue Kisses. The members of the Farmwomen's Market enjoyed them, but the next day I wondered what readers of a column in the paper thought about my cooking, for the columnist in writing about the party had mentioned my serving Sour Milk Kisses—which somehow didn't sound very appetizing.

··· *xiii*

Visiting Royalties

When royalty was entertained at the White House the procedure was much the same as for a state dinner. Perhaps the table decorations were a bit more lavish and possibly a favorite dish of the royal guests was part of the menu. But, as on other occasions, the guest list and the nature of the musical program that would follow the dinner were kept confidential, which added a highly speculative air to the evening.

At the end of the dinner in honor of Her Majesty the Queen Mother of Great Britain, Mrs. Eisenhower led the way to the Red Room, where a few of the guests, of whom I was one, were introduced to the royal visitor. I certainly shall never forget "the few moments" that I sat beside the Queen Mother on the little sofa as she told me how much she was enjoying her visit to the United States. She resembled an exquisite porcelain figurine which barely seemed to come alive and which, for me at least, was just as hard to converse with.

She was to be an overnight guest in the White House and I had, at the request of a friend in New England, asked Mary Jane Mc-Caffrey, Mrs. Eisenhower's secretary, if it would be possible to place a beautiful little hand-hooked rug in the royal guest's bedroom. It was the workmanship of a craftsman, and the design was a single beautifully executed rose on a plain background. It was intended to be a gift for the Queen Mother, but I was told the State Department decided it shouldn't be offered to her. So the little hooked rug stayed in New Hampshire.

The Queen Mother of Great Britain was, in due course, followed by many other royal visitors. The next to come to Washington, a month later, were King Paul and Queen Frederika of Greece. I again wore my inaugural gown. My escort for the evening was Congressman Vorys from Ohio. As we joined the procession on the way to the dining room I had a few bad moments when someone stepped on the hem of my skirt, bringing me to a quick halt. It happened again when we reached the dining room. It worried me but it amused my partner, for it reminded him, he said, of another White House gathering some years before when Vice-President Garner's sister, Dolly Gann, was at the height of her glory. During the procession down the hall someone stepped on her train, but Dolly kept going. There was a sound of ripping and those nearby who saw what was happening held their breath. A crisis was averted as the buxom Dolly halted. One gentleman was heard saying to another (both of whom had been concerned about where Mrs. Gann was going to sit at the banquet), "Gee, I thought for a moment we were going to see where Dolly sits."

With Congressman Vorys on my left and Senator Alexander Smith of New Jersey on my right I couldn't help but enjoy myself. As the Senator spoke of his interesting travels around the world as a member of the Senate Foreign Relations Committee, I rather wished my husband had a similar job. Congressman Vorys was, for the moment anyway, more interested in what Mamie Eisenhower and Queen Frederika were wearing. He said he must write his wife back in Ohio all about the affair she had to miss. We easily agreed that the Queen was wearing cream-colored satin, lavishly beaded, but what was the material of Mrs. Eisenhower's gown? I couldn't help the Congressman with that and he looked as if he had lost faith in me. That it was of a salmon color with an overlay of lace we both agreed, but his wife would want to know the kind of material it was made of, who had designed it, and whether it was short or long.

A day or so after the dinner I received a letter from Congressman Vorys. Utilizing the ability of congressmen to ferret out information, he had been able to give his wife answers to all the questions she would be most interested in. And for my own information he wrote, "Mrs. Eisenhower's gown was made of coral peau de soie, covered by black lace, made with strapless bodice, and waltz length. The designer was Nettie Rosenstein."

From where I was sitting at that dinner I could easily observe the Eisenhowers and their royal guests. Queen Frederika, warm and friendly, looking like a young girl in her size-ten gown, was captivating. Her tiara, sparkling with diamonds, seemed to rest lightly on her dark curls. The gorgeous emerald-and-diamond necklace detracted nothing from her beauty and added a considerable air of regality to the occasion.

Across the table from me sat Jane Weeks. A product of the South, with a luscious drawl, she had won everyone's admiration, and I am speaking particularly of Northerners now, by her ability to adjust to her husband's home in the near-polar regions of New Hampshire. To all appearances she loved that part of the country and certainly everyone loved her.

My eyes traveled to the portrait of Abraham Lincoln on the west wall above the fireplace. It was a wonderful likeness showing him with chin in hand, elbow resting on his bony knee, and as always he seemed to be looking down on the assemblage. If he could have spoken, would he have said, "You are not very different from those who enjoyed the hospitality of these hallowed rooms with me. There is only more of everything now"? It is such a dignified, appealing, and somehow necessary portrait. I was sorry when it was later relegated to the Red Room and replaced by a landscape completely lacking the character and rightness that the Healy portrait of Abraham Lincoln seemed to lend to the room. The Lincoln painting reminded visitors of the Gettysburg Address and the man who made it. It was a painting full of greatness and, at the same time, humbleness. It was particularly fitting, I thought, that it should hang in a room where so many Americans and guests from other lands were entertained.

To digress for a moment, I remember another painting in the White House that hung exactly where I thought it ought to hang. It wasn't the painting itself that I was worked up about—it was what was under it. On the lower floor, where the China Room, the library, the little theater, the kitchen, and several other rooms are, is a long hallway. Portraits of early Presidents hang on the broad expanse of the south wall. There was a very large painting hanging on the opposite wall. The space is really too small for such a big painting but still it had to be large to cover up what was underneath. The first time I noticed it was when I was on tour of the lower floors of the White House with friends. I stopped and wondered at the too-large painting for the amount of space. Then I thought I remembered something I had seen on the marble wall behind it months earlier when I visited the building during the Truman Administration.

"What is back of that painting?" I asked the aide who was in charge of our group.

"I was afraid you were going to ask that," he said. What was back of it, and what I remembered, was an inscription in the marble wall of the hallway. It covers several square feet and informs the viewer of the identity of the many well-qualified gentlemen connected with the renovation of the White House, headed up, in large letters, by the name Harry Truman. I wished someone in that group had insisted instead on a bronze tablet of much smaller proportions to acquaint all interested persons with the names of the members of the Commission on Renovation. The painting, "Signing of the Peace Protocol between Spain and the United States, August 12, 1899," covered up the inscription during the Eisenhower Administration. Someone else apparently felt as I did.

Tearing my attention from the wonderful Lincoln portrait I concentrated again on my dinner partners and Mamie Eisenhower's dress. As the dinner neared its end, and the champagne glasses were filled, the conversation died down. Most of the dinner guests were looking in the direction of the President.

He fingered the delicate stem of the champagne glass, glanced around the room, then as a waiter pulled his chair back, he stood up. Putting on his glasses and directing his words to His Majesty, he read a citation, and then presented the Legion of Merit to King Paul, saying as he did so, "Your Majesty, as I hand this to you, I am going to ask the company to rise and with me drink a toast to Your Majesty the King," and then looking across the table to the Queen and nodding, "and to Your Majesty the Queen of Greece." "To the King—to the Queen," mingled voices responded as the toast was drunk.

Everyone sat down again except the King, who gave thanks to the American people for their aid and timely support during and following the war. He also reminded those present that his country of Greece was the first democratic country completely to defeat Communist aggression.

With the toasts and the speeches over, the monogrammed napkins were laid on the still-beautiful table. Shortened candles burned as bravely as when they were tall and new. The corps of waiters stood around the sides of the room with their hands behind their backs, their faces completely expressionless. As the President and Mrs. Eisenhower rose with the royal guests, chairs were pushed back all around the huge table and another White House dinner was becoming history.

In the Red Room Queen Frederika settled herself regally on the little sofa above which would later hang the painting of Lincoln. Mary Jane McCaffrey introduced some of the guests to the Queen. When it was my turn to sit on the other end of the sofa and speak to Her Majesty—a privilege I did not expect—I told her of all the wonderful people in New Hampshire who are of Greek descent. She was natural and gay and interested and not at all hard to talk with. All too soon my allotment of time ran out and someone else was introduced to her.

Over in one corner of the room a couple of former Radcliffe girls were talking about archaeological excavations, skeletons, and interesting bowls. Mrs. John Foster Dulles, in blue satin, sat on the little sofa in front of the marble fireplace. Next to her was Mrs. Humphrey, wearing a gown of peach-colored lace. Mrs. Eisenhower circulated, for the most part, among the out-of-town guests, having talked to the Cabinet ladies earlier in the evening when they and their husbands were presented to the King and Queen before dinner. As she came up to me she exclaimed, looking at my necklace, "Isn't that a Trifari piece, Rachel?" I said that it was. "I have one very similar upstairs and I just love it." Then she lifted her head a bit, and, fingering her necklace of diamonds and pearls, told me she had bought it in England and went on to explain how it could be changed into pins, or even a coronet. And then she was off to show interest in some other guest.

The royal couple spent that night in the White House, King Paul in the Lincoln suite and the Queen across the hall in the more femininely decorated pink suite. The red guest room (which my husband occupied a few years later when we were overnight guests of the President and the First Lady) was given to the master of ceremonies to the King, and the yellow room (which later I was to sleep in) was taken over by the lady in waiting to the Queen. On the following day the royal entourage moved to Blair House, across Pennsylvania Avenue, the official guest house of the President, authentically and beautifully furnished with pieces typical of the period in which the delightful old house was built.

It had rained hard the evening of the dinner for the Greek King and Queen, and I think my husband's New England conscience got a little watering down, for the next evening he rather sheepishly announced that he had ordered a car from the White House garage to take us to the reception the King and Queen were giving at the Army-Navy Club. It was the beginning of his concession that perhaps after all it was better to order a car when we had to go to official events, especially if it was raining. I agreed heartily, though he still had doubts about its being the most sensible thing to do.

Neither of us was looking forward to another night out. We had already attended three dinners that week and were scheduled for still another the next evening. It was too much of a good thing, the Governor felt, for he liked to arrive at his office early and in good form for whatever problems the day had in store. So I wasn't surprised to learn at the end of the week that he had told his secretary, Ilene Slater, that he would fire her if hereafter she signed him up for more than three evenings a week. Ilene knew she wouldn't be fired, but as a result of his decree we had to regret a number of invitations.

On the evening of the reception given by the King and Queen we were ready when the car-with-driver arrived at our door a little before 5:30. Five-thirty is about the middle of the Washington rush hour. Our driver, helped by a few back-seat directions from the Governor, finally got onto Route No. 1, in preparation for crossing the 14th Street bridge. All lanes were full of trailer trucks, private cars, and taxis, and the lines were making extremely slow progress. In fact, in more than half an hour we had covered very little distance. Sherm began to be surer than ever that he should have driven himself. In time we crossed the bridge and went in the general direction of the Army-Navy Club, and finally found a back entrance which we hoped would be less crowded than the front entrance. It was then 6:45 and at seven we were supposed to be at the Italian Embassy back in the city, for a reception in honor of John Davis Lodge, the Governor of Connecticut. But the back driveway, too, was congested with cars, none of which seemed to be moving, and it was raining hard.

The Governor had no intention of sitting there in the rain for an indefinite period waiting to get inside where there would be another long line of guests being received by the royal couple. Sure that we wouldn't be missed in such a crowded room, he instructed our driver to get out of line if he could and take us to the Italian Embassy, adding that he hoped the driver knew where it was. Yes, the driver was sure he knew right where the Italian Embassy was. The Governor relaxed a little on the way back to Washington but he came to with surprising quickness when he noticed we were entering the driveway across the street from where we wanted to go.

"Where in thunder are you going now?" he demanded.

"Isn't this the Italian Embassy?" asked the driver.

"The place we want to go is right across the street," my husband said firmly.

We finally arrived at our destination a bit late but the guest of honor and his wife were much, much later.

After the presentation of the citation to Governor Lodge, there were cocktails and pizza pie. Then we went out to see if the driver had remembered where he left us. He had, and in a few moments we arrived home without any detours. Of that the Governor made certain. Taking no chances, he instructed the driver at every turn.

The following week we attended another state dinner at the White House given by the Eisenhowers in honor of members of the Cabinet and their wives. I remember it particularly because a waiter dropped a soup spoon which disappeared under the table and the voluminous folds of my gown. He quickly put his tray on a nearby table, said, "Excuse me, Mrs. Adams," as he went in search of the piece of silver.

After dinner there was the usual interlude as the ladies and gentlemen separated for coffee and liqueurs before going to the East Room for the concert that usually followed a formal White House dinner. Fred Waring and his Pennsylvanians had been engaged to entertain on that particular evening. President Eisenhower and the First Lady sat in the middle of the front row of gilded chairs. Cabinet members and their wives occupied the seats nearby. The remaining dinner guests, and the staff members and other government officials who had been invited for the concert, easily filled up the rest of the chairs.

Waring and his group were in great form. The concert began with "Bless This House," followed by "Mamie" and "Ike, Mr. President." The next selection was from the Nutcracker Suite. Fred then told the audience how the Governor used to join the Waring singers during the early Ike campaign in New Hampshire. He said he was going to ask the Assistant to the President to come up front and help them with "Sweet and Low." The group soft-pedaled their voices so that the audience would be sure to hear the Governor. He looked perfectly angelic, as he always did when singing, and though he was out of practice he sounded wonderful. I think that was the last time he ever sang in public.

Fred Waring's gaiety always infects his audience. The Governor thoroughly enjoyed singing with the group again, and there were many in the room, including the President and his wife, who were reminded of the campaign trail and the pleasure Fred Waring and his Pennsylvanians had given to so many Eisenhower supporters. After the singing of "Ol' Man River" the concert ended with "The Lord's Prayer," both of which had been favorites when the campaign train was making its last run from the Boston Garden rally back to New York the night before election.

The royal visit that created the greatest stir was that of Her Majesty Queen Elizabeth and His Royal Highness Prince Philip, Duke of Edinburgh. They arrived in Washington on a dreary day but the inclement weather in no way discouraged the throngs of people who lined the streets to get a look at the Queen as she rode by. People watched almost with reverence, waved, hoisted small children aloft for a better view. The guards were insistent that the crowd keep at a respectful distance and they had little trouble enforcing their wishes.

Our place on the precedence list which the State Department issued that year was just below the Cabinet, so we were invited to all the events connected with the Queen's visit. On the night of her arrival we attended the state dinner at the White House. I found it hard to keep from looking at the Queen all the time, and the men on either side of me were having the same trouble.

The concert that evening was both surprising and successful. It wasn't a group of operatic virtuosos, nor yet a performance by some well-known group of instrumentalists. It was, once again, Fred Waring and his Pennsylvanians and it was a truly American program for the most part.

The next evening the British Embassy held a reception for Her Majesty. Everyone was amazed at the transformation of the terrace, where, to make room for the large number of guests, a huge white tent supported by high posts encircled by wreaths of flowers had been set up. The red carpet that the Queen strolled along with Ambassador Caccia added a touch of regality and warmth to the gray October evening. The Queen was led unobtrusively to various prominent government officials. As the greetings and curtsies took place everyone watched with undisguised interest, wondering if perhaps she would come their way. Most of the women and many of the men were lined up along the edge of the red carpet, anticipating that age-old thrill of youngsters, "to be near enough to touch a queen!"— especially one so young and attractive.

My husband, seemingly oblivious to what was happening along the red carpet, was off in a corner talking to an elderly senator's wife who, unable to stand comfortably for any length of time, was sitting in a chair in a corner. This kind of thoughtfulness was characteristic of him, and because of his interest in that charming little lady with the cane he was not in evidence when the Queen asked for him.

The royal guest had met many of those present and at last her host quietly guided her back toward the foyer of the embassy. But the Queen wanted to meet someone else.

"Where is Sherman Adams?" she inquired of her host. Ambassador Caccia looked around but couldn't see the Governor in his far-off corner. His reply to the Queen's question was inaudible. I wanted to cry out, "There he is, over there," but I could only smile as the Queen drifted slowly past.

We met many other interesting foreign guests during those Washington years but of them all, for a not important reason, I especially remember the visit of Prince Bernhard of the Netherlands. A good friend in India had sent me a magnificent sari of red and gold, with small figures of elephants and birds in the design. I took the material and went to the best dressmaker I could find, and afford. If the figures in the material promised luck for the wearer, as I was told they did, my good fortune started with the finding of an exceptionally gifted seamstress, one who knew how to translate my ideas into a gown that had both charm and individuality.

I first wore it to the Centennial Festival of Music in the Academy at Philadelphia, at which my husband had been asked by the President to represent him. Though I had entertained a faint hope that my new gown, which contained the colors of the festival, would be admired, I was unprepared for the attention it did receive. To have a number of Philadelphia gentlemen come and tell me how beautiful it was and ask if by chance it was designed from a sari, and to show by their obvious interest that I hadn't been mistaken about its beauty, made my evening quite complete. When asked who the designer was, I tried to be nonchalant as I answered that I had designed it myself. I removed the gown quite tenderly that night, wondering how soon I could try it out at a Washington affair.

A week later a state dinner at the White House gave me a chance to wear it again, and again it was much admired. During that month of February I wore it to a number of large dinners and always it drew compliments. The climax was the evening I wore it to the Netherlands Embassy at a dinner in honor of Prince Bernhard. The Prince walked across the room to where I was standing to tell me how beautiful he thought my gown was. "May I ask what kind of material that is? And where did it come from?" It is a trivial thing to recall, I realize. It was just that it was so unexpected—and appreciated. I felt then that I was ready to lay the gown away for posterity.

xiv

On "Person to Person" with Mr. Murrow

As time went by it became apparent that Washington was an unwelcome change for a few of the wives who had followed their husbands to the capital city. They had little or no interest in either the political or the social scene; Washington life was a tolerated interim between frequent trips back home. There were yet others who refused to make the break at all, and came to the city only for very special occasions. But for the most part wives came with their husbands determined to enjoy the change and fully resolved to keep their sense of balance—on the edge of the whirlpool.

It was easier for those who had had some indoctrination in public life. Our previous experience with long lines of handshakers made the occasions in Washington a lot easier when we were asked to help out, or "to stand in line for a little while." Shaking hands is an old New England custom, and meeting friendly people and introducing them to the next in line is a pleasant task—if one is wearing comfortable shoes. Once in a while, though, there came down the line the kind of person I could do without. With a sly smile he or she would say, "You don't remember me, *do* you?"

"*How* could anyone forget *you?*" I would answer, smiling benignly as I tried desperately to remember the name.

It was generally easy for the Governor to remember the names even of those he didn't know well. Once in a while, though, he would hesitate as someone he hadn't seen for some time looked hopeful of being recognized. Then he would get a certain gleam in his eye and, turning to me would say, "*You* remember who this is, *don't* you, Plum?" He would wait for what seemed like an eternity for my reply.

Often I was of no help, but more than once I had a definite urge
to say, "No, I'm sorry I don't remember. Who *is* it, Governor?"
However, I could never quite bring myself to put him in such an
embarrassing position.

Perhaps it was as well that now and then someone tested the extent
of our memory. It helped to keep us on our toes, for as wives of
government officials we were expected to know people as well as the
answers to many and varied questions. Acting as guides to visitors
from our home state or, indeed, from anywhere who were seeing
Washington for the first time could be rather embarrassing if we
hadn't stored up some knowledge about the shrines and historical
spots in the Washington area.

There were countless other demands on the time of a Washington
wife, especially in the spring when the various charities put on all-
out campaigns. Luncheons and bazaars, the first at big hotels accompanied by a fashion show and the latter at colorful embassies,
were popular ways of raising money. They had to be well-planned
affairs to bring in the thousands of dollars which were hoped for
and usually gathered, but almost any kind of fashion show preceded
by a luncheon would sell every available chair and inch of floor space.
I for one was content with about one fashion show a year, having
little inclination to spend my afternoons watching a parade of exquisite gowns which I couldn't afford, but sometimes I found myself
a part of the event in one way or another.

I'll never forget—and I doubt if the store owner will—the time I
was invited to pose for a photograph that would be used to publicize
a forthcoming fund-raising campaign. I accepted, glad to be of help
and thinking at the same time that it would be fun to add a little
zip to the usual runway fare. I arrived at the large department store
where the pictures were to be taken and was introduced to the store
model with whom I was to be photographed. She was quite a picture
by herself. The lower half of her good-looking figure was clad in a
pair of tight velvet lounging pants. I have forgotten the details of
the exotic creation that adorned her upper half, but I do remember
strings and strings of costume jewelry cascading down toward the

velvet pants. Having in mind the skiing the Governor and I hoped to be doing soon, I took courage and suggested to the manager that it would be nice to be photographed with a model in the latest ski pants and parka—after all, that was one of my favorite costumes. Everyone looked at me as if I were quite out of my mind. In quiet tones I was told that there wasn't anything in that category in the store. I registered due consternation and regret and moved into focus with the glittering model, smiling at the thought of the effect on certain Washingtonians if, when they looked at the runway, they saw a parade of ski costumes instead of the ever-popular cocktail dress or lounging ensemble.

(Recently I was pleased to learn that a change had finally taken place on a fashion show runway in Washington. A friend who knew I would be interested informed me of the addition of smart ski costumes. I wish I had been present.)

One fashion show I did enjoy, however, was when I appeared at a Republican Women's Luncheon with other government wives who were modeling the gowns of former First Ladies. Mine was a copy of one worn by Angelica Van Buren when she was official hostess for her father-in-law. It was a charming cameo-type creation of blue velvet with a lace bertha and trailing skirt. With good reason it was vastly admired, and I was loath to take it off.

The way Washington women in general dressed made an impression of a kind on at least one distinguished visitor, who expressed his dismay in no uncertain terms: "Mink stoles—Frederic hats—but their *shoes!*"

Perhaps he was kin to the person who said of the dear old Boston ladies: ". . . but their hats!"

There was one appearance for charity that I shall never forget, and I might have been less enthusiastic about participating if I had known all that would happen as a result of my husband's acceptance of Edward R. Murrow's invitation to be on his "Person to Person" show. The event was to benefit the Crippled Children's Association and Sherm could hardly refuse to help an organization so deserving, particularly since he had been its state president some years back when he was governor of New Hampshire. At the time neither of us had any idea of the domestic upheaval necessary for the production of a "Person to Person" performance. We learned a lot before it was over.

A preview of the house for Mr. Murrow's advance men gave them ideas for the highlights of the show. Since the Governor was busy, it fell to me to expound the historical virtues of our interesting Tilden Street home. I was getting along all right until they spied what I insisted were dinosaur tracks in the hearthstone of the fireplace. They weren't going to believe that without a lot of explanation, so I had to spend some time finding the data to satisfy them. They found my claim more credible when I explained later that the stone with the tracks had been discovered in Virginia and placed in the house at the time it was converted from an old barn.

Along with the factfinders came a cameraman to take some preliminary shots of the house and grounds. These would help in planning the show—what would be highlighted, what would be left out.

A few days later Mr. Murrow kept an appointment with the Governor in his office. I was asked to be present. As the interview progressed, I presumed the gentleman behind the bushy eyebrows and the busy cigarette was trying to evaluate my potentiality as a performer. I was quite sure that he had no qualms regarding the Governor's ability to bring credit to the occasion, but I think he decided that in the best interests of his show he had better keep me in the background as much as possible—which was quite all right with me. Perhaps those penetrating glances in my direction were occasioned by some uneasiness about my ability to stick to the facts in connection with the dinosaur tracks.

From then on for about a week Mr. Murrow's forces were at work. A big piece of equipment which someone said was a TV booster was parked in the nearby picnic area. More telephone lines were connected. An extra transformer was installed to take care of the heavy load needed for the powerful equipment. Then, on the day of the broadcast, twenty men appeared, as well as a number of trucks, one of which belonged to a caterer.

That morning I had halfheartedly considered doing some errands downtown. When I entered my dining room and saw twenty men standing around my dining table listening to orders regarding the the installation of three very large TV cameras, the laying out of a tangle of cables, wiring and chalk marks, and the plans for moving out most of the furniture, I hurriedly shut the cat in the back bedroom and with unusual enthusiasm headed downtown.

When I returned in time to dress for dinner at the Statler with friends, the first floor was hardly recognizable. Television cameras were being checked and rechecked. There seemed twice as many men around. Pictures had been switched. Furniture had disappeared. I could barely pick my way to the stairs in the hope of finding some degree of normalcy on the second floor. Later, as we left the house, we were reminded to be back at 8:30 for rehearsal.

We arrived back at the house with about twenty minutes to spare before the first rehearsal. Sometime during the early part of the evening a flower arrangement had arrived. Accompanying it was a note— the thoughtful gesture of one who hoped to put his performers at ease: "Good luck and I'm sure it will be fun. Ed Murrow."

Mr. Murrow's voice (he was in the studio in New York) could already be heard on the monitor and men were everywhere with earphones, testing, testing, testing. The Governor was ready, or so he thought, until the make-up girl cornered him with her assortment of equipment. I had been sent upstairs by the same girl to change as quickly as possible and told not to put on a rustly petticoat—it would make unwelcome noises on the show.

After the Governor was finished, I received my No. 5 Pancake treatment and a wisp of eye-shadow. Then the same make-up girl secured two batteries around my waist—under my full skirts. A wire was left to dangle about ten inches below the bottom of my skirt. I wondered how they had "hooked up" the Governor but I was much too busy trying to keep my wires from getting crossed to think much about anything else. Besides, I had been warned. "You are now 'live,'" I was told. Anything you say will be heard by the boys at the controls here and in New York." Such an admonition would generally suffice for the average woman—in fact, those words carried such an element of foreboding that I hardly dared think.

We rehearsed without any hookup and then we went through the same process again at 9:30 connected with the studio in New York. Mr. Murrow's questions came through the monitor on top of the buffet, a rather small box containing the loudspeaker. We had been cautioned to keep our eyes on this when answering his questions, so that it would look on television screens across the country as if we were in the same room with him. I was definitely nervous though I tried hard not to be. After the last rehearsal Mr. Murrow said, "Fine." We then were told to relax until show time at 10:30. The Governor went upstairs to read the paper. I went to the kitchen for a drink of water, and a couple of cameramen followed. They were interested in the labeled bottles I removed from the refrigerator and thought it fine water. They wanted to know if it was really much better than the city water. I told them that for a number of months my husband had thought so. "After the crystal-clear unadulterated drinking water we have been used to in the hills of New England, the District of Columbia product is a little hard to swallow," I said, "and the Governor suggested I keep a never-ending supply of Mountain Valley Water on hand." After a number of months I decided it was a needless expense and when the Governor wasn't looking I filled the bottles from the tap and put them in the refrigerator where, after a bit, the unpalatable flavor disappeared. I went on to tell them how he had served some to Sam Goldwyn, the motion-picture magnate, one hot and sultry Washington evening, explaining that he just couldn't drink city water and expounding the virtues of bottled water. I admitted to the men I had felt a little ashamed as I listened.

At this point I suddenly realized with great consternation that I was still "live" and on a rather extensive hookup! I had forgotten the admonitions at the beginning of the evening and had talked too much. My ever-present make-up friend tried to be consoling. It was her fault, she said, for not remembering to remind me.

"I expect you've had some interesting experiences with other people who, like me, can't remember to keep quiet," I offered hopefully.

"Oh, my yes!" she answered. "The best one I remember was when Mrs. —————— was on Mr. Murrow's show. After rehearsal she took me upstairs to her bedroom. She thought maybe she would look better if she put on some falsies, and we discussed the subject for quite a few minutes—neither of us remembering she was on a live circuit!"

Finally 10:30 came and we were in our places. Sylvia, our Siamese cat, was purring contentedly in our daughter Sally's lap in front of the fireplace which no one had remembered to light. The Governor and I were in the dining room ready for Mr. Murrow's voice to come from the monitor. The chalked dinosaur tracks were ready for inspection by the enormous television audience. Every technician, every cameraman, the script writer, and all the others in attendance awaited almost breathlessly the signal to start. There was a hush throughout all the rooms; the only animation noticeable came from the electrically controlled blinking eyes of a stuffed elephant sitting on top of our television set. A few seconds passed, then one of the men wearing headphones gave the signal, and the show was on, from coast to coast.

When we went off the air the Governor lost no time in getting to bed. I watched the other half of the show as the cleanup crew went to work, quietly and quickly, and then I started wearily up the stairs too. The sound of the telephone halted my progress and I returned to the living room to answer it. The voice on the other end of the line belonged to Mr. Murrow. He expressed his appreciation of our cooperation and said sometime he "would learn." We "should have been on for the whole show." I didn't agree with him. It was getting late and I could hardly wait to put the day behind me as the furniture was replaced and the equipment dismantled. The crew expected to be all cleaned up and out of the house by 12:30. I was too tired to wait for their departure.

In the morning as I looked through the rooms to see how well they had remembered where the furniture belonged, I observed with a great deal of satisfaction and high regard for Mr. Murrow's well-trained crew that the only item not in place was a magazine rack. Passing through the dining room into the kitchen, I glanced at the dinosaur tracks. They were still there and still full of chalk.

XV

The President Visits Our Town

In June of 1955 I left the Washington scene for important days in New Hampshire. The President, having missed stopping in Vermont and Maine during the campaign of 1952, had with my husband's help planned a special trip to get better acquainted with those states. Our home town of Lincoln would be one of the scheduled stops.

I arrived in Lincoln a week before the great day. The whole town was busy with preparations. The lumberyard, with its many years' accumulation of old bark, rotten boards, and other debris, had been bulldozed. Down in the West End the biggest change took place. The empty bottles and cans which the lumberjacks had for many years been tossing among the young hardwoods had been shoveled onto trucks and the whole area made neat and clean. Everyone received a reminder in the mail or with their pay envelopes at the mill to please have their grass cut by the time the President arrived. Almost everyone did. One or two barely finished in time.

A professional decorator did a good job hanging bunting on the principal buildings. And he got extra work when an idea of mine caused the route for the presidential motorcade to be changed. I thought the President's party should be invited to stop at our house for refreshments and a break in the morning's schedule. It seemed like a very long time from 8:30 A.M., when the President was to leave Laconia, to 1:00 P.M., when he was due at Whitefield. Anyway, when would a President be coming our way again?

So I paid a visit to the Secret Service men at the State House in Concord. First, I suggested they change the route through Lincoln from Maple Street to Church Street, in order that the motorcade could pass the churches, hotel, schools, and library. Then, before I had a chance to mention my next plan, they said they were a bit concerned about a place for the President to stop on his way! So the rest was easy—except when I telephoned my husband in Washington to let him know what I planned to do. He said very firmly, "I positively do not want to hear about the President's making *any* stops not already scheduled, whether for an ice-cream cone or for *anything else*." I never argue with my husband. I just went ahead with my plan.

Since I had been at home only occasionally during the past eight years there was much that needed attention. I kept one man busy for three evenings on the lawn. Another man fixed the loose brick on the front steps. A carpenter had the job of getting the doors, which stuck, to work better. I covered up the result of his scrapings with new paint. I put up new curtains in our room and bought new guest towels marked "Top Brass" for the powder room downstairs. I was busy every minute of Tuesday and Wednesday, all the time not knowing for sure if the motorcade would stop.

On Monday the steps in front of the well-made speaker's stand by the high school were moved to the left side, for the Secret Service had said the motorcade would arrive by way of Maple Street. On Tuesday the steps were changed to the right side, for the Secret Service now said the motorcade would arrive by way of Church Street. The carpenters began to wonder whether the Secret Service really knew *where* they wanted the blank steps! Naturally, I didn't tell them I was responsible for the last change.

By Wednesday evening everything was ready at our house. Freda Wilson would be in the kitchen. A neighbor would lend her silver service, another neighbor her napkins. A lady from Church Street would deliver fresh doughnuts; another would furnish cookies. There would be Vermont cheese, lemonade, milk, and coffee. Furthermore, my sewing club would get together and have a party if the President *didn't* stop—and they would also have a party if he *did*. I went to bed hoping I could sleep.

Thursday was a beautiful day. I made an early trip to the beauty shop to have my hair done. At 11:45 I was off to Concord, where I found many people already gathered at the State House and along the streets. The crowds seemed very happy. The Reception Committee was especially busy in the Governor's Chambers. In addition to members of the press there were many legislators there as well as representatives of the Secret Service.

At 3:45 I was escorted to my seat in front of the speakers' stand by a member of the National Guard. Someone came out and announced that the President and his party had just left the airport. In a few minutes there he was, riding along Main Street! I hoped my husband was with him—I hadn't seen him for about a week.

A few minutes more and Sherm appeared on the platform and was introduced. He looked around and finding me in the front row said softly, "Where did you get *that* hat?" (I had just finished saying to Betty Dwinell, wife of the Governor, who sat by me, "The first thing he'll notice is this new red hat!")

When the President was introduced, "the biggest Concord crowd ever" gave him a hearty welcome. He launched into his now famous remarks about the education the staff received regularly from the Assistant to the President regarding the glories of New Hampshire.

When the ceremony was over I rode to Laconia with Bernard Shanley. I was bursting to know whether the Secret Service had informed him of my plan to have the President stop at our house in Lincoln. It wasn't until later that I was told it "looked as if" my invitation was going to be accepted. There were hundreds of excited people all along the way, the President trying to look at and say hello to each one. And that is the impression so many had—that he was waving and speaking to them alone.

Charlie Stafford met us at the door of his tavern in Laconia. The little elevator was busier than it had ever been. Our room, and those of the President, General Snyder (the President's physician), Elizabeth and Richard Cooper (the latter Republican National Committeeman of New Hampshire), Bernard Shanley, Secretary to the President, and the Secret Service men were on the third floor. They were newly painted and papered, newly furnished, and hung with oil paintings borrowed from the local art gallery. There were big baskets of fruit, an air conditioner, and a television set. We had about thirty minutes to change and appear for the next event, which was to be at the Guilford Recreational Area, some miles away. There would be barbecued chicken—and speeches.

Lib Cooper and I got ready and waited for someone to tell us to present ourselves for the motorcade. No one did. Then, at the very last minute, her husband telephoned from the lobby: "You girls better come down; everyone is ready to leave." We rang for the elevator three times. Nothing happened. The elevator man must have been out watching the President leave. By the time we had walked down the three flights of stairs, the motorcade was far away. We hopped into the sheriff's car, and with the aid of his siren arrived in Guilford only a couple of minutes after the others.

After the barbecue we were escorted to the speakers' stand. The crowd seemed small in such a huge area—acres and acres of land. The bawling heifer, a gift for the President, added much to Senator Bridges' oration. The two New Hampshire Red hens and rooster in their cages beside the stand looked up at the President, then clucked to one another, then looked again and did some more clucking. The press and photographers got a big kick out of watching the Secret Service man standing beside the cage of fowl. Everyone was wondering whom he was guarding—the hens or the President.

Following the speeches and the presentation of the livestock, we were entertained by New Hampshire talent and folk dancing. Then the band played "Onward, Christian Soldiers," as a signal for the President's party to leave. I waited for the President to go, but he took my arm saying, "Why aren't you singing?" So we walked to the cars singing. I have since learned that it was a favorite hymn of the President's.

The trip back to the tavern in the soft New Hampshire air and with a fine sunset was beautiful. There were more than a hundred people waiting to greet the President in the dining room. It was quite an ordeal after what he had been through for the past few days, but he was a good sport, and it wasn't too late when we finally separated for what everyone hoped would be a good night's sleep.

Because so many people wanted to speak privately with the Governor, I went into the bathroom and locked the door as I prepared for the night. But when I tried to unlock the door, nothing happened. I tried again; nothing happened. I looked out the window, hoping to find a fire escape, but there was none nearby. I searched the bathroom for something to pound loose the pins in the hinges—there wasn't a thing, and anyway the President was trying to sleep across the hall. Finally I decided I might as well give my husband the bad news, and after his callers left, I was able to make him hear me. He went to the telephone and called Charlie Stafford, our host, and that made two men who didn't know what to do. I could clearly see that I was going to spend the night in the bathtub unless I figured out something. "Sherm," I whispered, "give me your nail file." He slid it under the door, and with it I coaxed the screws out and the doorknob fell to pieces. And the President slept on.

I woke about four o'clock and couldn't seem to fall asleep again, maybe because of the changing of the guard in the corridor. Later I ate breakfast with some other New Hampshire women while my husband was eating with the President, Governor Dwinell, and the New Hampshire senators and congressmen.

We women were the first ones in the cars that morning, having no intention of being left behind again. Earlier I had finally found enough courage to say to my husband, "I expect the President's party to stop at the house for coffee." He only asked if I had someone looking after things at home.

There was a slight drizzle, but we fervently hoped that the Great Stone Face in Franconia Notch would be clear. Almost everyone along the route was outside their houses and places of business, cheering and waving, thrilled to see the President. We entered Lincoln by way of the old iron bridge. The President and my husband waved to a group of woodsmen, then passed under the huge sign that was stretched across the road. "Lincoln Welcomes IKE and SHERM." On Pollard Road, which is the street we live on, all the neighbors were out. The Walshes' dog even had a big red bow on his collar. The cars slowed down and stopped at our house. I was in the sixth car, so by the time

I reached the house the President and the others were inside, having been greeted by Marian, our daughter, and Tommy, our oldest grandson. Then the Governor escorted the President to his study on the first floor.

A few moments later the President came into the dining room and sat down in an old Hitchcock chair between the windows. Marian filled his coffee cup three times. I was told later that when he entered the house he said, "My! That coffee smells good!" Everyone had something to eat or drink. One of the guests said, "Don't forget to have the President sign your guest book." I told them it was in Washington, and anyway I thought we had better give him a rest from autographs. But the temptation was too great, and finally I asked him to leave his signature on the wall over the plate rail, above where he was sitting. The Governor heard us talking and raised his brows: "What's going on?" The President grinned. "Oh, your wife and I have a little project in mind," he said.

Time was passing, and practically everyone but the President had left for the cars. Jim Hagerty came in and suggested to the President that perhaps he too was ready to go.

But the President said, "Now, don't rush me! This is the most relaxing place I've found. And I am going to have another cup of coffee." When he was ready the Governor went out with him, and the motorcade disappeared down the street in the direction of the speakers' platform at the high school. It was exciting to see the crowd and the Lincoln Committee meeting the President for the first time. Sherm paid him a wonderful tribute in introducing him, and the President's speech, mostly about his top assistant, was very moving. I was presented with a spray of roses, the Governor with a bag for carrying fish, and the President with trout rods.

After the meeting we drove to Franconia Notch. The pageant depicting the region's early history was over when we arrived, but the Indians, stagecoaches, horses, and men with beards wearing buckskins and carrying rifles were still around.

We lunched at the Mountain View House at Whitefield and later the President played golf and was treated to a New Hampshire thunderstorm. Then we went to Secretary Weeks' farm for dinner. The President was given charge of charcoal broiling the steaks. He called for a platter to catch the drippings from one burner; for butter and lemon to make a gravy; for salt and pepper and oil to rub on the steaks for the second burner. On the third burner he laid the steaks directly on the coals—his favorite way—and asked someone to time them.

Inside the old rambling house there were fires in both fireplaces. It was a most relaxing and enjoyable evening. The President went to bed about 9:30 and so did we.

The following day the President's party went on to the Dartmouth Grant and Parmachenee Lake after a stop in Berlin. I returned to Lincoln. It was quite a letdown after so much excitement. But I found my neighbors still talking of nothing but the President's visit to our town. And as I wandered around the house, looking at the autograph on the dining-room wall, the chair in which the President had sat, the cup he had used, and even the napkin, I too became excited all over again.

A few days later I was back at Tilden Street in Washington, where we took up once more the chain of never-ending events. Everything went along smoothly for several days; and then one beautiful, quiet evening, as we were having a dinner of succulent roast lamb on the porch while the ravens were lazily drifting in the calm air above the zoo, and two young bunnies were enjoying their patch of clover, we heard something that sounded very much like the bleat of lambs. We looked at each other and put our forks down. We listened, and the sound was rebleated. I rushed to the door by the street entrance and saw a Railway Express truck, its driver advancing toward me with a COD slip to sign. Pointing at two spring lambs with black faces, he looked at me curiously, and asked, "Ma'am, were you expecting these? Shall I unload them?"

"Certainly," I answered, trying to give the impression that such deliveries were a daily occurrence in Washington.

The Governor arrived on the scene. We looked at each other again and we looked at the lambs. The driver gave us a queer look, I thought, as he pulled himself up into the cab and started off.

"Good old Sinny!" said the Governor, as he seized a lead rope which Sinny had thoughtfully provided.

"Yes, good old Sinny!" I mimicked as I fastened a rope to the other bundle of wool. Ever since our trip to Sinclair Weeks' home at the time of the President's visit to New Hampshire, I had twitted Sinny about the lambs he had said he was going to send me from his farm to help me keep the two acres of grass mowed. I now wondered how we were going to induce such determined creatures, whose intentions were exactly the opposite of ours, to travel around the house to the field out back. The Governor wasn't worrying about anything like that. He simply opened the door to his office and took the shortest and most direct route to the back yard. The lamb, being a product of the New Hampshire hills, apparently recognized good old granite determination and followed, as a lamb should, through the office, down the steps into the living room, across the Oriental rug, and out the big doors onto the spacious lawn and field, with never a pause. I followed with my charge. The bleatings didn't subside even with all the tender grass to be had. The newcomers to the Washington scene were definitely unhappy. We wondered what the neighbors would think.

Sinny had kept his part of the bargain but the sheep did little to make my task of grass cutting any easier. In fact, they upset our routine considerably. It was hard to find anyone to look after the house while we were away on vacation or official business. They would come to take care of our Siamese cat—but lambs, no. One couple undertook it once but nothing could induce them to come again. No matter how we tried to make the top of the hill attractive in every way with shelter and food, the lambs took every opportunity to come down to the patio. It wasn't always convenient to have lambs around the patio, so we put up a fence on the hill.

During the early part of their Washington residence they missed the rest of the flock, I think. In the daytime, when they could see each other, it wasn't so bad but about midnight they apparently became extremely lonesome and their loud bleats could probably be heard as far as Connecticut Avenue. I would hurry out to tie them a little closer together, hoping they hadn't awakened the Governor. If he was awake, I was apt to be reminded that *my* lambs were upsetting the peace of the neighborhood.

Nevertheless, we grew very fond of those sheep. They presented a restful and pleasing picture as they grazed on the hill near the big mimosa tree. I was always going to do a Corot-type of painting of them, full of lights and shadows, but I never got around to putting them on canvas—nor into the freezer, as the Secretary of Commerce expected I would.

President Coolidge must have been fond of sheep too. He had some on the White House grounds ostensibly for the same reason—to help keep the grass short. Perhaps, though, that really wasn't the reason— perhaps it was simply that to New Englanders they represented something missing in the Washington scene—watching them, I used to think of rock pastures, shady lanes, and quiet, clear pools, and the lovely New Hampshire hills.

The sheep continued to grow and every day they became more attached to us. After several months I decided they would be happier on a farm and suggested to Mrs. Eisenhower that they would make a nice addition to their farm in Gettysburg. It was during the President's convalescence in Denver from his heart attack that I received her answer to my suggestion.

"The sheep sound like a wonderful addition to our farm," she wrote. "I'll mention it to Ike when he is stronger."

Whether the President didn't feel up to getting into the sheep business or didn't receive the message, I never knew. I finally took them to a friend's farm in Maryland.

Emerson said, "I like the sayers of 'No' better than the sayers of 'Yes.'" But there are a number of people in Washington and across the country who wouldn't agree. When they asked for something they expected to get it—or did until Sherman Adams came on the scene. Because of his unswerving determination to do the right thing, to make the right decision, regardless of consequence, he sometimes won enemies. He never worried me with the hundred-and-one troubles and burdensome problems that it was his job to try to solve and take the blame (and less frequently, the credit) for. I don't know how many times he said "No" in order to win the title of no-man but I am sure it wasn't anywhere near so often as certain members of the press implied. In spite of all the adverse criticism, he kept going, apparently oblivious to the arrows. At a dinner that the President of Pakistan gave in honor of John Foster Dulles, Charles Wilson, then Secretary of Defense, said during a conversation regarding the bombardment the Assistant to the President underwent almost daily, "The water drips on Sherm all the time. It never lets up."

There were, and still are, countless people throughout the country who were thoroughly cognizant of the fact that Sherman Adams was a deeply dedicated man. He was, first and foremost, dedicated to his boss, the President of the United States; second, he was dedicated to his job. His family and friends ran very close competition but were never accorded quite the devotion that the President and the job received.

With a job such as the Governor's there was little time or opportunity for relaxation. He had to do what he could in the few hours available to him to keep from getting overtired both mentally and physically. Undoubtedly the most restful period of each week was the Sunday morning service at St. John's Episcopal Church near Lafayette Square. "The Church of the Presidents," it was called. Unlike the expanse of the Washington Cathedral, where we worshiped while my husband was a member of Congress, St. John's had a more personal friendliness about it. In making the decision to attend the smaller church the governor said a bit wistfully, "I'd like to go back into the choir at the Cathedral but it just wouldn't work out. I would miss rehearsals and undoubtedly there would be some Sundays when I would be tied up at the White House."

The first time we attended St. John's we were early and took seats in one of the pews fairly well up in front. I remember being vaguely conscious of a certain tenseness in the air as we settled down for one of Dr. Glenn's meaty sermons, but "the glory all about" as the sunlight, taking on colors from the stained-glass windows, shone on the altar and the flowers, kept me from giving it much thought. As the hour for the service approached, and the church filled up, I felt, more than saw, someone come down the aisle and stand beside the pew we were occupying, and then leave. A moment later an usher, plainly embarrassed, asked us kindly to move to seats in the back of the church. "This is the Admiral's pew," he said in explaining his regrettable duty. We picked up our coats and retreated to the rear as the Admiral and his lady sailed down the aisle. We hadn't been told that most of the pews in St. John's were rented, but we learned from that encounter that we shouldn't trifle with an admiral's possessions, not even his pew in church.

Later, when we were in our own assigned pew at St. John's, President and Mrs. Eisenhower attended a morning service there. It is customary for a President to go to at least one service in the "Church of the Presidents" while he is in office and generally it is a yearly event, even when he is a member of another church.

But that day in October the first family didn't get all the attention of the congregation. Neither did the lay reader who had the pulpit that morning. Quite unexpectedly, two ladies who were sitting next to each other were the focus of amused glances for, while kneeling, the veils on their hats had become entangled and when they arose they were astonished to find they were quite securely fastened together. Neither one, apparently, thought to take off her hat, so there were a number of anxious moments until they had separated the offending veils.

On another Sunday morning it was I who was embarrassed and amused too. As the service progressed I noticed my husband wasn't kneeling in accordance with the order of worship. I slyly glanced at his face to see if I could ascertain the reason. His expression suggested he had decided to sit it out. I leaned closer when I got a chance and asked what the matter was. "I am not going to put my face in that wheatfield!" he said, nodding toward the sumptuous fur collar of the lady's coat which cascaded over the back of her pew practically into his lap.

Peaceful as those Sunday morning interludes were, however, they hardly took the place of the vacation that by now the Governor really needed. Consequently, I was delighted when some time after the Lincoln visit, the President persuaded Sherm that he should take a European trip. It was the first time either of us had ever been out of the country except for several trips to Canada, and the first time in his life that the Governor had taken even more than ten days away from his work, except for the few times he had been hospitalized. To add to our pleasure, General Goodpaster and his wife Dossy were to go with us. Andy Goodpaster, who had previously been stationed at SHAPE, was now a member of the White House staff.

It was almost noon, on one of Washington's typical August days, when we took off from the airport in General Gruenther's plane. The temperature of 68 degrees inside the cabin was a welcome relief from the 96 degrees outside, but it was almost too much of a change. The Governor had borrowed my red wool stole and presented quite a picture as he studied maps and booklets in preparation for getting the maximum enjoyment out of that first real vacation. Well aware of his usual attention to detail and thoroughness in planning, I knew it would be a busy trip with no time wasted on what he would call foolishness. Mountains, music, and historical spots would get priority. (I was right.)

At 9:20 the next morning we were flying over the red-tiled roofs of Paris and slowly descending toward Orly Field. It was the beginning of several wonderful and exciting weeks. One person's first trip abroad is much like another's, I suspect, and we followed what I imagine is a familiar routine, from France to Germany and Austria, then Italy and Denmark, and finally England and Scotland. We crowded in as many sights as we could, made numerous side trips, ate some delicious food and some not so delicious, saw much fine art and many beautiful buildings and breath-taking views. We heard magnificent music and tramped the museums until we were weary. We also went up a number of mountains and even got in some fishing and, in Scotland, a game of golf. As we arrived at the Prestwick airport for the return trip home we were given the startling news that the President had had a heart attack the day before. The Governor was on his way to the hospital in Denver almost as soon as we landed in Washington, and I saw very little of him for the next few weeks. For the remainder of the President's illness he journeyed back and forth between that city and Washington, doing to the best of his ability what he believed the President would want him to do.

The President's faith in my husband, as he lay in his hospital bed, was emphasized in a letter which I received from Mamie at the time.

Denver, October 6, 1955

Dear Rachel,

Many, many thanks for your warm and encouraging letter. I read it to Ike today as we were having luncheon, and both of us were much cheered to know of your sincere prayers and good feelings.

We are quite encouraged by the progress Ike seems to be making right now. I am confident that it will not be long before he will be able to enjoy painting in bed as you did during your recuperation—when I described the wonderful things you could do with a canvas in this position, he could hardly wait to get out his brushes and begin!

It is good to know that Sherm is here to take things over. Ike is so relieved to know that the burden is being lightened so capably by your husband.

Ike joins me in sending you warm regards,

MAMIE DOUD EISENHOWER

xvi

A Montana Vacation

The Republican Convention of 1956, which was held in San Francisco, lacked the excitement of the 1952 convention in Chicago, though there was plenty of bustle and agitation in the days preceding, and indeed during, the convention.

For almost a year the President's health had been a favorite topic of conversation across the nation and around the world. His heart attack in September of 1955 and the operation in June, 1956, to relieve an intestinal disorder had the whole country, Republicans in particular, wondering whether he would be able to stand another four years in the White House.

Not until July 10, only a few weeks before the Convention, did the President let it be known he was still a candidate for a second term. He had been convalescing at his farm in Gettysburg since leaving the hospital and my husband frequently journeyed there by helicopter to confer with him. I haven't any doubt that he knew of the President's decision to run again somewhat before he made his formal announcement. The President's decision was received by many of his followers with a great sigh of relief because in so deciding he had announced to the world that he had, once again, fully regained his health.

Five weeks after the President's statement, the Governor and I were on our way to San Francisco. We had been there during the 1952 campaign and we were glad to be going back. Our flight ended at the Oakland airport about 10:15 in the evening, West Coast time, and we delayed our departure from the plane until all the other passengers were off, for we could see a sizable group of photographers and

newsmen waiting for the Governor to appear. After the news conference we went directly to the St. Francis. Our room was on the sixth
floor which was the headquarters of the San Francisco White House,
the President's suite being at the end of the main corridor.

Every morning we were up at our usual hour of 6:15. The Governor's days were long and full. There were staff meetings, private meetings with individuals, and meetings with groups of Republicans
concerning the convention and all its aspects. It was an intensely busy
period for the Governor but nothing at all like the tension-filled days
of the 1952 convention in Chicago.

On Sunday we attended the morning service at Grace Episcopal
Cathedral where Governor Knight of California read the first lesson.
The second lesson was delivered by my husband, who never felt more
at ease than behind a pulpit, the reason being perhaps his close association, when young, with his preacher grandfather. Late in the afternoon he felt a need to get away for a few hours from the pressure of
events and the never-ending line of visitors. We filled the car with
friends and drove to the Muir Forest. It was almost as if we were
attending another church service. The spires of those huge redwoods
were the steeples of the forest, the massive trunks like the tremendous
supports of a cathedral; the quiet and peace were a blessed change
from the feverish pitch of the convention; the pushing, the hurrying,
the planning, the unexpected and the expected.

I had been thoroughly indoctrinated during the previous campaign
in regard to sharing our quarters or, as was more often the case, finding another place to sit while our rooms were being used for meetings.
Many times I shut my bedroom door as the living room filled up with
high-ranking Republicans or other noteworthies. Sometimes it was a
temptation (which I never yielded to) to leave the door ajar and
listen to what must have been, in many instances, history-making
arrangements.

San Francisco and its environs were full of charming and gracious
people who entertained lavishly for the convention participants and
visitors. The Governor and I accepted very few of the many invitations that we received, though we did try to appear at a few gatherings

for a little while. However, the Governor found it hard to mix business with pleasure and he was always relieved when I didn't try to encourage him to attend social functions. We did promise to appear at Governor Knight's reception and ball at which someone said there were eight thousand people. It was more than a ball for me. It was an evening to remember with a considerable amount of personal satisfaction, for the ball gown I wore was a size 12. For two weeks I had dieted, and exercised, and concentrated in order to fit into the black silk taffeta creation. The two staff wives who were called in to help with the zipper early in the evening said something about my having "just made it." Anyway, once securely inside the gown I felt years younger, and perhaps the feeling showed, for after the ball was over I heard I had looked "stunning" and "petite." Words which, when one has passed the fifty-year mark, and is a grandmother, are as wine to the soul.

Another of the several affairs I attended was the Women's Luncheon in the Venetian Room of the St. Francis. It was a decidedly pink affair in honor of Mamie. Table decorations were pink, as were the many arrangements of roses. The champagne was pink and so was the raspberry sherbet.

While I was shopping or sightseeing or attending women's gatherings the Governor was tied up with meetings or giving a speech. One talk was delivered to the forty-two Republican state chairmen at a closed-door luncheon session in the Sheraton-Palace Hotel. His remarks, which were heard in the outside corridor by newsmen, gave evidence of his faith in Nixon. In speaking of the Vice-President the Governor said, "He is one of the most effective campaigners in the party and has established a great record as Vice-President in both ceremonial and constitutional duties." He also expressed his belief that Nixon could be as popular with voters as Eisenhower.

Some things went well, like the way Harold Stassen gave up in his fight against Nixon for Vice-President and seconded his renomination. But something went wrong at the end of the second day's session. The Governor's principal part in the convention program was that evening, and it was assumed that a large television audience was watching with interest, as he introduced, with a few well-chosen words, each member of the Cabinet, all of whom were present except John Foster Dulles, who was in London attending the International Conference on the Suez crisis. The floor of the Convention Hall was full of delegates and alternates but the visitors' galleries were quite empty, for many had gone to the airport to watch the arrival of the President. However, as soon as the President's plane landed, all television programs were switched to the airport where the television audience was treated to fleeting glimpses of the President and the large crowds out to greet him. Meanwhile, back at the Convention Hall, the Governor continued to introduce the Cabinet members, who responded with short campaign speeches directed especially to the television audience, unaware that no one was seeing or hearing them. There were other miscalculations and mixed signals that evening. A TV announcer said Presidential Assistant Sherman Adams was at the airport when the President's plane landed; and the band got a wrong signal and struck up with all stops open right in the middle of the Governor's introduction of Secretary of Commerce Weeks. It was quite an ending to an otherwise well-planned session.

The next evening the convention ended with a bang—repeated many times as hundreds of balloons floated down onto the crowded convention floor and were popped by lighted cigarettes throughout the hall as the President, acknowledging the ovation following his acceptance speech, grinned broadly. So, with what sounded like a Fourth-of-July celebration, the Republicans left the Cow Palace with their sights set on the November election and another victory for the Republican party.

After the shouting and the fanfare in San Francisco, we took a plane for Missoula, Montana, where we had stopped several times during the 1952 campaign. It was a part of the country we had taken a great liking to.

Besides wanting a few days' vacation after the past strenuous weeks, we were looking forward to seeing our son, who was spending the summer working in the Bitter Root Mountains of Idaho, just across the state line from Missoula.

An old forester friend, James Vessey, who was the supervisor of the national forests where we would camp, had for years been insisting we come to Montana and let him show us some really fine rugged country. It proved a rare experience by which we will feel forever enriched.

Arriving in Missoula, we found our one suitcase to be missing. Our convention clothes had been sent directly home and we had packed only our outdoor clothes and personal items for the Montana trip. Luckily the duffel bag containing our hiking clothes landed with us, otherwise the following day's schedule would have been upset. Apparently our suitcase had not been put on our plane, or maybe had been put on another flight going in some other direction. No one could tell us when we might expect to receive it. Consequently, we went on a little shopping expedition in the Missoula Mercantile Store, where we bought gaily printed pajamas, a couple of toothbrushes, and a few other necessary items for our trip into the deep woods. The manager gave me a box of assorted flies, which he promised were just what I would need to catch the cutthroat trout we were hoping for.

At dinner that evening our host told us of the plans for the next three days. It all sounded wonderfully exciting. Washington and the recent convention hullabaloo already seemed far, far away.

At eleven o'clock the next morning we climbed into a battered, noisy, trimotor Ford airplane—vintage of 1927. The pilot was Bob Johnson, a veteran flyer who, as much as anyone, has made smoke-jumping practical through his skillful bush piloting. The plane shook and creaked as it rambled down the runway so I was surprised that it held together as it took off with a shudder. Once it had leveled off it was much quieter but we had to shout to each other to be heard. The plane was one generally used to fly the smoke jumpers, whose headquarters were nearby, to the scene of a forest fire, but Bob Johnson told us that on one occasion it had been used to deliver two horses far into the deep woods. All the seats were taken out and the horses were "given the needle." After they had fallen asleep they were slid into the plane on a canvas—and they slept until after landing. I thought to myself that the inside of the plane looked as if the horses had awakened and bitterly resented being transported in such a manner.

We climbed to about eight thousand feet and traveled ninety miles an hour. The weather was perfect and our pilot took us on a two-hour ride over the Rockies which formed the Great Divide. The Governor sat in the cockpit, taking pictures and studying a map. We were especially interested in the Chinese Wall, about forty miles long and a part of the Great Divide. Some of the party saw mountain goats far below, and most of us had frequent glimpses of elk.

Close to 1:30 we landed at Black Bear Ranger Station—seventy miles from the nearest habitation. There were no roads to this isolated spot in the wilderness. One had to hike or ride horseback or fly in as we did.

Three rangers, the superintendent, and the cook greeted us. The cook had an excellent lunch ready as soon as we had carried our gear from the plane to the cabin. Afterwards most of us went down to the river with our rods. We were not disappointed.

At five o'clock I went over to the corral to see if the pack train had arrived. It had, and the packer, Adam Funk, and his helper (our son Sam, who had been loaned from his trail job for the first few days of our visit), were about to take the mules and the horses up to the landing strip to graze for the night. The horses wore bells—similar to cowbells—to make it easier to find them if they strayed. The mules didn't need bells for they always stayed close to the horses.

Contentedly I leaned against the old fence. It was a pleasant sight on that late afternoon: a glowing sunset was shaping up and all was quiet save for the peaceful, familiar noises inside the corral. The animals were munching their oats, the bells were tinkling, and the spurs of the packer jingled as he moved among the horses. The only other indication of activity was the column of smoke spiraling out of the chimney of the cabin. The cook was busy with preparations for the evening meal.

While I was trying to impress every bit of the scene upon my mind so that I would never forget it, the Governor arrived from the direction of the river. By his step and expression I knew he had been successful—we would have trout for breakfast.

There was plenty of time before supper, so we set about getting our bedrolls ready for the night. For many weeks we had been looking forward to sleeping in the open under the Western skies. The signs of rain clouds on the horizon didn't change our minds. We found a spot near the cabin, inside the fence, and went to work blowing up the air mattresses. The Governor seemed to be having a little trouble with his and I politely suggested it was no wonder—he had done so much bragging about the fish he had caught he probably had no wind left.

Just as we finished arranging a canvas to keep the rain off, the call for supper sounded. We gathered around the large table in the one-room cabin, near the big square camp stove. The heat felt good that August evening as the sky slowly filled with somber-colored clouds. The large steaks and numerous other dishes one would hardly expect to find in such an out-of-the-way place disappeared swiftly.

As the rest of the group became involved in a game of bridge, the Governor and I sought out our spot by the corner of the cabin. Before many hands had been bid and played we were asleep. During the night a big-eared woods mouse kept investigating my hair, which stuck out from under the scarf I had tied around my head. When I awoke he would jump up on the fence rail and sit there looking at me. It did rain a little but except for a slow drip from the canvas near my shoulder we were cozy as could be.

Shortly before six I was awakened by the bells on the horses. Sam was bringing them in for their oats. It was a foggy dawn, but the kind that promises a beautiful day. Everything was damp and still—everything except the bells and the anxious cloppity-clop of twelve horses and mules as they trotted toward the corral. Following behind was Sam on his big red Ranger, his Western hat adding a fitting touch to an early-morning picture I knew I could recapture only as a memory. It was another one of those rare moments one instinctively knows will never be repeated.

Before we had finished breakfast the saddle horses were ready and the packer was loading the mules for the seven-mile trip up the South Fork of the Flathead River, where we would camp for the night. As soon as a picnic lunch was ready we were on our way, leaving the packer to come along later. I had a good trail horse named Brownie. The Governor was on Cricket, also an intelligent, experienced mount. We traveled along the river through beautiful woods of Douglas fir and larch. Twice we stopped to cast a fly into the busy water and added to our growing mess of trout for the evening meal.

We arrived at the campsite, which was at the junction of the Little Salmon and the South Fork of the Flathead, at one o'clock. After lunch we went in quest of more trout, for there were eleven healthy appetites in the making.

A trail crew had set up three tents a couple of days before we arrived. Kimmel stoves were used for cooking and for heat in my tent, which I shared with two other women. Neat stacks of firewood were ready. Everything was in apple-pie order. Both the Governor and I were a little concerned about the rather lavish outlay of comforts which we had never before enjoyed on any of our trips into the deep woods. I was even a bit embarrassed to find a *stove* in our tent. Did these Westerners think we were such tenderfeet? But I was most grateful for the warm comfort of that little Kimmel heater, for earlier, intent on catching my share of trout for breakfast, I had been incautious enough to go under the clear, cold waters of the Little Salmon River. It had been a warm day, but as the cool shadows gathered my wet clothes felt less and less comfortable.

In the morning some of us rode up to Big Salmon Lake to bring back the horses from their night's grazing. After breakfast, at which stacks of huge pancakes, trout, warmed-up potatoes, scrambled eggs and bacon disappeared in no time, the Governor started fishing the seven miles back to Black Bear camp. He wasn't an ardent horseman, usually preferring to hike and explore each pool along the river.

After getting our duffel together, I watched the process of packing the supplies and equipment in large squares of canvas, called mantas. Those bundles would give each mule about 160 pounds to carry. Our host and his wife elected to return to camp in a rubber boat, fishing on the way, and urged me to accompany them. It was a great temptation but I preferred the trip by horseback. (At least I kept dry that way, while they appeared in camp some hours later soaked from shooting the rapids.)

Those of us who were riding broke camp about ten o'clock. We stopped to wait for the boat and its occupants at two places on the trail and to hear about the fishing and the negotiation of the rapids. Several miles further on, when we next met them, they said they had seen the Governor, who was enjoying the best fishing he had ever had. He arrived at camp about the middle of the afternoon looking completely happy and relaxed. That night we felt more adventurous and put our bedrolls farther from the cabin, under a big Douglas fir. It rained during the night but heavy canvas covers kept us dry and warm.

Our outing was to end the next morning. When we awoke, however, a very low ceiling with intermittent showers made it doubtful that the plane could come in for us. A radio hookup told us that Bob Johnson had left Missoula and would try to get in. Everything was packed. Some of the men were playing cribbage as the showers came and went, some were reading, others were just spinning yarns as the hours went by. Every few moments someone would go to the door and look out at the low, heavy clouds while listening for the sound of the plane's motors. All of a sudden everyone jumped up as we heard the roar of the plane, coming in low over the cabin. The clouds had lifted slightly and we hurriedly caught up our packs and rushed to the landing strip in order to get off before the weather closed in again.

After flying about twenty-five miles the weather improved greatly and we had an excellent close-range view of Hungry Horse Dam, the Mission Range, and the 40-mile-long Flathead Lake. Early in the afternoon we landed again in Missoula. Our introduction to the Flathead National Forest had far exceeded our expectations, and we couldn't have had a more able pilot than Bob Johnson.

The next morning we hired a Hertz car and left Missoula. Our destination was Glacier Park, long a "must" on the Governor's list of parks yet unvisited. Unfortunately the weather had worsened, and it seemed unlikely that we would be able to hike or even fish the streams.

We reached the entrance to the park in the early part of the afternoon and found the superintendent, Mr. Emmert, waiting for us. He showed us where to fish in case the weather improved, and then took us to the motel at one end of MacDonald Lake where we had reservations for two nights. The clouds were low—almost touching the lake —but after unpacking we decided to go out in the drizzle and try a little fishing anyway. We drove to the Middle Branch of the Flathead River, then walked through the woods until we came to the "good pools" we had been told about. The Governor went off upstream and I went in the opposite direction. The trout weren't taking and after about an hour's casting we left for the motel to get into dry clothes.

That evening we drove to the MacDonald Hotel, eight miles farther up the lake, for dinner with Mr. Emmert. Adorning the walls of the lobby was a large display of stuffed animal heads. Most of them looked familiar, but one exhibit caught our special attention. We had had no cocktails—but it did look queer. Our host offered little help, intentionally. Finally the Governor and I decided that the head had once belonged to a solemn-looking cow moose, while the antlers had at one time been the property of a reindeer!

The next morning we were up at six o'clock in order to get an early start for the trip through the park which would take most of the day. It was a beautiful morning. The huge lake was like a mirror, reflecting the towering mountains with their new fall of snow. With Mr. Emmert as our guide, we were soon on our way enjoying the spectacular views from the "Going-to-the-Sun" Highway. After many stops to inspect park setups, lakes, and gorges, we arrived at the Many Glacier area. Mr. Emmert unlocked the gate to the huge garbage pit belonging to the hotel farther on. He hoped there would be some grizzly bears feeding, but though we waited several minutes none appeared. After lunch, however, we took binoculars and watched a group of fifteen big-horned sheep high up on the mountainside.

I decided to ride horseback in that area rather than accompany the men to the Canadian side of the park. The manager of the hotel introduced me to a guide named Blackie, a big, sun-browned fellow with a bushy black beard. We started out, Blackie and I, while the Governor and Mr. Emmert watched from the car. Before we were out of sight they drove away. I tried to make conversation but Blackie had little to say. He sat half turned in his saddle, appearing to scan the upper slopes of the mountains. I followed behind on a gray horse, wondering where he was going to take me.

We went over the worst trails I ever saw. We went through mud up to the horses' knees, we went over rock piles, we went along the sides of steep, slippery hills, and we forded some rivers. We went down steep banks where the horses all but sat down and slid. All the time there was not a word from my companion, but I suspected he was watching me out of the corner of his eye, while pretending to look for mountain sheep up on the high slopes. Perhaps he was trying to find out how much this Easterner could take. I wondered what else he would try. I didn't have to wait long for an answer. All of a sudden our trail led into the garbage pit!

"You stay here and maybe you'll see some bears," he said. "I'm going back along the trail a minute," he added as he disappeared.

Frankly, I had not the slightest interest in seeing a grizzly bear while I was on a strange horse, or any horse; but I couldn't let on that I was shaking as much as my mare, who knew she could smell bear and didn't like the situation any better than I did.

I don't know whether Blackie was trying to scare up a bear or two or whether he had a cache of firewater back there in the bushes. I do know that he seemed more talkative when he returned. He had been gone a long five minutes during which no bears appeared, for which I was most thankful; otherwise I and my horse would have lost no time in streaking toward the wide-open spaces of the Blackfoot Prairies.

Blackie led the way again out through the gate and across the highway to a little grave made long, long ago. There was a crude, ageless stone wall around the lonesome mound. Above it stood a weather-bent old tree with its few gnarled limbs stretching out over the resting place of the first white woman to enter that territory.

My companion reined up his horse near the tree and waited. I was trying to imagine what it must have been like for that adventurous soul so long ago and I was a little slow to realize that Blackie expected me to take a picture of him, but I finally returned to the present and reached for my camera. I pressed the shutter release and nothing happened. I had apparently taken the last picture on the film, but Blackie didn't know that. He put on his Western hat again with a flourish and led the way back to the hotel.

The following day we were back in Missoula, regretfully packing our outdoor clothes, and a day later Northwest Airlines deposited us and our luggage in Chicago. Capitol Airlines picked us up and landed us at midnight in a sweltering, steaming Washington.

I asked the Governor where he would rather be and he said, "Anywhere but here!" I felt the same way but I was thinking especially of those cool and quiet nights in the mountains of Montana.

With November, 1956, came the last feverish preparations of the Republicans to keep President Eisenhower in the White House for another four years. On the Sunday before Election Day the Governor appeared on the "Meet the Press" show. After he had returned home following the broadcast the telephone rang. It was the President calling to tell him what a wonderful job he had done.

"I've got a roomful of folks here," said the President. "A while ago I was wondering who they ["Meet the Press"] were going to put on for the last broadcast before election. When I learned it was you I didn't worry any more!"

James, the colored boy who lived with us and helped with all kinds of work, wasn't doing any worrying either. He explained his feeling that "ev'thin' is goin' to be okay."

"Ev'body up at Pine Forge School [which he had attended in Pennsylvania the previous year] is wearin' IKE buttons, an' ev'body at church says they is fo' Ike, an' today I went down to see my old boss and they-all is goin' to vote right!"

On election night we listened to the returns in the Sheraton-Park ballroom in Washington. As the evening wore on and the news kept getting better and better, the crowds were jubilant. The final victory converted the ballroom and most of the rest of the hotel into a happy and hilarious mob scene. The Republicans had won again, and by a record vote. And, as was expected, the President, as in 1952, ran well ahead of the rest of the Republican ticket. Precisely how much my husband had to do with that second GOP victory is something I know little about, but I would assume it was plenty.

A few weeks after election we left the bright lights of Washington and the continuous succession of parties and drove to New Hampshire, reaching Lincoln just in time for Christmas Eve. The sky was full of stars, and lighted candles shone from the windows of our red house. The air outside was crisp and the snow was crunchy. Inside, the glow from the fireplace lighted up the faces of our children who were waiting for us. In the corner stood a beautiful little Douglas fir tree. It was the tree the cook at Black Bear Ranger Station in Montana had said he was going to send for our Christmas.

That Christmas our children and I had decided to give the Governor a golf bag, which he certainly needed. There was much telephoning back and forth as the children and I talked the matter over and finally placed a special order with an interested store owner up in New Hampshire. Delivery for Christmas Day was guaranteed. We were all set. *That* Christmas we would really surprise the Governor. We could hardly wait for him to unwrap what we knew would please him. He carefully untied the ribbons, and patiently took off the wrappings. He put on a really fine show of appreciation and we were well pleased with ourselves—but not for long. Later in the day he finally got up enough courage to say, "I didn't tell you, Plum, but just before I left Washington I learned the President had given me a golf bag." He added, "I feel terrible not keeping yours, but I don't need two bags!"

Well, we all enjoyed the joke on ourselves. Of course we insisted that he keep the one from the President—it was much nicer than ours.

We were always glad to get back to New Hampshire, especially at Christmastime, if only for a few days. To be with the family again, to have an abundance of clean snow, and to be able to enjoy together the exhilarating freshness of the air as we skied the slopes of Cannon Mountain or skated on Profile Lake was pure happiness. The 600-mile trip from Washington to New Hampshire was something we usually tried to negotiate as quickly as possible. There were many times, however, when a late start made it necessary to find a place to stay for the night. One year, knowing we would be late getting off, we made a reservation at an inn in a little New York village which we would be passing through. When we arrived after dark on a cold evening we were told there was no reservation—and there was no available room.

"But I am sure you were notified I wanted a reservation," said the Governor, unable to believe the discouraging news. He had no idea where else to go. The hour was late, and it was just two nights before Christmas.

"Can't you find us something?" he implored.

The innkeeper shook his head. At that point I nudged the Governor, "Maybe they would have a stable?" I asked innocently. The Assistant to the President gave me a look that suggested it was no time for one of my quips. He picked up his briefcase and followed me out the door. It was some time and several miles later that we finally found a hotel that could put us up.

A month or so after we returned to Washington that winter the Governor and I were pleasantly surprised by a heavy fall of snow. The seventeen inches that fell in the middle of February caused the usual tie-ups in traffic that even a few inches seemed to bring about. The trees and shrubs throughout the city and its environs drooped under their white weight. The picnic benches, the tables, and the seats of the swings in the park areas were piled high. Along Rock Creek the heavily laden branches bent down and dipped their fingers into the brown waters.

Downtown the snow-removal equipment was making slow work of clearing the streets. For three days they were in better condition for sleigh-riding than traveling by auto, or even walking. Returning from church one very white Sunday morning, we saw two horse-drawn sleighs cross Connecticut Avenue, and I was inspired to try to find one. As usual, Sherm had work to do and couldn't accompany me, so I called the wife of a member of the White House staff, who was at once delighted by my proposal. The horse we found for the job was a well-behaved animal but the sleigh was rather decrepit; however, it held together miraculously. The sleigh bells announced our approach to pedestrians who found it necessary to be out on that windy and very cold day. Our ride through downtown Washington was uncomfortably chilly but hilarious. Shovelers and stuck motorists shouted and waved as we drove past. The bells jingled merrily, silenced only at traffic lights. We even considered calling on Mrs. Eisenhower and headed momentarily for the White House. But then we decided, probably wisely, that the guards would have trouble deciding what to do about clearing a horse-drawn vehicle through the gate with two staff wives in control. Still, it was one of the most memorable sleigh rides of my life.

I think it was also that winter that the Governor and I decided to investigate the possibilities of ice skating. Surely, we thought, there must be a rink somewhere in the vicinity. I hunted through the yellow pages of the directory and found what I wanted. The Uline Arena offered quite a program, and feeling as if we were really going to enjoy *that* winter in Washington, we jubilantly gathered up our skates and took off for the "Open House" program. It was a wettish, too-warm day but once we got inside we expected to forget all that. What fun it would be sailing around the ice in that huge place!

To our sorrow we found there were limitations which interfered with our free-style enjoyment of the sport. Always having had a whole lake or pond pretty much to ourselves, we didn't fully appreciate the well-organized program. The intricate figures being executed by the professionals and their expert pupils were nice, but we weren't interested at our age in taking up figure skating. Quite cautiously it was suggested that we join a class for beginners, and our attention was directed to one of the corrals on that large cake of ice. Somehow it left us cold, and we never went back.

We didn't give up hope, however, that there would be some good freezing weather and we could still have a little unregimented fun. We watched the temperature hover around the upper thirties and then for a few nights it took a drop—not very far but enough to satisfy the anxious watchers of the reflecting pool in front of the Lincoln

Monument. There would be skating that evening. The Governor and I arrived as crowds of children and adults were happily skimming along the length of the pool, or in little groups hazardously trying out their skates after many years of disuse.

We sat down on the cement wall to remove our shoes and lace up the skates. We could hardly wait to get out on the ice. With anticipation high, we placed our shoes side by side on the bank, noting the exact spot, and stood up, anxious to be off. We got about four feet from the edge—and along came a guard motioning everyone off the ice. It had begun to crack up. We returned to the house and hung up our skates—for good.

xvii

The Storm Breaks

June of 1957 was a month of honorary degrees and speeches for my husband. He accepted an invitation from the University of Maine for a certain Sunday, and an invitation from President Stratton of Middlebury College in Vermont for the next day. We took turns driving the many miles between colleges, arriving in Montpelier, Vermont, late Sunday evening and getting up at 6:30 the next morning in order to finish the distance to Middlebury in time for the Commencement Exercises, which were to start at 10:30.

In the middle of the ceremonies, a man tiptoed onto the stage where President Stratton and the recipients of degrees were sitting. He whispered in the Governor's ear and waited for a reply, then tiptoed off again.

From my seat in the audience I had noticed the interruption and immediately wondered what had happened to the President—or to someone in our family. The Governor didn't leave the stage, so I presumed—correctly as it turned out later—that it was nothing urgent. As the exercises came to a close I saw the Governor leave quickly, without waiting to take part in the round of congratulations. As soon as possible I returned to the car and waited for him.

Finally he appeared, looking worried. "The President has had another upset. We may have to go right back."

We had planned on a couple of days' fishing in Maine with our son, whom we had seen too little of during our years of political life. It would be a keen disappointment to have to return to Washington, but it wouldn't be the first time the Governor had been called back from a much-needed few days of change and rest.

After lunch at President Stratton's house the Governor called the White House again, as he had agreed earlier to find out how the President was feeling before we returned to New Hampshire to pick up our son and go on to the fishing camp. General Snyder seemed to think the attack was nothing to worry about and he advised the Governor to continue on and get a little rest, if possible. So, relieved that the President was in no apparent danger and that we would be getting away to Parmachenee Lake the next morning, we enjoyed our ride back to Lincoln through the rolling hills of Vermont, and thence through the rugged Franconia Notch as only a June day in that kind of country can be enjoyed. To both of us, as to countless others who "have been away," the hills, the clear streams, the pockets of little peaceful villages, and the open road were a benison. We drove in silence, not missing a single beautiful scene.

The following morning, with Sam, we made one last check to be sure none of the necessary fishing gear, clothing, or other essential items had been forgotten. Then we locked up the Lincoln house and eagerly set out for the drive to Parmachenee Lake in Maine. At lunch time we stopped at a small roadside eating place. The service was slow. Ordinarily the Governor would get impatient if the waitress wasn't reasonably active, but that day he had already begun to relax. There weren't a hundred and one decisions to be made. There weren't appointments around the clock. There weren't any people around finding fault. There weren't any people at all—except the waitress, the Governor, Sam, and me. But, being Sherm, he had to be doing something, so reaching into his change pocket he took out a nickel, put it into the jukebox, took a casual look at the list of records, and pressed a lever.

The sounds which resulted made Sam and me stare at each other in complete wonderment, and then I instinctively glanced around to see if anyone else had come in. Relieved that we were still the only patrons, I turned my eyes on Sherm. He looked as he always did when he had a chance really to relax. In fact, he looked absolutely impish as Elvis Presley shook out the words to "I'm All Shook Up." Never in all the time I had known my husband had he ever put a nickel in a jukebox. If possible he always avoided eating in a place where there was one.

Sam and I now knew he was going to enjoy the next couple of days. He had been told there was no need to worry about the President. The weather was perfect. For a short time he had dropped the heavy load of his job, and the only thing of any immediate consequence was how good the fishing would be. We ate our hamburgers and the Elvis Presley record played on to the end. We didn't enjoy it, but we enjoyed the humor the Governor was in. He didn't enjoy it either, but he enjoyed the effect his selection had on his wife and son.

In a few days we were back in Washington. The 97-degree temperature on that June day set a new record. If we thought of the cool shadows along the edge of Parmachenee Lake or the quietness of the evenings, broken only by the call of a loon, we didn't speak of them.

Back in the saddle again, the Governor tensed up, as if summoning all his strength, his courage, and his patience against the unending siege of politicians wanting this or that. While he had been away, new problems had arisen. Some of the old problems were still smoldering. The lightheartedness he had exhibited when he put the nickel in the jukebox was replaced by a grim determination to work out the many pressing issues that accumulated each hour, each day, each week. Under the strain and stress of his job there must have been many times when he wished wholeheartedly that he was back down in Maine fishing. The glory of his position—if glory there was—took quick flight in the face of harassing and hard decisions. He could only do the very best he knew how.

That he had a passion for getting things done, and quickly, had early become known to staff members. One of them, Jim Lambie, talking with the Governor in his office one day, was an interested and amused bystander when the telephone rang. The Governor picked up the receiver and after listening to the voice on the other end said, "I'll be right there!" and hung up.

Seconds later the telephone rang again. The same person said he thought the Governor was coming right in. The Governor exploded,

"What the hell do you think I am—a goddam antelope?" Quite obviously the staff member on the other end of the wire was thoroughly enjoying his little joke.

Laurence Whittemore, often called "Mr. New Hampshire" by some of his scores of friends, told me he once thought he would have a bit of fun with my husband. He called him on the telephone, said a few words, and abruptly hung up. In a matter of seconds his own telephone rang. It was the Governor who said, "Say! You aren't any damned old Adams—you can't hang up on me like that!"

The Administration went into its sixth year with the Governor doggedly keeping the machinery of the White House staff functioning with precision. When, I wondered, was he going to have a let-up from the day-after-day tenseness, a vacation that would be long enough to let him get unwound. I tried on several occasions, most unsuccessfully, to get him to stay away from Washington until he had had a really good rest and change. He was always adamant to my pleas for a longer vacation. "I've got a job to do, Plum," was his usual answer. Nevertheless, I knew he felt he could function more efficiently if now and then he could have more than a two- or three-day respite from Washington, in the woods or along a stream, though he never showed any exasperation when time and again as the years went by our few days' vacation were interrupted.

More than once we were called back just as we were setting out. One time we had hardly boarded the plane at the Washington airport when a summons came: the President had had an ileitis attack. The plane waited while we gathered our belongings and got off. There were other occasions, like the time we went up to the Miramichi River in New Brunswick, Canada, for a weekend of spring fishing. We had unpacked quickly upon reaching camp and were soon out on the river hoping for a strike from one of the many black salmon on their way back to the ocean after spawning and wintering in the upper reaches of the river. Sherm finally landed a good-sized specimen and we returned to camp for a hearty meal, and an early departure to bed.

At midnight there was a loud knocking at the door of our cabin.

Sherm awoke from a deep sleep and groped his way toward the door. As he opened it his eyes settled on a wide black belt which girded a scarlet jacket, then traveled up about two and a half feet to the face of a Canadian Mountie. I never knew what went through his mind; perhaps he wondered if he had remembered to get his fishing license, or perhaps he had visions of a catastrophe in Washington. But the Mountie merely said the Governor should call the White House as early as possible in the morning.

Before breakfast Sherm drove to a little store a few miles from camp to put in the call. When he returned he said quietly that he would have to get to St. John, New Brunswick, in a hurry in order to catch a flight, for he had to return to Washington. General Paul T. Carroll, a member of the staff, had died suddenly and the President, who was in Denver, wanted the Governor to represent him at the funeral. We didn't talk about it. We just packed quickly and drove to the airport, which was over a hundred miles distant.

General Carroll had been one of the finest men on the President's staff. We were greatly saddened, as were all who knew him. Here was a young man struck down with a fatal heart attack, a man full of vigor who worked full time and much extra time also.

After leaving Sherm at the airport I continued on alone for the 500-mile trip back to our home in New Hampshire. I thought of him and of how disappointed he must be—he had looked forward to those few days of fishing for so many months. I wondered how long he could hold out. Could even he, with his unrelenting devotion to the President and the job, despite his seemingly endless amount of energy, keep up the rigorous pace indefinitely?

The following June I took our station wagon and drove to New England to visit the children and some friends. The Governor would join me later. Only a few weeks before he had said, "I think I can get away for a couple of days after the speech at Holderness School. I'm just about all in."

A station wagon was new to our way of life. The Governor had always taken a dim view of any such conveyance. The last one he had ridden in many years before had given him cause for regret. Then, too, he surmised, and rightfully I might add, that I would probably have it full of things most of the time. So, after years of absolutely no encouragement, I had been completely surprised one day to hear him ask, "How would you like a station wagon, Plum?"

"I'd love to have one, if you would," I answered, trying not to have an I-told-you-so look.

We tried out a green model the following weekend. The Governor was surprised to find how comfortable it was and that it was "a honey to drive."

"And just look at all the room there is for my painting equipment, and our fishing gear, and golf bags, and skis, and grandchildren, and . . ."

"I'm glad we got rid of those sheep!" said my husband.

My trip back to New England was full of joy at the prospect of seeing the children and old friends. I was in no great hurry.

"*What* were you doing all that time?" asked my husband when I told him it had taken me eight hours to drive to New York.

"Having a leisurely trip," I answered.

"You certainly were," answered the man who can't bear to take longer doing something than is absolutely necessary.

It was wonderful to get away from the busyness of Washington and out on the far-reaching turnpikes. But every once in a while my mind went back to something the Governor had said recently about an investigation. I kept dismissing the intrusion on an otherwise enjoyable trip. There had been a number of occasions, I reminded myself, when someone had tried to get the Governor on the stand in connection with this or that investigation. This new agitation was undoubtedly the attempt of some frustrated or jealous person to launch another attack. There was nothing to worry about, I told myself firmly. They might give the Governor a bad time for a bit but it would undoubtedly die down as quickly as it had sprung up.

Within a couple of days I had renewed old friendships and spent all too short a time with our children. Then I felt I must visit the familiar hills around Belmont where I spent so many happy days as a child. I drove along the country roads where many years before I had scuffed the dirt into little clouds with my bare feet. I gazed across the sunlit lake—the "stars" were still there. The water still spilled joyously over the dam into Mill Brook. The cattails nearby still nodded in the breeze or swung to and fro under the weight of a red-winged blackbird.

I spent the night in my log cabin, high on a hill, and a mile from the village. The site had been a favorite picnic spot for our family, relatives, and friends for over half a century. The cabin, which is rustic and lacks many of the modern conveniences, would probably prove uncomfortable over any length of time. But for a night or two it provides a peaceful refuge from counterfeit glitter and the hubbub of continually restless people rushing in all directions.

There are those who have never known the tranquillity of such a place as my cabin. But there are others who will understand my feeling for that inviolate sanctuary. Such a place does something for one that no other place can do. The mere whiff of fir balsam and the plaintive notes of the white-throated sparrow take me thousands of years away to an enchanted land. Then, as the sun reluctantly slides behind the distant Adirondack Mountains, a hush shrouds the valley below, only accentuated by the faraway tinkle of a cowbell. I feel renewed in soul, in body, and in mind. That night the Washington scene and all it implied seemed far, far away.

The next morning when I arose the lake was covered with a restless mist, and I had to scrape a film of ice from my windshield before starting out. I was to meet the Governor at the Lebanon airport in New Hampshire. I knew how glad he would be to be back in New England for a few days.

After a trip to southern Vermont to pick up some heirloom plates, which we tucked carefully in the back of the station wagon, we followed the Connecticut River north to the foothills of Moosilauke Mountain, and then took the road over the hills to Lincoln and our little red house. Once more we were home for a few hours.

In the morning we were off again to Holderness School for the Commencement exercises at which the Governor was to speak. As soon as we could we returned to Lincoln and packed for what we hoped would be three days of fishing at Parmachenee Lake in Maine. The packing didn't take long. We had had plenty of experience with tight schedules on the campaign train and other political tours. In short order we were off on the 120-mile trip into the woods.

Dick Noyes, the genial guide and caretaker, was at the wharf to meet us. In a matter of minutes we were crossing the lake toward the little island where log cabins stood close together in a row as if to reinforce each other against the elements. We were the only guests and were doubly welcome for that reason. It was good, Dick told us, after weeks with hardly a visitor, to have someone to cook for, to guide, and to talk to. He led us to our cabin, one that the President had used when he visited New England in 1955 and that we had also used on other occasions.

As we finished unpacking, the bell for the evening meal sounded. Generally speaking, guests were seldom far away at that time of day, but if by chance they had lost all thought of time in their absorption in the art of fly casting, or what my husband called "the pernicious, obnoxious, nefarious practice of trolling," the penetrating sound of that venerable locomotive bell would remind even the deafest ones that they were hungry.

The fare was as sumptuous as on our previous visits. Nellie Noyes in her immaculate white uniform was able to provide a tremendous meal of superb home-cooked food without any apparent fuss or bother. After indulging in more calories than we needed, we returned to our cabin for our usual evening game of rummy. I kept thinking of an article I had seen in a paper only the day before, and though I had promised myself to forget its unpleasant implications I found it hard to keep my mind on our game. However, the Governor didn't seem to be worried so I presumed that everything would eventually come out all right.

The article that troubled me was only one of several that the papers had been printing for the past few weeks about an investigation soon to be launched by the House Subcommittee on Legislative Oversight. Some of the members of the committee hoped they could prove that Sherman Adams had asked certain agencies to make exceptions in favor of his friend Bernard Goldfine. The very suggestion was utterly ridiculous. I, and anyone who ever knew Sherman Adams at any point in his life, in any connection, from the President on down, knew his absolute integrity and dedication.

I consoled myself with the thought that surely a number of his old colleagues on the Hill would at least give him moral support. I found out later that my thinking had been wrong. My misconception and thoroughly naïve reflections regarding the columns of smoke rising from the newspapers had lulled me into a state of unwarranted optimism.

As I tried to improve my score in our rummy game, my mind kept drifting back to the accusations that I had seen in print. The Governor's mind must have been as full of anxiety as mine, but we didn't discuss the storm on our horizon. There had been other in-vestigations. It was what someone in public life could expect. After an hour or so of rummy the Governor said he thought it was time to go to bed. I was glad to agree, and soon the lapping of the waves and the wind that breezed in and out among the cabins were all that could be heard. The occupants of Cabin No. 7 were deep in sleep.

The next morning, after a big breakfast, we sank heavily into the boats and were off for a whole day of fishing at Rump Pond. The fishing wasn't very good but there were compensations, like the several deer that were feeding along the shore, the picnic lunch we ate in the cove, and the eerie cries of a loon on the other side of the pond. Otherwise all was a deep and wide quietness.

Arriving back at camp late in the afternoon we found Pat Herr and his wife Ethel waiting for us. Pat had driven all the way from Berlin, New Hampshire, just to try to beat the Governor at pitching horseshoes. Ethel and I sat in front of a maplewood fire, for the early June evening was very cool, and talked about our families and the good times we had had in past years. I presumed the Herrs, like everyone else, had read the papers and knew of the pressure that was being put on the Governor. The hospitality that we had innocently accepted from the Goldfines was making headlines. The gifts which, over the years, we had exchanged, were being enumerated. After the horseshoe pitching contest was over, the Herrs left, wondering how many deer they would catch in the headlights of the car between the camp and their home.

The Governor said that in lieu of our usual evening game of rummy he was going to give Dick Noyes a few pointers about cribbage. Maybe they played for the camp, or maybe a Parmachenee Belle Fly. The Governor had already "won" the bank in Plymouth, and the Pemigewasset River from some of his cribbage-playing friends back in Lincoln. Maybe he was hoping to enlarge his holdings to include part of Maine.

We again retired early in order to be ready for another long day of casting, and thought how lucky we were to have two more days ahead of us. But when I awoke the next morning one of my eyes was badly bloodshot. I felt weary from the previous day's activity in the open air and decided to stay in out of the wind and cold. The Governor was disappointed. He could generally count on me to be a part of any out-of-doors activity in which he was interested, but even the trip to my favorite fishing spot, Little Boy Falls, couldn't persuade me to go out into the damp and chilly weather.

"Will you come up at noon for a steak cookout?" he wanted to know. I told him I surely would if my eye was better. However, the infection didn't clear up and I spent the hours resting and feeling sorry that I had to miss a whole day of fun on the river. Tomorrow I told myself, I'll make up for all this lost time.

"Tomorrow" didn't come for us at Parmachenee Lake. The Governor came back in the latter part of the afternoon with three nice trout. He had caught many others but, as was his custom, had returned them to the pools. His delight is in outsmarting the inhabitants of those dark waters and keeping only what he needs. If the fish aren't taking, he still has a good time being in the woods and on the water. No, tomorrow on that clear, winding river with a fly rod didn't materialize. A different kind of tomorrow—the kind that only Washington knows how to produce, with all its innuendo and sensationalism, was in the making.

It wasn't until after supper, when the Governor had gone to the office to give Dick Noyes a chance to redeem himself at cribbage, that the old wall telephone emitted a sputtering ring. The call was from Washington and it was for the Governor. Whoever was calling —and I never asked who it was—suggested that the Governor might want to return immediately since the Committee on Legislative Oversight had disclosed some information that was making the headlines.

The Governor returned to our cabin with a determined look on his face. I knew it was not because of any cribbage game. The soft terseness of the six words he spoke as he went to the bedroom to pack indicated clearly that a storm was really brewing in Washington.

"We've got to leave right away," he said. I didn't have to ask any questions. It took only about fifteen minutes to pack. Dick Noyes was ready to help load our gear into the boat. After the last good-bys were said we sped across the water in the last glow of the sunset toward the wharf where we had left our car.

The journey to Lincoln seemed interminable but we finally arrived shortly after midnight. I knew the Governor must be greatly upset. He wasn't concerned about himself. It was "the boss" he was thinking of. After doing all he possibly could, over a period of years, to make things easier for the President, he was faced with a situation that could put the Administration in a bad light, and nothing, of course, would please the opposition more.

In the morning I drove him to Concord, where he took a train for Washington, since weather conditions were against flying. Then I returned to Lincoln and visited an old woodsman who, many years before, had worked in the Lincoln woods with the Governor. I wanted to talk with him about his experiences in the lumber camps.

Joe Boyle was eighty-two years old but his mind was as clear as a spring on Loon Mountain. He enjoyed telling me about the early days in and around Lincoln. He was one of the few remaining grand old men of the forest. His tremendous frame was weathered and stooped and gnarled from bucking a long, hard life in the woods, but the inner man, like the heart of a sturdy pine, was sound and true. Reminiscing about Sherm's logging days, he said, "Of course he was young and rugged. By God! You got goin' with him and you had to tell him to stop. We got in lots of arguments but we got along. By

God! He'd make Billy [Joe's brother] mad! It tickled him to get Billy's goat!"

If, when the chance came for my husband to enter politics, he had refused and continued on in the logging industry, life for us would have undoubtedly been far less interesting and exciting, though probably more tranquil. There would have been no governorship, no Washington experience, no campaign train, and no association with those who live and work in the White House. All too few men of ability are willing to give up a good job to enter the unpredictable field of politics, but my husband "took the road less traveled by, and that has made all the difference." Inevitably his intense determination to get things done and to see that others did too earned him enemies among the less industriously inclined. At the same time it brought him the esteem of many thoughtful people throughout the country and the world, who knew what a terrific load he was carrying and recognized his remarkable ability.

He acquired other enemies, as people will who have definite conscientious objections to saying yes to any proposal just "to keep everybody happy." My husband had little patience with pretenders. He was particularly adept at spotting anyone intent on slowing down the tempo of the work. There were others whose feathers became ruffled when they were eased out of his office before they were quite ready to depart though they had used up too much valuable time already. Then there were those who never got in at all. In such a large organization as the federal government, there were, naturally, a tremendous number of people from all corners of the land who had a personal ax to grind, or who longed for and sometimes insisted on a job for themselves or a friend in the higher echelons of government. Their qualifications weren't always what the Governor thought they should be. It hurt some to be brushed aside, however politely, and some it made mad. The Governor took the blame in his stride. It was a part of his job as the Assistant to the President. He certainly didn't enjoy the farfetched accusations that every now and then appeared in the press but he was well aware of the type of person responsible for some of the charges.

Our north country can produce storms and blizzards with little, if any, warning, but down in Washington a squall is nearly always brewing on Capitol Hill. One of those squalls blew our way in the summer of 1958. Storm warnings had been hoisted off and on during the spring and we had decided if there was going to be a turbulent change in our political climate we would weather it to the best of our ability.

That summer I learned a number of things about political attack that I hadn't known before. One of those lessons was the destruction of the myth that "a man's home is his castle." During the days when the Governor was under fire I had no protection against intrusion, especially by news gatherers and photographers. There were a few members of the press who didn't seem to enjoy their assignment and who apparently had little taste for adding to the troubles of my difficult days; but they all tried to get in. Finally I became so over-alert I found myself unwilling to let anyone cross my threshold. Dora, my cleaning woman, was my strongest protection. She looked up from her work one day to see a clergyman standing in the room. *"Who* let *you* in here?" she somewhat menacingly wanted to know. She did not realize that I had returned from an errand and had invited him in.

I attended my first Congressional hearing the day that my husband volunteered his testimony, and it was later, on my birthday, that the President told the world he believed in Sherman Adams and needed his help. A few weeks after that we celebrated our thirty-fifth wedding anniversary, and in August we attended our son's wedding. Altogether it was quite a summer. Between gusts from Capitol Hill we tried to go about our duties and pleasures with as little interruption as possible.

September came, and the Governor went to Newport to talk with the President about his resignation. Members of the press kept a vigil in front of our house. A few days earlier when he had mentioned to me that he was considering resigning, I had replied, "Okay, Sherm, and there is something else you are going to do. You are going on television and tell your side of the story." The evening he returned from Newport I stayed home and watched the TV screen as my husband gave a superb presentation. Then I returned to the kitchen and finished preparing dinner. Before the Governor had left for the broadcasting station I had endeavored to lighten the atmosphere.

"Sherm, don't you want me to go down to the dog pound and pick out a mournful-looking pup for you to take along to the broadcast? We could name it Scrabble or Gin Rummy!" The Governor smiled, remembering the Nixons' dog Checkers. At that time, when others wanted to dump Nixon from the GOP line-up, the Governor had said, "Let's wait and see."

On the way to St. John's Church, one Sunday after his resignation, the Governor told me of the several interesting offers he had had from a number of publishers for a book.

"I have plenty of chances to write condemning things about a lot of people—but I couldn't do it without hurting people and I don't want to do that."

That was the way he thought when things looked darkest to him. That was the man whom men of less character called the "no-man"; that was the man some said had ice water in his veins. Those persons really didn't know Sherman Adams.

Back in 1956 my husband had handed me the little red leather-bound Bible saying, "I got this for you, Plum." I was deeply touched and wondered what had prompted him to buy it.

The Bible generally went to church with us and the Governor followed the reading of the lessons. He also carried his red leather-bound hymnal to every service of morning worship. It was the one he had used while a member of Congress, when singing with the choir of the Washington Cathedral. He kept track of the occasions when certain hymns were sung by writing the dates in the margin.

In June of 1958 the little red Bible came into almost constant use. Many of the hundreds of messages that I received from people throughout the country professing complete faith in my husband suggested that I read this or that verse or psalm to give me courage to face the hard days while he was under fire, and to help me be tolerant in my thinking about his persecutors. I have no doubt that the little red Bible did much to help me through those unhappy days.

...
xviii

Return to Lincoln

If it had not been for the unfortunate so-called "Goldfine episode," and my husband's subsequent resignation from his position as the Assistant to the President, our return to a quiet life in a small community might have been postponed for several years. The heartaches that we suffered, and that family and friends endured, have to a great extent been eased. There are still times, however, that I have to push out of my mind a feeling of bitterness as I recall the people who assisted, one way or another, in the decision that my husband found it necessary to make.

From the first I have repeatedly told myself that, somehow, what happened was all for the best. I have always possessed the ability to make the best of things (or perhaps it is simply an aptitude for ignoring the unpleasant); even so, I arrived back at our little red house with a heavy heart. I knew it was even harder for my husband.

As those first days at home passed, the heavy shroud of discouragement began to lift. There were many things to do. The house was in need of repairs after having been neglected for many years. We were concerned with stone walls which needed rebuilding, with lawns which plainly showed the results of neglect, and with the necessity of getting many other things attended to before winter set in.

Foremost in my husband's thoughts were plans for writing his book. He had, at first, little interest in the idea, as I have said, but after several publishers and friends had impressed him with the necessity for such a book he began to think more favorably about it.

After that first Christmas back home he sat down in front of the typewriter (which the staff in the White House had given him for just such a purpose) and began work in earnest on *Firsthand Report*. Some things were fun to write about. Some things came hard. For over two years the tapping of the typewriter keys could be heard for the better part of each day, sometimes clearly and sometimes almost inaudible, as the hi-fi or records provided a classical background to the story of the Eisenhower Administration and the part the author had played.

There were interludes when he simply couldn't stand being indoors for another minute. Often a partly filled sheet of paper would be left in the typewriter as we changed into the appropriate clothes and went in search of ski slopes. Later, in the spring, we would intersperse the long hours of writing with fishing trips, and when summer came the Governor found that mountain climbing still held a great appeal for him. There were many children eager to accompany him on those expeditions; children who had never climbed a mountain or slept out in the woods overnight. They now have a sizable list of peaks which they have climbed and many memories which will stay with them forever—memories of experiences and good times they might not have had if the Governor had not returned to Lincoln.

Those same children had never slept in a sweet-smelling haymow until ours gave them the opportunity. And the red pung that was made by hand over a hundred years ago can be seen almost any winter's afternoon as, full of children with bright-colored caps and mittens, it is pulled around the field by a big gray mare named Polky.

During that first summer as we worked in the gardens, cleared trails and boundaries in our nearby woods, and entertained several grandchildren, we began to feel the heaviness lighten perceptibly. Now I began really to believe that perhaps what had happened to end our Washington life had, after all, been for the best. Would the Governor ever have written his book if we had continued on in Washington? Most likely not. Would his health have held out under two more years of such merciless pounding? I doubted it. As the pages of his manuscript continued to pile higher and higher we found ourselves becoming, once again, well-established residents of the little village we had called "home" since our marriage thirty-six years before.

Two things happened that summer that have substantially changed our way of life—or at least the kind of quiet, retired existence we had certainly anticipated. The Governor, knowing of my love for nicely weathered old barns, and the absence of any spot I could call a studio in which to paint, in an unguarded moment suggested that I buy an old barn and build a studio. Perhaps he had cause during the subsequent months to regret such a casual suggestion.

The other event was the result of more planning on my part. I suggested to the Governor that it would be nice to have a saddle horse, and instead of buying one I thought it would be better to take a camp horse at first and see how we got along. Surprisingly enough, he thought it was a pretty good idea. I waited a couple of days and announced it would be advisable, I thought, to have two horses so we could ride together. It wouldn't cost much more to feed two horses and it would be silly to build a stable with only one stall. The Governor laughed and said something about my having things pretty well thought out.

That was a busy summer. I found an old barn and had it torn down. The huge hand-hewn timbers were marked with chalk so it would be easier for the builder to put them together again in the fall.

I found a summer camp that had two good horses we could have during the months the camp was closed. They arrived during the last week of August—just before the stable was finished. A shelter had been quickly built in the field across the road from our house and a small fenced-in area added. A group of neighbors' children watched the unloading of the two animals, little realizing what changes those horses would make in their young lives. Doubtless the neighbors too watched the changes taking place on Pollard Road and had a few misgivings as the stable took shape and a horse pasture was added. If they had looked out their windows that first cold, rainy night after the horses arrived and had seen me sitting on a bench in a fur coat, softly admonishing the horses to keep quiet, they might have been more worried, for soon after we had retired that night I heard loud noises of splitting wood as the flimsy shelter shook and in some places gave way under the determined kicks of both horses. Apparently, I thought, they don't get along very well. I tiptoed out of the house so as not to disturb the Governor, wondering if I could quiet the animals before they completely demolished the lean-to and woke all the neighbors.

I settled myself at what I hoped was a safe distance at the rear of the two horses. After one look at me in the fur coat, holding a golf umbrella in one hand and a horsewhip in the other, they settled down and quietly munched on the unfinished pile of hay. The next day the stable was finished—at least finished enough to put the horses into for the night. I saw to that.

It was November before the builder finally arrived to start putting the timbers in place for my studio. I'll never forget that particular day. A cold rain was coming down as the Governor, the builder, and I, with umbrellas, stood looking at the soaked pile of timbers. Most of the markings had been washed away.

With considerable Yankee ingenuity the builder was able, during the ensuing days, to get the framework of timbers in place. The measurements were the same as the original barn had been—but I doubt if any of the timbers were in the same location they had known for almost a hundred years.

The Governor suggested I had better hire an architect, but nothing was further from my mind. There were days when I made up my mind about certain details of construction just before the carpenters were ready to start pounding the nails. At other times I had something all planned out days ahead of the workers. It was great fun trying to think of ways to make the building more interesting for the grand-children, and usable for grownups. Generally I was only a few hammerings ahead of the carpenters in my plannings.

We hunted far and wide for old materials that would lend the atmosphere I was hoping for. Paul Mansur of Concord was of invaluable help. He knew of many buildings throughout the state that were being demolished, and he helped me in many ways to find the materials and fixtures I thought I had to have. Old Bissel Hall, long a landmark on the Dartmouth campus, provided the hardwood floors and most of the thousands of bricks that went into the fireplace and chimney. From the old boardinghouse in Lincoln, which was torn down that same year, came the windows. The paneling on the lower floor had been part of the Abbott house in Concord, one of the oldest houses in the state. I was especially insistent that the plumbing for the downstairs bathroom be different and I knew exactly what I wanted. The Governor, after hearing my plans, wasn't so sure, and the carpenters and the plumber gave me a second look when I made my wants known. Here and there I found the pieces I hoped for; a little white porcelain tub with feet that had been part of the "excellent accommodations" of a nearby summer hotel half a century ago, and a pull-chain, copper-tank toilet which also had been in the Abbott house for many years. Later, when the Governor found me painstakingly painting pink roses on those two pieces of antiquated plumbing, it was almost too much for him. However, it wasn't long before he was showing the bathroom first to all visitors. "This is Rachel's Victorian Room!" he explains.

After the last workman had left I wondered how on earth I was going to find enough of the right kind of furniture to fill up the large main room which ran the length of the barn, or any of the other rooms, for that matter. I needn't have worried, for neighbors and friends found "Fieldhouse" was "just the place" for some family heirlooms—for example, a spool bed or a "buffalo" rifle which had been carried by a scout back and forth across the plains three times. There were countless other interesting items that found their way to what had been intended as a "place to paint." And, too, I found our attic in the main house afforded more appropriate furnishings than I had thought possible.

Almost as soon as the building was finished it became a guest house, a community gathering place for arts and crafts classes and other organizations. The huge fireplace takes four-foot wood, which the local children, eager for the reading of a story by the Governor, cheerfully bring in from the woodshed. One of the back rooms, with its black potbellied stove, often prompts a feeling of nostalgia as I pass through or watch granddaughters playing school at desks I used in the district school where I grew up in Vermont. A rope coming through the ceiling rings the very school bell that I used to ring over fifty years ago.

One of the old beds on the second floor has a feather mattress—something the visiting ski enthusiasts good-naturedly vie for when the temperature is low and the wind howls across the big field. The "scoot-through" for youngsters from one room to the other is next to the fireplace. The "scoot-up" is a ladder leading to a small opening in the second floor. (We don't tell visitors about the stairs until they have successfully negotiated the ladder.)

Though only four years old, Fieldhouse is already full of warm memories of the fun and happy times we have had there with family and friends. The local children are welcome to find a book to read and often invited to stay overnight—and even to learn to paint on canvas. (My studio, by the way, is in the basement, taking up only such room as is not needed for something else.)

There are other ways in which the young people are encouraged to share in our many projects. There is haying to be done, there is the care of the horses, and each week children take turns coming to help with the stable work before going to school. On dark, way-below-zero mornings in winter it is almost unbelievable to open the door to those children at 6:30 or earlier. Sometimes they stop to warm their hands or their feet, but generally they can hardly wait to get out to the horses. Practically every morning throughout the winter months and well into the spring children on "work detail" have breakfast with us. They are more than willing to help, and because of their interest and endeavors we have enlarged the stable so it will accommodate more horses; one is a pony which belongs to all the Lincoln children and which they raised the money to pay for.

When we left Washington for Lincoln we didn't have any idea we would be getting up early to look after horses. We didn't have any idea a group of youngsters would be our almost constant companions —nor that that old dream of mine of a little place to paint would develop into a place like Fieldhouse.

Now we find ourselves in constant readiness for grandchildren's visits. (The local youngsters keep us in good condition.) Being the kind of man he is, the Governor is never idle. The same drive that he put into haying as a boy, building trails as a college student, rounding up men for the lumber camps, and later into many years of government service, he still possesses in abundance. Younger people find it hard to keep up with him. He is always glad to take time out from his many daily projects to talk with college students who come for help with their theses or with men in government and community affairs who seek his advice.

As for me, the days are not long enough for all the interesting things I would do.